Keep from Stumbling!

Bible Basics
for Spiritual Stability

Eugene Priddy

DEDICATION

This book is lovingly dedicated to my wife,

Monna Dean Priddy

a faithful companion since 1954
and mother of our five children.

"House and wealth are an inheritance from fathers,
But a prudent wife is from the LORD."

Proverbs 19:14

Jude 1:24-25

[24]Now to Him who is able to keep you from stumbling,
and to make you stand in the presence of His glory
blameless with great joy, [25]to the only God our
Savior, through Jesus Christ our Lord, be glory,
majesty, dominion and authority, before all time and
now and forever. Amen.

3

ACKNOWLEDGMENTS

My thanks goes to all who have given much time and effort to make this book a reality. Several missionary staff members and volunteers at Bible Basics International helped in proofreading and making suggestions for this edition to whom I owe a debt of gratitude: Karen Anderson, Isabel Bowen, Vida Burgess, Marilyn Dunn, Travis Mitten, Monna Dean Priddy, Gerald Pruden, and Sharon Pruden.

It is impossible to give credit to all who have had an influence on this book. Many ideas have been gleaned from classrooms, sermons, and books whose sources have long been forgotten. I am very grateful to the Lord for the bounty of Christian teachers who have taught me through the years.

TABLE OF CONTENTS

7. Man and God's Law

8. Salvation

9. Prayer

10. The Church

11. The Future

12. Judgment to Come

13. The Eternal State

PREFACE

These studies were originally written to teach the basics of Scripture to missionary radio listeners. Radio versions have been translated and broadcast in more than a score of languages. Many have trusted Jesus through these studies and others have grown in faith.

This book is an extensive revision of the radio material to make it suitable to publish for reading, studying, and teaching. I believe you will find this book easy to understand. A number of language and formatting styles have been employed to accomplish that purpose:

- **Chapters are divided** into shorter sections, each marked with a "✝" sign for easier reading and study.

- **Easier vocabulary and sentences** are used to make the subjects more quickly understood.

- **Boldfaced subject headings** can give the reader a rapid understanding by scanning them.

- **The NASB uses capital letters** to indicate a quote from the Old Testament in the New Testament.

- **Bible Text Formatting Features:**
  Ample references are used so those who wish to do further study can easily locate verses in their own Bibles.
  Italicized Scripture text makes it easy to distinguish words directly from the Bible.
  Boldfacing is supplied by the author to emphasize certain words of Scripture.

Ellipses (...) have been used to indicate partial verses in indented Bible quotes, but *not* at the beginning or end of those quotes that flow within the text itself.

Brackets [ ] indicate an explanation added by the author.

Please use your Bible to read entire verses within their contexts. Every Christian should be as diligent as the Bereans: *"they received the word with great eagerness, examining the Scriptures daily to see whether these things were so"* (Acts 17:11).

These studies have formed the basis of Bible classes with each section containing sufficient material for a stimulating class discussion. I trust you will find this book very helpful in your life. May God use it to keep many from stumbling into a failed spiritual life.

Eugene Priddy
November, 2007

Chapter 1

God
† His Identity Revealed

God! – Who is He? What is He like? How can I know Him? We must begin here to get right answers about God in order to not stumble spiritually. Therefore, we begin our study with God Himself and how He has shown Himself to us through creation and through the Scriptures. Two ways we can come to know about God are through general knowledge and revealed knowledge. First, let us see how God reveals Himself through the things He has created.

GENERAL REVELATION

God Reveals Himself through Creation

The Scriptures teach that mankind has some knowledge of God apart from the Bible. The Apostle Paul wrote in his letter to the Romans that God has made some things evident to men:

Romans 1:18-20
18 For the wrath of God is revealed from heaven against all ungodliness and unrighteousness of men who suppress the truth in unrighteousness,
19 because that which is known about God is evident within them; for God made it evident to them.

20 For since the creation of the world His invisible attributes, His eternal power and divine nature, have been clearly seen, being understood through what has been made, so that they are without excuse.

Paul taught in these verses that we can know God exists because of the things He made. The world's systems work together like a finely tuned instrument which required an intelligent designer. The human eye alone is a marvel of construction, to say nothing of the rest of the body. It takes more blind faith to believe that all these things just happened than it does to believe that an intelligent God designed them. The same goes for hundreds of thousands of other things on earth and in the heavens. Romans 1:20 says that by *"the creation of the world His invisible attributes, His eternal power and divine nature, have been clearly seen, being understood through what has been made."* When you stand before God on the day He judges mankind, you will be without excuse if you did not believe the evidence. God said that you may learn of His eternal power and divine nature through what He created.

God Reveals Himself within Men

The Bible never tries to prove the existence of God. It starts with a simple statement: *"In the beginning God created the heavens and the earth"* (Genesis 1:1). Thus, the Bible assumes two facts: first, there is a God – that is, He exists – and second, the knowledge that He exists is in the hearts of men, even though some men willfully reject that knowledge.

It has been said that no one has ever been born who did not believe that God exists. Some have been taught to believe there is no God, but they were not born with that belief. The Scriptures support this idea. Solomon, the great and wise king of Israel, tells us that God Himself did something special for men. He said, *"He has also set eternity in their heart"* (Ecclesiastes 3:11). How is it a man can say in the deep recesses of his own soul, "There is no God"? The Scripture plainly tells us the contrary. It tells us men have a sense of eternity placed in their heart by God. Whom are we to believe – God, who says He has *"set eternity in their heart,"* or the atheist who says he does not believe in God or in an afterlife? Obviously, we must believe God.

There are people who deliberately suppress the truth about God within their own heart. The Apostle Peter told us about things as they would be in the last days, the days in which we are living. Speaking about the truth of Jesus' coming again to earth, he said in his second epistle:

2 Peter 3:3-5
3 Know this first of all, that in the last days mockers will come with their mocking, following after their own lusts,
4 and saying, "Where is the promise of His coming? For ever since the fathers fell asleep, all continues just as it was from the beginning of creation."
5 For *they are willfully ignorant of this fact, that by the word of God the heavens existed long ago and the earth was formed out of water and by water. [*Marginal reading]

Peter teaches that people who deny that God is the Creator are willfully ignorant of the fact that He created the heavens long ago. Often, they claim to be open minded, better educated, and more scientific. However, they willfully ignore the facts, according to Peter. The mere fact that Peter wrote that this would happen almost 2,000 years ago is another proof of the reliability of God's Word.

Thus, the Scriptures teach that we may know God exists because of the things He has made. All we need to do is examine the facts with an open mind. Furthermore, God said that He has put a witness to His existence within every man. The problem is that many men, because of sin, willfully fight against the truth and will not receive the truth God has given through creation.

SPECIFIC REVELATION
THROUGH HIS NAMES

God Reveals Himself in the Bible

Even though man has a sense of eternity planted in his heart, he can never understand God simply through creation or find Him by searching. Creation does testify to His existence, but it is woefully limited in telling us who He is. Thankfully, God did not limit Himself to creation as a way to show us that He exists.

We must have the special knowledge God gave about Himself in the Bible in order to come to know Him personally. God, therefore, chose to tell us personally about Himself in specific details through His written word. For example, the Old Testament contains several different names for God which teach us much about His relationship to us.

Elohim: Mighty God

The very first mention of God in the Bible is in the book of Genesis where it is written, *"In the beginning God"* (Genesis 1:1). The word for God there is "Elohim" in the original Hebrew. Elohim is made up of two words. One word means mighty, strong, and prominent. The other word means to declare or to swear. When one swears, he binds himself by an oath. Putting these meanings together, we know God as the mighty One who binds Himself to mankind by His own word and promises, known as covenants. A covenant is a binding agreement between at

14

least two people. In this case it is God who binds Himself by His word to do certain things for us.

"Elohim," the covenant-keeping God, is also the Creator God. He is spoken of not only as the God who made the physical creation in Genesis 1, but also the God who created the angels mentioned throughout the Bible. So, from God's scriptural name Elohim, we learn that He is the all-powerful Creator of spiritual and physical life and that He obligates Himself to mankind by covenant for our good and for our benefit.

El Elyon: God Most High

God revealed Himself to Abraham by His name "El Elyon," which means "God Most High." Melchizedek, a priest of El Elyon, blessed Abraham in this way:

Genesis 14:18-20
18 And Melchizedek king of Salem brought out
*   bread and wine; now he was a priest of God*
*   Most High.*
19 He blessed him and said,
*   "Blessed be Abram of God Most High,*
*   Possessor of heaven and earth;*
20 And blessed be God Most High,
*   Who has delivered your enemies into your*
*   hand. ..."*

This name of God shows that He is the possessor or owner of heaven and earth. God, who created heaven and earth, is the same one who is the rightful owner of that which He made. What does that mean for us now in this modern era? It means that God is able to supply every need we have, both physically and spiritually, because He has His entire creation at His command. The Bible says that God owns the cattle on a thousand hills (Psalm 50:10); He is never short of provision for His people.

Adonai: Master

"Adonai," another name by which God calls Himself, is used some 300 times in the Old Testament. It means "owner" or "master" and shows us that God owns all things. God said to Job, *"Who has given to Me that I should repay him? Whatever is under the whole heaven is Mine"* (Job 41:11). That last phrase includes us, whom He made. Therefore, we owe Him our complete obedience.

It's interesting to notice in passing that both "Elohim" and "Adonai" are plural words. "Adoni," is the singular form of "Adonai." It is often used in the Old Testament in reference to men. However, it is used only one time in the singular in reference to God. That single reference is in Psalm 110:1, which says, *"The LORD says to my Lord: 'Sit at My right hand Until I make Your enemies a footstool for Your feet.'"* The way it is used there strongly implies that God is a trinity. The words, *"The LORD says to my Lord,"* are, in the Hebrew, *"Jehovah says to my Adoni."* Jesus Christ applied this striking passage to Himself in Matthew 22:41-45. It is clearly significant that David, when referring to one member of the Trinity as speaking to another member of the Trinity, used the singular form rather than the plural as is normal when speaking of God. The *"Adoni,"* to whom the LORD said, *"Sit at My right hand, Until I make Your enemies a footstool for Your feet"* refers to Christ, one member of the Trinity!

El Shaddai: the Almighty

"El Shaddai" is the name often translated "the Almighty." For example, God revealed Himself to Abram by that name:

Genesis 17:1-2
1 Now when Abram was ninety-nine years old the LORD appeared to Abram and said to him, "I am God Almighty;
Walk before Me, and be blameless.

16

> 2 *"And I will establish My covenant between Me*
> *and you,*
> *And I will multiply you exceedingly."*

It may be based upon a similar Hebrew word for breast and refers to the one who is the sustainer of those who put their trust in Him. As a young infant feeds at his mother's breast and receives life-sustaining milk, so you and I rely upon the Almighty to be the sustainer of life, particularly of spiritual life.

Another possible meaning is that God is strong and powerful, with power to set aside nature, that is, to perform miracles. For example, Abraham and Sarah were well beyond child-bearing age and yet, contrary to nature, they had a son according to God's promise. God is able to fulfill all His promises!

✝ God – His Special Name Jehovah

The name of God used most often in the Old Testament is Jehovah, especially in His relationship to mankind and our need of salvation. When the name "LORD" is printed in capital letters, it is a translation of the Hebrew name, Jehovah. The book of Jonah tells us plainly that, *"Salvation is from the LORD"* [Jehovah] (Jonah 2:9). Now, we will find out more about the salvation God has provided for us by understanding His name "Jehovah."

The Name Jehovah – I AM
This name comes from an Old Testament word which means "to be" or "the state of being." When God called Moses to lead the Israelites out of Egyptian slavery, He appeared to him in the burning bush that was not consumed with fire. This is an account of God's revelation of Himself at that time:

17

Exodus 3:13-14

13 Then Moses said to God, "Behold, I am going to the sons of Israel, and I will say to them, 'The God of your fathers has sent me to you.' Now they may say to me, 'What is His name?' What shall I say to them?"
14 God said to Moses, "I AM WHO I AM"; and He said, "Thus you shall say to the sons of Israel, 'I AM has sent me to you.'"

God's name, *"I AM WHO I AM,"* is an English translation of a word that is related to the name Jehovah. In the KJV it is translated: *"I AM THAT I AM."* It shows us that God is completely independent of His creation. This name alone is enough to show that the widespread idea that everything in nature is part of God is wrong. He needs no one else and nothing else in order for Him to exist. If everything in the universe vanished into nothing, God would still be there. Nothing came before Him and nothing caused Him to come into being. He exists simply because He exists.

THE COMPOUND NAMES OF JEHOVAH

God has bound Himself in a covenant of personal salvation to all who trust in Him and in His Word. In His relationship to man as Savior, God has revealed Himself to us by using at least eight compound names made up of Jehovah in combination with another name. Each of these eight names of Jehovah God shows us a different aspect of the salvation He has provided.

Jehovah-Jireh: The LORD Will Provide

Jehovah-Jireh was the first compound name God used to reveal Himself to Abraham. It means *"The LORD Will Provide"* (Genesis 22:14). God made the meaning clear to Abraham: *"God will provide for Himself the lamb for the burnt offering"* (Genesis 22:8).

Isaac was Abraham's only son by Sarah, the wife whom he loved. In order to test Abraham's faithfulness, God ordered him to sacrifice Isaac on an altar. The New Testament says Abraham had faith to believe God would raise his son from the dead (Hebrews 11:17-19). Therefore, he obeyed His command. Abraham took Isaac to Mount Moriah, built an altar, bound him, and laid him on it. As he raised the knife to sacrifice him, an angel of the Lord stopped him with a call from heaven. Then God provided a ram caught in a bush for the sacrifice. Thus, Abraham experienced firsthand Jehovah's provision of the necessary sacrifice for his offering.

John the Baptist said about Jesus, *"Behold, the Lamb of God who takes away the sin of the world!"* (John 1:29). Thus God, who provided the sacrifice for Abraham on Mount Moriah, also provided the sacrifice for the sins of the world in the person of Jesus Christ. It is more than chance that the Mount upon which Abraham started to sacrifice his son is the same one upon which Jesus was crucified some 2,000 years later. It is God who takes the first step in our salvation by providing the necessary sacrifice for our sins in the person of Jesus.

Jehovah-Rapha: The LORD your Healer

God also revealed Himself to mankind as the one who heals. Jehovah-Rapha means, *"I, the LORD, am your healer"* (Exodus 15:26). God promised the children of Israel that they would not have the diseases of Egypt if they would listen to Him and do what was right in His sight (Exodus 15:26). It is clear that God was speaking primarily of physical healing. In Psalm 103 David blesses the LORD because He is a healer of those who put their trust in Him.

Psalm 103:1-3
1 Bless the LORD, O my soul,
And all that is within me, bless His holy name.

*2 Bless the L*ORD*, O my soul,*
   And forget none of His benefits;
3 Who pardons all your iniquities;
   Who heals all your diseases.

Throughout Scripture, God is active in healing both spiritually and physically. Jesus Christ healed time and time again in response to faith and in answer to prophecy concerning Him in the Old Testament. Matthew wrote about the healing of Peter's mother-in-law by Jesus:

Matthew 8:14-17
14 When Jesus came into Peter's home, He saw his mother-in-law lying sick in bed with a fever.
15 He touched her hand, and the fever left her; and she got up and waited on Him.
16 When evening came, they brought to Him many who were demon-possessed; and He cast out the spirits with a word, and healed all who were ill.
*17 This was to fulfill what was spoken through Isaiah the prophet: "*HE HIMSELF TOOK OUR INFIRMITIES AND CARRIED AWAY OUR DISEASES.*"*

We should not make the mistake of saying that we do not need doctors. God has given us natural means of healing through the practice of medicine and through the efforts of science and research. However, there are times when the best that the wisdom of men can produce is not enough. God is the only one who can heal what is to us an incurable disease.

Jehovah-Nissi: The LORD Is My Banner

God also revealed Himself as the source of victory in the believer's life. To Moses, Aaron, and Hur, God revealed Himself as Jehovah-Nissi, meaning, *"The L*ORD *is My Banner"* (Exodus 17:15).

They were in a war with Amalek, a picture of the sinful nature of man. As long as Moses held his hands high with the rod of God, the battle went in favor of the Israelites. When he grew tired and his hands dropped, the battle went in favor of Amalek. That is when they found the value of mutual support in the struggles of life. With Aaron and Hur holding up Moses' hands, Israel won the victory. When the battle was over, Moses built an altar and named it, *"The LORD is My Banner"* – Jehovah-Nissi.

A banner is a battle flag. It was very important in war because the troops united around it. If the flag were dropped, another man would quickly pick it up and hold it high so that the troops would not be scattered. *"The LORD is My Banner"* means God is my Defender, my Deliverer, and my Victory. He is the one around whom we rally when life gets hard. This fact puts fear to flight because victory is certain with God.

Jehovah-M'kaddesh: The LORD Who Sanctifies

Jehovah-M'kaddesh, *"the LORD who sanctifies,"* is revealed in Leviticus 20:8. Sanctify means to set apart for God, or to make holy and pure. We hear much teaching about deeper Christian life and sanctification. Sanctification is shown in this name of God to be a work of God Himself. It is God who sets us apart for Himself and enables us to live a life pleasing to Him. He is the one who makes us pure. It is not something we can do for ourselves. We should enter into it with thanksgiving and cooperation.

In another sense, however, we do have a part in sanctifying ourselves. We turn from sin to serve God. Sanctification is both instantaneous and progressive – when God sets us apart for Himself at salvation, it is instantaneous; as we set ourselves apart for Him on an ongoing basis through holy living, it is progressive. This subject will be dealt with in more detail later.

21

Jehovah-Shalom: The LORD Is Peace

God revealed Himself in the book of Judges as Jehovah-Shalom, *"The LORD is Peace"* (Judges 6:24). God offers peace to mankind in two ways. First, He offers peace with Himself through the sacrifice which He has provided. When we accept that which God did for us in Jesus Christ, then we have peace with God. But there is another aspect of peace which we need – peace of mind, heart, and soul. God is absolutely supreme over all, nothing ever takes Him by surprise, nothing can ever change Him. Therefore, He is at perfect peace within Himself. He offers us that same kind of personal peace if we will trust Him. Paul tells us in Philippians:

> Philippians 4:6-7
> *6 Be anxious for nothing, but in everything by prayer and supplication with thanksgiving let your requests be made known to God.*
> *7 And the peace of God, which surpasses all comprehension, will guard your hearts and your minds in Christ Jesus.*

Jehovah-Raah: The LORD Is My Shepherd

Because God offers us personal peace, Psalm 23 takes on deeper meaning. There, He is revealed as Jehovah-Raah, *"The LORD is my shepherd"* (Psalm 23:1). God calls those who love and serve Him *"the sheep of His pasture"* (Psalm 100:3). We are His sheep. The Good Shepherd is Jesus Christ who leads His flock and calls each one by name (John 10:1-18). You and I are known personally by God. In fact, Isaiah tells us that God has engraved our names on the palms of His hands (Isaiah 49:16).

Jehovah-Tsidkenu: The LORD Our Righteousness

In Jeremiah 23:6 God is called Jehovah-Tsidkenu, *"The LORD our righteousness."* When Jesus died on the Cross He did more than pay for the guilt of our sins. He provided a positive righteousness which is ours because the LORD is our righteousness. That which we cannot obtain for ourselves is provided for us by Jesus Christ our Lord. Because God gives us His righteousness, we are fit for heaven.

Jehovah-Shammah: The LORD Is There

Finally, Ezekiel reveals that God is Jehovah-Shammah, *"The LORD is there,"* or the LORD who is present (Ezekiel 48:35). God is with us even when we do not feel His presence. Jesus promised, *"lo, I am with you always, even to the end of the age"* (Matthew 28:20). We can count upon the presence of Jesus Christ in every circumstance, at all times, without exception. He is always with us to help us. Do not rely upon how you feel to determine if the LORD is or is not present. Instead, rely on what He has told you in His Word – the LORD who is present is His name.

† God – His Triune Being

God is a complex being. That fact gives many people difficulty in trying to understand Him. While we cannot completely understand everything about Him, we can know about His three-in-one nature because the Bible tells us about it. The word "trinity" refers to the one God existing as Father, Son, and Holy Spirit, all at the same time, One in essence, but all distinct persons.

God – Three-in-One

The Bible is clear that while God is one God, He is revealed in three persons called the "Trinity." The word "trinity" is not in the Bible, but it does describe His nature. God is a three-part unity; but He is not three individual beings. There are some illustrations which help us understand a three-part unity, though they cannot fully explain it, because there is nothing in our earthly experience like it.

However, here are two illustrations that can give us limited insight into the nature of the Trinity: First, in the Old Testament (Numbers 13), twelve men were sent to spy out the land of Canaan and came back with a large bunch of grapes. Each grape drew life from one stem, but together they made just one bunch of grapes. Second, scientifically, water can be steam, liquid, or ice, all made of the same thing. It illustrates unity of being with differences in expression. Nevertheless, no illustration can really describe God in a way that can be easily understood.

The biblical teaching may be stated this way: the Father, the Son, and the Holy Spirit are each God, each having personality, and yet there is only one God. God is a tri-unity, each person being equal to the others in power, nature, and eternity.

THE TRINITY IN THE OLD TESTAMENT

Here, briefly, is the biblical teaching about the three-in-one nature of God. The Old Testament uses many plural words when referring to God. The very names of God in the original language, "Elohim" and "Adonai," are plural rather than singular, as was pointed out earlier in this chapter.

Creation of Man

As God started to create man, He said, *"Let Us make man in Our image, according to Our likeness"* (Genesis 1:26). Notice that He used the plural *"Us"* and *"Our"* speaking of Himself. Some people teach that God was speaking to angels. However, angels had not yet been mentioned in the Bible. Furthermore, though angels are spirit beings (Hebrews 1:14), they are never said to be created in God's image as men are. When God said *"in Our image,"* He meant in His own personal image because verse 27 says, *"God created man in His own image, in the*

24

image of God He created him; male and female He created them."

Expulsion from Eden

Another indication of God's three-in-one nature is in the passage where He expelled Adam and Eve from the Garden of Eden because of their sin:

Genesis 3:22-23
22 Then the LORD God said, "Behold, the man has become like one of Us, knowing good and evil; and now, he might stretch out his hand, and take also from the tree of life, and eat, and live forever" –
23 therefore the LORD God sent him out from the garden of Eden ...

Notice the plural pronoun *"Us."* It is clear that God is discussing with Himself the expulsion of Adam and Eve from the Garden.

Confusion of Languages

Genesis tells about the erection of the tower of Babel against God's wishes. Seeing that, God said, *"Come, let Us go down and there confuse their language, so that they will not understand one another's speech"* (Genesis 11:7). Verse eight shows that God had been talking with Himself when He said, *"let Us go down."* Verse eight does not say "God and the angels scattered them," but *"the LORD scattered them."* Again, here at the tower of Babel, the Lord refers to Himself as *"Us."*

Isaiah's Call

Isaiah 6 is another place where God refers to Himself as *"Us."* Isaiah the prophet discusses his call to the ministry and his vision of the Lord high and lifted up. Isaiah 6:8 says, *"Then I heard the voice of the Lord, saying, 'Whom shall I send, and who will go for Us?' Then I said, 'Here am I. Send me!'"* Once again, God is speaking and He is saying, *"who will go for Us?"* Isaiah did not seem to have any problem with that, even though he lived in Old Testament times and was seeing God high and lifted up on His throne. A few verses before, the prophet wrote that it *"is the LORD of hosts, The whole earth is full of His glory"* (Isaiah 6:3). It is obvious that God referred to Himself using plural pronouns and gave a clear declaration that He is one God.

The Pierced LORD
One important Old Testament passage indicating the trinitarian nature of God is found in Zechariah 12. The discussion of that verse is being reserved until the next section about the nature of God.

THE TRINITY IN THE NEW TESTAMENT

At Jesus' Birth
Luke 1:35 refers to the Father, Son, and Holy Spirit in one verse. An angel says to Mary, the mother of Jesus, *"The Holy Spirit will come upon you, and the power of the Most High will overshadow you; and for that reason the holy Child shall be called the Son of God."* Notice all three members of the Trinity were involved here: the Holy Spirit, the Most High God, and the Son of God.

At Jesus' Baptism
At the baptism of Jesus: *"the Holy Spirit descended upon Him in bodily form like a dove, and a voice came out of heaven, 'You are My beloved Son, in You I am well-pleased'"* (Luke 3:22). Again, we find Jesus, the Holy Spirit, and the voice of God the Father from heaven claiming Christ as His own beloved Son.

Unity of Father and Son
The relationship between God the Father and Jesus is brought out clearly in John's Gospel. Jesus said, *"I and the*

26

Father are one" (John 10:30*)*. The meaning of the word "one" shows that they are one in nature and being. This relationship also shows when Philip asked, *"show us the Father"* (John 14:8). Jesus responded, *"He who has seen Me has seen the Father ... Do you not believe that I am in the Father, and the Father is in Me? ... the Father abiding in Me does His works"* (John 14:9-10).

God the Holy Spirit

Acts 5:3-4 shows that Peter regarded the Holy Spirit as a member of the Godhead. He called Him *"God"* when he said to Ananias, *"why has Satan filled your heart to lie to the Holy Spirit ... You have not lied to men, but to God."*

Paul Mentions the Godhead

And, of course, Paul's epistles are filled with references to the Trinity. Look at just one example, the blessing given by Paul in 2 Corinthians 13:14, *"The grace of the Lord Jesus Christ, and the love of God* [the Father], *and the fellowship of the Holy Spirit, be with you all."* Once again, Father, Son, and Holy Spirit appear together in one verse.

The Entire Godhead Participates in Salvation

God the Father is active: Jesus said, *"No one can come to Me unless the Father who sent Me draws him"* (John 6:44). God the Son is active: because He said, *"no one comes to the Father but through Me"* (John 14:6). God the Holy Spirit is also active: Paul wrote, *"no one can say, 'Jesus is Lord,' except by the Holy Spirit"* (1 Corinthians 12:3; see Romans 10:9-10).

The Godhead is also at work in choosing God's people and enabling them to live a godly life. We are: 1) loved by the Lord Jesus, *"Just as the Father has loved Me, I have also loved you"* (John 15:9); 2) chosen by God the Father, *"So, as those who have been chosen of God, holy and beloved* (Colossians 3:12); and 3) sanctified by the Holy

Spirit, *"that my offering of the Gentiles may become acceptable, sanctified by the Holy Spirit"* (Romans 15:16).

Christians may be: 1) filled with all the fulness of God, *"that you may be filled up to all the fulness of God"* (Ephesians 3:19); 2) filled up with the fulness of Christ, *"until we all attain to the unity of the faith, and of the knowledge of the Son of God, to a mature man, to the measure of the stature which belongs to the fulness of Christ"* (Ephesians 4:13); and 3) filled with the Spirit, *"but be filled with the Spirit"* (Ephesians 5:18*).*

The Lord God Almighty – Father, Son, and Holy Spirit – is the object of our faith. No man truly understands the idea of the Trinity, but it is clearly taught in the Bible. It is truth beyond the range of human experience; therefore, it is difficult, if not impossible, for man to understand. However, the Trinity is the perfect balm for the healing and perfection of the soul; a lesser god is never adequate.

✝ God – His Awesome Nature

No one can come to have true knowledge about God simply by searching or by reasoning. He must turn to the Bible, only real source of true knowledge about God. He clearly declares to be speaking in the Scriptures and therein gives us information about Himself that we cannot find elsewhere. Now, we will examine the nature of God, including His natural and moral qualities, which some like to call His perfections.

God Is Spirit

One of the first things we must understand about God is that He is spirit. In John's Gospel, Jesus discussed with the Samaritan woman where and how to worship God:

John 4:23-24
23 "But an hour is coming, and now is, when the true worshipers will worship the Father in spirit and truth; for such people the Father seeks to be His worshipers.
24 "God is spirit, and those who worship Him must worship in spirit and truth."

God Is a Trinity
The entire previous section was about the trinitarian nature of God. It is very much an essential part of what He is like. One important passage we did not discuss from the Old Testament is found in Zechariah; it refers to the pierced LORD. Its wording is unique in all the Scripture. It is a very interesting prophecy concerning the second coming of Jesus Christ. The LORD God is speaking and says, *"I will pour out on the house of David and on the inhabitants of Jerusalem, the Spirit of grace and of supplication, so that they will look on Me whom they have pierced; and they will mourn for Him"* (Zechariah 12:10). How very important this verse is! The chapter is a declaration of *"the LORD who stretches out the heavens, lays the foundation of the earth, and forms the spirit of man within him"* (Zechariah 12:1). It is the LORD God who is saying, *"they will look on Me whom they have pierced."*

Notice something very different about this verse. Right in the middle of the sentence the pronoun is changed from *"Me"* to *"Him."* It reads, *"they will look on Me whom they have pierced; and they will mourn for Him."* This verse is a beautiful Old Testament illustration of the fact that while the Lord is One, He was to come in the flesh and be pierced with a spear (John 19:34).

The fulfillment of this prophecy is shown to us in the New Testament book of the Revelation. The Apostle John wrote about the second coming of Jesus Christ to earth, *"BEHOLD, HE IS COMING WITH THE CLOUDS, and every eye will* see Him, even those who pierced Him; and all the tribes of the earth will mourn over Him. So it is to be. Amen" (Revelation 1:7). Zechariah's prophecy made over 500 years before Christ will be fulfilled at least 2,500 years after it was written. It will not be long, if I understand prophecy correctly, before this verse will literally come to pass.

God Is the Source of Life

In John 4:24 quoted above, Jesus declared that God is spirit. But not only is God spirit, He is a living, personal spirit being. Jeremiah 10:10 says, *"the LORD is the true God; He is the living God and the everlasting King."* In Revelation 4:10, the heavenly creatures worship God as *"Him who lives forever and ever."*

The only self-existent, living God is the One who gives life to all things. Within His very being is the essence and source of all life. Paul wrote to Timothy, *"I charge you in the presence of God, who gives life to all things"* (1 Timothy 6:13). Everything that has life, including you and me, owes its life to God.

God Is the Supreme Being

Not only is the living God an eternal, life-giving spirit, He is also the only Supreme Being. By definition the word "supreme" allows only *one* God without equal, above and beyond all other so-called gods. God was quoted by the prophet Isaiah as saying, *"I am the first and I am the last, And there is no God besides Me"* (Isaiah 44:6).

In the New Testament, Paul made a similar statement about God when he wrote,

1 Corinthians 8:4-6
*4 Therefore concerning the eating of things sacrificed to idols, we know that there is no such thing as an idol in the world, and that **there is no God but one.***

30

5 For even if there are so-called gods whether in heaven or on earth, as indeed there are many gods and many lords,
6 yet for us there is but one God, the Father, from whom are all things, and we exist for Him; and one Lord, Jesus Christ, by whom are all things, and we exist through Him.

Thus, there are declarations, both in the Old Testament and in the New Testament, that God is the one and only supreme and sovereign God.

HIS SOVEREIGN ATTRIBUTES

God's attributes expressed in His being are both non-moral and moral in nature. His non-moral attributes are His intrinsic abilities; His moral attributes have to do with His character. We will deal with His non-moral abilities first.

God Is All-Knowing (Omniscient)

The Bible teaches that God knows everything about all things. He knows everything about you and me. Solomon wrote, *"the ways of a man are before the eyes of the LORD, And He watches all his paths"* (Proverbs 5:21). He also wrote, *"The eyes of the LORD are in every place, Watching the evil and the good"* (Proverbs 15:3). In the New Testament, Hebrews 4:13 says, *"there is no creature hidden from His sight, but all things are open and laid bare to the eyes of Him with whom we have to do."* Yes, God knows every thought, word, and deed of all His creatures.

God Is All-Powerful (Omnipotent)

God likewise has all power in heaven and on earth. For that reason He is called the Almighty God. The LORD said to Abraham in Genesis 18:14, *"Is anything too difficult for the LORD?"* Job said to the LORD, *"I know that You can do all things, And that no purpose of Yours can be thwarted"* (Job 42:2).

31

God Is Present Everywhere (Omnipresent)

Not only does God know all things and is all-powerful, but He is also present everywhere at all times. There is no place one can flee from Him, for He is there. In Jeremiah, God said:

Jeremiah 23:23-24
23 *"Am I a God who is near," declares the LORD,*
    "And not a God far off?
24 *"Can a man hide himself in hiding places*
    So I do not see him?" declares the LORD.
    "Do I not fill the heavens and the earth?"
    Declares the LORD.

God is present with both you and me even though we may be separated by a great distance.

God Is without Beginning or End (Eternal)

Paul wrote in praise of God: *"Now to the King eternal, immortal, invisible, the only God, be honor and glory forever and ever. Amen"* (1 Timothy 1:17). An Old Testament prophet asked the question, *"Are You not from everlasting, O LORD, my God, my Holy One?"* (Habakkuk 1:12). One of many places where that question is answered is Psalm 90:2: *"Even from everlasting to everlasting, You are God."* We have difficulty with this concept because everything in our experience had a beginning.

God Does Not Change (Immutable)

One of the most comforting things about God is that He does not change. He is perfection itself. If He were to change, He would become less than perfect. Because He is perfect, He will not change. He Himself proclaimed, *"For I, the LORD, do not change"* (Malachi 3:6). James 1:17 says, *"Every good thing given and every perfect gift is from above, coming down from the Father of lights, with whom there is no variation or shifting shadow."* We can always count on God because He does not change His mind from one minute to the next. He is completely reliable.

32

HIS MORAL ATTRIBUTES

The intrinsic moral attributes of God that express His character are also shown to us in the Word of God.

God Is Holy

Perhaps the most outstanding characteristic of God is His holiness, because it stands out in sharp contrast to what we know of human nature. Because God is absolutely holy, He is without sin. Peter exhorts us to holy living because God is holy:

1 Peter 1:15-16
15 ... like the Holy One who called you, be holy yourselves also in all your behavior;
16 because it is written, "YOU SHALL BE HOLY, FOR I AM HOLY."

God Is Righteous

Jesus called Him *"righteous Father"* in His prayer in John 17:25. Righteousness is a direct result of being innately holy. Because God is holy, He will always do the right thing. It is very reassuring and comforting to know that the God of all the earth always does the right thing without fail. We can say with Abraham, *"Far be it from You to do such a thing, to slay the righteous with the wicked, so that the righteous and the wicked are treated alike. Far be it from You! Shall not the Judge of all the earth deal justly?"* (Genesis 18:25).

God Is Faithful

God always keeps His word. He is faithful to His own nature and to His people. Again, He never fails to keep His promises to mankind. Paul wrote, *"If we are faithless, He remains faithful, for He cannot deny Himself"* (2 Timothy 2:13). He is also faithful to provide us a way of escape from temptation: *"No temptation has overtaken you but such as is common to man; and God is faithful, who will*

33

not allow you to be tempted beyond what you are able, but with the temptation will provide the way of escape also, that you will be able to endure it" (1 Corinthians 10:13).

God Is Merciful

Mercy is God showing His goodness, compassion, and love toward those who deserve His wrath and punishment. Someone has said, "What we need is mercy, not justice!" If we were to be judged and sentenced solely on the basis of justice, every one of us would be in trouble! Actually, both justice and mercy are an essential part of God's character. God can, therefore, meet both needs for mankind. The great psalmist of Israel, King David, spoke of the mercy of God. He wrote: *"But You, O Lord, are a God merciful and gracious, Slow to anger and abundant in lovingkindness and truth"* (Psalm 86:15). And in Psalm 145:8 he wrote, *"The LORD is gracious and merciful; Slow to anger and great in lovingkindness."* Jesus instructed us: *"Be merciful, just as your Father is merciful"* (Luke 6:36).

God Is Loving

The most famous verse in all the Bible expresses the love of God for a lost world: *"For God so loved the world, that He gave His only begotten Son, that whoever believes in Him should not perish, but have eternal life"* (John 3:16). The Apostle John tells us: *"The one who does not love does not know God, for God is love"* (1 John 4:8).

MAKE GOD PERSONAL

God is the only holy, righteous, loving, supreme being. He created all things; therefore each of us owes Him our life and devotion. Because He is God, He is a very complex being who has revealed Himself as a Trinity – Father, Son, and Holy Spirit.

Peter wrote that God's *"divine power **has granted to us everything pertaining to life and godliness**, through the true knowledge of Him who called us by His own glory and excellence"* (2 Peter 1:3). He has provided for our salvation, healing, defending, and sanctifying. He is our peace, our shepherd, and our righteousness. He is always with us.

As believers, we can be at peace knowing that He is absolutely good. We rest in the sure confidence of His willingness and ability to help us. On the one hand, He is all powerful, and on the other hand, He is loving and merciful. It does not matter what your personal need may be, He is more than willing and able to meet it.

It is important to serve the one true God of heaven and earth. That is the only way to keep from stumbling spiritually, for He alone is the covenant-making and covenant-keeping God.

God in the flesh, the Lord Jesus Christ, was crucified on the Cross for your sin and mine. If you will receive Him as your own Lord and Savior, He will free you from the guilt and burden of your sins, and give you eternal life, guaranteeing you an abundant entrance into heaven.

Won't you confess your sins to God and ask Him to forgive and cleanse you because Christ died for you on Calvary. He was resurrected, and now sits at God's right hand. You can trust Him completely. He will never fail you.

Ephesians 2:4-5
4 But God, being rich in mercy, because of His great love with which He loved us,
5 even when we were dead in our transgressions, made us alive together with Christ (by grace you have been saved).

Chapter 2

Jesus Christ
† A Unique Person
WHO IS HE?

What you believe about Jesus Christ is crucial to your eternal salvation. If Jesus were only a man, He would have been born a sinner like the rest of us. If He were only God, He could not have died. In either case, we would still be in our sins. He had to be both God and man! The virgin birth, His substitutionary atonement, His bodily resurrection, and other basic doctrines are extremely important. They cannot be shrugged off lightly as though they do not matter. Many people are being led astray on these issues and, as a result, are stumbling spiritually. We will be discussing Jesus in the next several sections and answering questions such as: "Who is Jesus?"; "Why did He come?"; and "What is He doing now?"

The single most important question you and I face in life is: Who is Jesus Christ? As a matter of fact, Jesus spent most of His ministry teaching His disciples the answer to that question. He did not begin by saying to them, "Follow Me, I am the Son of God." He approached them and said, *"Follow Me, I will make you fishers of men"* (Matthew 4:19). During the following three and a half years or so, Jesus taught them, performed miracles, healed the sick, and cast out demons in their presence. Slowly but surely, the apostles came to realize just who He really was.

JESUS, SON OF GOD

We find Jesus and His disciples in Caesarea Philippi. The Scripture reads, *"He began asking His disciples, saying, 'Who do people say that the Son of Man is?'"* (Matthew 16:13). It should be noted that the term *"Son of Man"* is a Jewish term referring to the Messiah. So He was asking, "Who do the Jews say Messiah is?" – *"Who do people say that the Son of Man is?"* The conversation continued:

Matthew 16:14-16
14 And they said, "Some say John the Baptist; and others, Elijah; but still others, Jeremiah, or one of the prophets."
15 He said to them, "But who do you say that I am?"
16 Simon Peter answered, "You are the Christ, the Son of the living God."

Jesus Is God in the Flesh

The first chapter of the Gospel of John says something very important about Jesus Christ. It cannot be said about any other man. John calls Him *"the Word"* that was with God in the beginning:

John 1:1-3, 14
1 In the beginning was the Word, and the Word was with God, and the Word was God.
2 He was in the beginning with God.
3 All things came into being through Him, and apart from Him nothing came into being that has come into being.

14 And the Word became flesh, and dwelt among us, and we saw His glory, glory as of the only begotten from the Father, full of grace and truth.

Verse one says, *"In the beginning was the Word, and the Word was with God, and the Word was God"* (John 1:1). In the original language, the word *"with"* in this sentence means "toward" or "facing." In the beginning, *"the Word"* was facing God or was "face to face" with God. It expresses a very close, intimate, personal relationship between the Word, who became flesh in verse 14, and God the Father. Verse two emphasizes that the Word was with God in the beginning!

Not only was He in close relationship with the Father, He was, in fact, God. The original sentence order is *"and God was the Word."* In that verse, *"Word"* has a definite article showing that it is the subject of the sentence. The word *"God"* is without the article and means God in His nature or being. Jesus, therefore, is God in the very nature of His being. In the original text, the word for God appears first in the phrase, even though it is not the subject, emphasizing that the Word **is** God. The main point is this: Jesus is truly God in the flesh – God with us.

Jesus Is Creator

John's Gospel goes on to say, *"All things came into being through Him, and apart from Him nothing came into being that has come into being"* (John 1:3). The Word, which later became flesh, was the Creator of all things, whether visible or invisible, whether they be thrones, principalities, powers, or dominions, or any other thing that can be named. They came into being through Him and for Him:

> Colossians 1:15-16
> *15 He is the image of the invisible God, the first-born of all creation.*
> *16 For by Him all things were created, both in the heavens and on earth, visible and invisible, whether thrones or dominions or rulers or authorities – all things have been created through Him and for Him.*

The entire Trinity was involved in the creation of everything that exists. However, the verses above put the emphasis on the part *"the Word"* (Jesus) played in creation.

Jesus Existed before His Human Birth

Look again at John 1:14, *"And the Word became flesh, and dwelt among us, and we saw His glory, glory as of the only begotten from the Father, full of grace and truth."* This verse teaches that Jesus existed before His birth in Bethlehem. *"The Word"* was from the beginning with God and became the man, Jesus.

Even Jesus Himself recognized this as He prayed to the Father in John 17. In that prayer, He said, *"Now, Father, glorify Me together with Yourself, with the glory which I had with You before the world was"* (John 17:5). Jesus clearly acknowledged that He was with the Father before the world was created.

Jesus Is God According to Paul

Paul taught that Jesus is God in such passages as Titus 2:13 in which he said we are to be *"looking for the blessed hope and the appearing of the glory of our great God and Savior, Christ Jesus."* In this verse, Jesus is called both great God and Savior.

Paul expanded on this truth in his other letters, such as Colossians where he wrote about Jesus Christ:

Colossians 1:15-17
15 He is the image of the invisible God, the first-born of all creation.
16 ... all things have been created through Him and for Him.
17 He is before all things, and in Him all things hold together.

As the image of God, Jesus is an accurate representation of God. If you want to know and understand God, study

39

Jesus! It is clearly stated that *"He is before all things"* and *"all things have been created through Him."* The term *"first-born of all creation"* refers to Jesus as the first man to be resurrected from the dead never to die again (Colossians 1:18). It does not mean that He was the first thing God created as some teach. Therefore, not only is Jesus Christ the Anointed Savior sent from God to save His people from their sins, but He is in every sense God Himself, not a created being.

Jesus Is God According to God the Father

Other New Testament writers make the same point. One of them was the writer of Hebrews. He quotes God the Father, who calls Jesus *"God"* in these verses:

Hebrews 1:8-9
8 *But of the Son He says,*
    "YOUR THRONE, O GOD, IS FOREVER AND EVER ...
9 *"YOU HAVE LOVED RIGHTEOUSNESS AND HATED LAW-*
    LESSNESS;
    THEREFORE GOD, YOUR GOD, HAS ANOINTED YOU
    WITH THE OIL OF GLADNESS ABOVE YOUR COMPAN-
    IONS."

In the same verses, His humanity is likewise recognized when God says, *"Therefore God, Your God, has anointed You with the oil of gladness above Your companions."* Here Jesus is said to have companions that have been anointed with the oil of gladness; but the anointing of Jesus was greater than that of His companions.

JESUS, SON OF MAN

Jesus Is Fully Man

In answering the question "Who is Jesus?" we cannot stop with the idea that He is fully God, because He is also fully man. He was born into the human race, *"born of a descendant of David according to the flesh"* (Romans 1:3).

40

He is not just a human body with God living inside; He is fully man because He has a human spirit, soul, and body.

The truth that Jesus is the Son of God is very important, but its companion truth is just as important for our salvation. If Jesus were only God, we would still be lost in our sins. We will look at the virgin birth and see what the Bible says about Jesus being fully man, and we will see why it was necessary for God to become a man.

Jesus – Born of a Virgin
The question is, "If Jesus Christ is God and existed prior to His birth in Bethlehem, then just how did He become a man?" The answer is found in the virgin birth, a teaching which has been ridiculed by many unbelievers. It is interesting that Luke, a physician, has a great deal to say about the virgin birth:

Luke 1:26-27
26 Now in the sixth month the angel Gabriel was sent from God to a city in Galilee called Nazareth,
27 to a virgin engaged to a man whose name was Joseph, of the descendants of David; and the virgin's name was Mary.

The next three verses of Luke are not quoted because they are not relevant to this particular study. We continue with verse 31:

Luke 1:31-33
31 "And behold, you will conceive in your womb and bear a son, and you shall name Him Jesus.
32 "He will be great and will be called the Son of the Most High; and the Lord God will give Him the throne of His father David;
33 and He will reign over the house of Jacob forever, and His kingdom will have no end."

Mary was very surprised by what the angel said and she replied:

41

Luke 1:34-35
34 ... "How can this be, since I am a virgin?"
35 The angel answered and said to her, "The Holy Spirit will come upon you, and the power of the Most High will overshadow you; and for that reason the holy Child shall be called the Son of God."

Verse 35 explains how the living Word of God came to be man. The Holy Spirit came upon the virgin Mary and the power of the Most High overshadowed her; she conceived the holy offspring by God, making Jesus the Son of God. God was the Father of Jesus and Mary was His mother through the Holy Spirit by the miracle of the virgin birth. Mary is the mother of Jesus from His human side; she is not the mother of God, for God was His Father.

A reference to the virgin birth is found as early as Genesis 3:15. God promised Eve, after she had sinned, that the *"seed"* of woman would bruise the head of the serpent, Satan. That was the first prophecy of the coming of Jesus and His victory over Satan. Interestingly, the Bible often speaks of the "seed" of man when telling of the birth of ordinary men. However, it speaks only of the *"seed"* of woman in reference to Jesus.* This is because He is the only man who was born without a human father. *(Note: in one place, 1 Samuel 2:20 KJV, at first glance *"seed"* seems to be used in connection with *"seed"* of a woman. However, it is used for children of Elkanah and Hannah, not for a *"seed"* produced by her. See 1 Samuel 2:20 NASB.)

Jesus Had a Human Body
It is clearly evident in the Bible that Jesus had a physical body. John declared in his first epistle:

1 John 1:1-2
1 What was from the beginning, what we have heard, what we have seen with our eyes, what we

42

> *have looked at and touched with our hands,*
> *concerning the Word of Life--*
> *2 and the life was manifested, and we have seen*
> *and testify and proclaim to you the eternal life ,*
> *which was with the Father and was manifested to*
> *us –*

John and the other apostles heard, saw, and felt with their hands the Word of Life, that is, Jesus Christ in the flesh. Hebrews 2:14 says, *"Therefore, since the children share in flesh and blood, He Himself likewise also partook of the same..."* Matthew 26:12 quotes Jesus as saying, *"she poured this perfume on My body."* These verses are sufficient to demonstrate that Jesus had a real human body. His resurrection body is also a human body, but a glorified one.

Jesus Has a Human Soul and Spirit

Though Jesus was filled with the Holy Spirit, He also had His own human soul and spirit. In Matthew 26:38, Jesus recognized His own human soul when He said, *"My soul is deeply grieved."* Finally, when He died on the Cross, He said with a loud voice, *"Father, INTO YOUR HANDS I COMMIT MY SPIRIT"* (Luke 23:46).

Jesus Had Natural Human Limitations

Jesus was subject to those limitations which bear no relationship to sin. Take note of some of the human experiences Jesus encountered:

He was hungry in the wilderness	Matthew 4:2
He was asleep in the boat	Matthew 8:24
He mourned over Jerusalem	Matthew 23:37-39
He desired companionship	Matthew 26:38, 40
He was weary from His journey	John 4:6
He wept over the death of a friend	John 11:35
He was thirsty on the Cross	John 19:28

Jesus experienced the total range of human emotion and temptation because He was *"tempted in all things as we are, yet without sin"* (Hebrews 4:15).

The fact that He is fully human, but without sin, qualified Him to be the sacrifice for sinful humanity. Since He is God, His death has infinite value so that He died for one and for all at the same time. He is the God-Man – both fully God and fully man. Both of these are equally true: one cannot reject the deity of Jesus without doing away with the all-sufficiency of His sacrifice; and one cannot reject the humanity of Jesus without doing away with the only satisfactory sacrifice for sin. Tampering with the biblical teaching about Christ leads to stumbling spiritually! Holding either of the two errors can keep a person from being saved. It is important to know that Jesus Christ is a complete human being because His humanity is made up of spirit, soul, and body like everyone else. As a human, Jesus is a faithful and merciful High Priest to represent us before God (Hebrews 2:17).

WHY JESUS HAD TO BE A MAN

Hebrews 1 gives seven reasons why Jesus Christ was God in the flesh. We pointed out some of these earlier. This time we want to see in Hebrews 2 the seven reasons why Jesus left heaven's glory and became a man:

Hebrews 2:5-8
5   For He [God] did not subject to angels the world to come, concerning which we are speaking.
6   But one has testified somewhere, saying,
"What is man, that You remember him?
Or the son of man, that You are concerned about him?
7   "You have made him FOR A LITTLE WHILE LOWER THAN THE ANGELS;

44

YOU HAVE CROWNED HIM WITH GLORY AND HONOR,
AND HAVE APPOINTED HIM OVER THE WORKS OF YOUR
HANDS;
8 YOU HAVE PUT ALL THINGS IN SUBJECTION UNDER HIS
FEET. "

The World to Come Is Subjected to Man

Jesus became a man because the world to come is to be subjected to man and not to angels. Man fell for Satan's temptation and sinned, thus subjecting himself to Satan's dominion. Therefore, it was necessary for God to become a man in the person of Jesus Christ. He defeated Satan and became the head of a new group of men whom He delivered from Satan's dominion (Colossians 1:13). Jesus then, as a true man, is the one to whom the world to come will be subjected.

To Bring Many Sons to Glory

Jesus became a man in order to bring many sons to glory. Hebrews 2 tells us why this is true:

Hebrews 2:9-10
9 But we do see Him who was made for a little while lower than the angels, namely, Jesus, because of the suffering of death crowned with glory and honor, so that by the grace of God He might taste death for everyone.
10 For it was fitting for Him, for whom are all things, and through whom are all things, in bringing many sons to glory, to perfect the author of their salvation through sufferings.

Here we see that God's intention is to bring many sons to glory. To accomplish this there had to be a Savior fitted for the task. He had to be taken from among men (Hebrews 5:1), i.e., one of the kind who was to be saved. Therefore, God became man that through the suffering of death on the Cross He might bring many sons to glory.

Prophecy Had to Be Fulfilled

Another reason Jesus had to become a man was to fulfill the Old Testament Scriptures. Hebrews refers to Psalm 22:22 and Isaiah 8:17-18 in this passage:

> Hebrews 2:11-13
>
> *11 For both He who sanctifies and those who are sanctified are all from one Father; for which reason He is not ashamed to call them brethren,*
> *12 saying,*
>
> *"I WILL PROCLAIM YOUR NAME TO MY BRETHREN,*
> *IN THE MIDST OF THE CONGREGATION I WILL SING YOUR PRAISE."*
>
> *13 And again, "I WILL PUT MY TRUST IN HIM."*
> *And again, "BEHOLD, I AND THE CHILDREN WHOM GOD HAS GIVEN ME."*

The Messiah was to proclaim in the midst of the congregation the praise of God and say, *"Behold, I and the children whom God has given Me."* God became the man Jesus in order to fulfill prophetic Scripture.

To Render the Devil Powerless

Hebrews 2:14-15 gives us a wonderful reason why Jesus became man! God had to become man to defeat Satan and rob him of the sting of death. The Scripture says,

> Hebrews 2:14-15
>
> *14 Therefore, since the children share in flesh and blood, He Himself likewise also partook of the same, that through death He might render powerless him who had the power of death, that is, the devil,*
> *15 and might deliver those who through fear of death were subject to slavery all their lives.*

Notice the past tense in, *"him who had the power of death."* Jesus took away the power of death from the devil. Elsewhere, the Apostle Paul wrote:

46

2. Jesus Christ – A Unique Person

1 Corinthians 15:56-57
56 The sting of death is sin, and the power of sin is the law;
57 but thanks be to God, who gives us the victory through our Lord Jesus Christ.

We may not want to die, but we have no reason to really fear death because we know what happens afterward!

To Deliver Us from Slavery to Satan
Jesus left heaven's glory so that He *"might free those who through fear of death were subject to slavery all their lives"* (Hebrews 2:15). Jesus delivers those who come to Him – those who had been in slavery to Satan because they feared death. Verse 16 goes on to say, *"For assuredly He does not give help to angels, but He gives help to the descendant of Abraham."* Paul tells us that those who belong to Jesus are the offspring of Abraham (Galatians 3:29). Believers need have no fear of death because the sting of death has been taken away by Christ (1 Corinthians 15:55-57). We can serve Jesus in peace and in joy because we are no longer in slavery to Satan.

To Provide Us a Perfect High Priest
The sixth reason why Jesus became man is that we need a perfect high priest – *"Therefore, He had to be made like His brethren in all things, so that He might become a merciful and faithful high priest in things pertaining to God, to make propitiation for the sins of the people"* (Hebrews 2:17). Jesus is a merciful High Priest because He understands us since He is one of us. He is a faithful High Priest because He is God in the flesh and He remains faithful to God.

To Aid Those Who Are Tempted
Our final reason is found in Hebrews 2:18. God became a man to deliver those who are tempted. The verse says this, *"For since He Himself was tempted in that which He has suffered, He is able to come to the aid of those who*

are tempted." If you need help in your temptation, Jesus Christ is the one who knows how to deliver you. He is the one who has suffered in all ways as we have, yet without sin. And He is able to deliver you from temptation. Paul wrote: *"No temptation has overtaken you but such as is common to man; and God is faithful, who will not allow you to be tempted beyond what you are able, but with the temptation will provide the way of escape also, so that you may be able to endure it"* (1 Corinthians 10:13).

✝ Jesus Christ — A Unique Mission
WHY DID HE COME?

Jesus Is the Savior Appointed by God

Peter's confession about Jesus was that He is the Christ, the Son of the living God. In those days, as it is in some places today, the name given to a person had a particular meaning. An angel said to Joseph in a dream, *"you shall call His name Jesus, for He will save His people from their sins"* (Matthew 1:21). The very name "Jesus" means "savior" and the word "Christ" means "anointed." To "anoint" in a religious sense is a ceremonial application of oil to set apart for a sacred service. Thus, Jesus Christ has been set apart by God for the sacred service of being the Savior of men.

He Came in Obedience to God

The question, "Why did He come?" implies a fact about Jesus which is not true of any other person who ever lived. He existed with God before His birth in Bethlehem (John 1:1). Therefore, He had a reason for coming into the world as God manifest in the flesh. Just what was His reason? Philippians 2 describes His leaving heaven's glory to become a man who was obedient to God:

48

Philippians 2:5-8
5 Have this attitude in yourselves which was also in Christ Jesus,
6 who, although He existed in the form of God, did not regard equality with God a thing to be grasped,
7 but emptied Himself, taking the form of a bond-servant, and being made in the likeness of men.
8 Being found in appearance as a man, He humbled Himself by becoming obedient to the point of death, even death on a cross.

The point of His coming to the earth is found in that last verse. He came in obedience to God, which led Him to Calvary. Why was obedience to the point of death necessary? The answer is in many books of the Bible, but we will look briefly at the Gospel of Mark to find the answer.

A RANSOM FOR MANY

Mark answers the question asked in previous section, "Who is Jesus?" as well as the question before us, "Why did He come?" The first eight chapters gradually reveal who Jesus is; the full answer is given in Mark 8:29. Peter confessed to Jesus, *"You are the Christ."* From that time on Jesus began to reveal why He came. Mark explained, *"And He began to teach them that the Son of Man must suffer many things and be rejected by the elders and the chief priests and the scribes, and be killed, and after three days rise again"* (Mark 8:31).

To Give His Life a Ransom for Many

As soon as the apostles recognized who Jesus was, He began to show them why He came into the world. The reason He came is clearly given in Mark 10:45 where He said, *"For even the Son of Man did not come to be served, but to serve, and to give His life a ransom for many."* A ransom is paid to gain the release or freedom of a person or property, in this case the release of a sinner from the guilt, penalty, and eventually, the presence of sin. The ransom that Jesus paid for us is not the same thing as one paying a ransom to a kidnapper to release a victim. It's the price He paid on Calvary to satisfy justice so that we could be set free.

Some early Church fathers taught that Jesus paid His ransom to Satan because he held us in bondage to sin. But that is totally unacceptable. One writer said that Christ does not recognize the right of Satan. Jesus simply overpowered him and now sets his captives free when they turn to God. That is what the writer to the Hebrews meant when he wrote:

Hebrews 2:14-15
14 Therefore, since the children share in flesh and blood, He Himself [Jesus] *likewise also partook of the same, that through death He might render powerless him who had the power of death, that is, the devil;*
15 and might free those who through fear of death were subject to slavery all their lives.

If the ransom Jesus paid was not to Satan, then to whom was it paid? It was paid to satisfy the eternal and universal justice of God. Since the penalty of sin is death, and all have sinned, then the ransom of death had to be paid to deliver the sinner. God could not simply forgive the sinner without having the penalty paid. Otherwise, there would be no basis of law and justice in the entire universe and moral chaos would result. That being so, there are several questions that naturally follow: 1) For whom was the

50

ransom paid? 2) Why did Jesus have to die? and 3) What are the benefits of His sacrifice for us?

For Whom Was the Ransom Paid?

The answer to this question is found in Romans 5, Hebrews 2, and 1 John 2, among many other places in the Scripture. The Apostle John says, *"He Himself is the propitiation for our sins; and not for ours only, but also for those of the whole world"* (1 John 2:2). This means that Jesus took our place and made a satisfactory, substitutionary, sacrifice [propitiation] for our sins, and John adds, *"also for those of the whole world."* Thus, the ransom Jesus paid was valuable enough to ransom every soul from Adam to the end of time because, as God manifest in flesh, His value is without limit. For this reason, His death covers your sins and mine as we trust Him.

The Ransom Was Not for Angels

The writer of Hebrews is careful to explain that the death of Jesus was for mankind and not for angels who sinned:

Hebrews 2:9-10, 14-16

9 But we do see Him who was made for a little while lower than the angels, namely, Jesus, because of the suffering of death crowned with glory and honor, so that by the grace of God He might taste death for everyone.

10 For it was fitting for Him, for whom are all things, and through whom are all things, in bringing many sons to glory, to perfect the author of their salvation through sufferings.

14 Therefore, since the children share in flesh and blood, He Himself likewise also partook of the same, that through death He might render

powerless him who had the power of death, that is, the devil,
15 and might free those who through fear of death were subject to slavery all their lives.
16 For assuredly He does not give help to angels, but He gives help to the descendant of Abraham.

The ransom that Jesus paid, therefore, covers only the human race. Each of us was born with a sin nature from Adam and is given the opportunity to receive help from Jesus as a descendant of Abraham by faith.

The Ransom Is Effective for Believers Only

Notice that verse 16 above says, Jesus *"does not give help to angels,"* but He does help the descendant of Abraham. Fallen angels are not being saved because they have no Savior. Each one, created directly by God, chose individually to sin against God while in a state of perfection. Each of us was born a sinner without a choice in the matter, so Jesus came to our aid. Galatians 3:29 says that believing Gentiles are also seed or offspring of Abraham: *"And if you belong to Christ, then you are Abraham's descendants, heirs according to promise."* This verse is in the context of a letter written to a Gentile church. Not only are Jews the offspring of Abraham, but Gentiles who have the faith of Abraham are spiritual descendants. While Jesus is able to redeem an infinite number of men, only those who have the same kind of faith as Abraham are actually redeemed. Perhaps you wonder what kind of faith that is. Abraham believed God's Word. He believed that what God told him would actually come to pass.

Thus, we have the answer to the first question, "For whom was the ransom paid?" It was paid for everyone. However, it is valid only for those who receive it and accept the payment that was made on their behalf. Therefore, while the ransom is adequate for every human being, salvation will come only to those who believe God.

There are two more questions that must be discussed about the ransom Jesus paid for our salvation: 1) Why did Jesus have to die? and 2) What is the result of His sacrifice for us?

WHY JESUS HAD TO DIE

Was there not another way salvation could have been purchased? Was it not possible for God save men in another way? Turn back to the beginning of the Bible, to Genesis where it reads, *"Then the LORD God formed man of dust from the ground, and breathed into his nostrils the breath of life; and man became a living being"* (Genesis 2:7). Following his creation, Adam was put in the Garden of Eden which is described in Genesis 2:10-15. Then, God gave him a command saying:

Genesis 2:16-17
16 ..."From any tree of the garden you may eat freely;
*17 but from the tree of the knowledge of good and evil you shall not eat, for in the day that you eat from it **you will surely die.** "*

The Wages of Our Sin
The penalty for Adam's disobedience to God's command was death – both spiritual death and physical death. When one understands death as the Bible uses the word, he can see that the penalty was immediate in the spiritual realm and began to be carried out in the physical realm. Death is not total destruction or cessation of existence, but rather, death is separation. Spiritual death is separation from God; physical death is separation of the soul and spirit from the body. The soul and spirit continue to exist after death, but apart from the body which eventually decays and returns to dust.

When Adam sinned he instantly died spiritually. He was separated from God, the source of all life. The biblical record says that Adam hid himself from God. It was not man who sought after God, but God who sought after Adam with the question, *"Where are you?"* (Genesis 3:9). God knew where Adam was; He simply wanted Adam to acknowledge where he was – separated from God because of his sin. Since God is the source of all life, to be separated from Him necessarily results not only in spiritual death, but in physical death also. Consequently, Adam began the downward path which resulted in his own physical death – and the death of all men after him, *"For the wages of sin is death"* (Romans 6:23).

Yes, death has come upon all mankind as the penalty for sin. Romans 5:12 says, *"Therefore, just as through one man sin entered into the world, and death through sin, and so death spread to all men, because all sinned."* In order for the death penalty to be paid and the sinner set free, Jesus had to die. He had to pay the penalty for our sin if we were to be forgiven.

The Shedding of Blood Necessary
When Jesus died on the Cross, shedding His blood, He was fulfilling the required payment for sin. This is in keeping with Hebrews 9:22 which says, *"without shedding of blood there is no forgiveness."* In the Old Testament book of Leviticus, God said to His people concerning atonement for sin:

Leviticus 17:11, 14
*11 '... the life of the flesh is in the blood, and I have given it to you on the altar to make atonement for your souls; for it is the blood by reason of the life that makes atonement.'
14 "For as for the life of all flesh, its blood is identified with its life. Therefore I said to the sons of Israel, 'You are not to eat the blood of any flesh, for the life of all flesh is its blood ...'"*

Why was Jesus' death necessary? It was necessary to pay the penalty for sin in order that you and I may be set free from sin's guilt, penalty, and bondage. Just as Romans 6:23 says, *"the wages of sin is death, but the free gift of God is eternal life in Christ Jesus our Lord."*

Jesus Died Voluntarily for Us

Some believe God was cruel to give His Son to pay for our sin on the Cross. That might be so if Jesus were not God. However, Jesus Himself said:

John 10:17-18
17 "For this reason the Father loves Me, because I lay down My life so that I may take it again.
18 "No one has taken it away from Me, but I lay it down on My own initiative. I have authority to lay it down, and I have authority to take it up again. This commandment I received from My Father."

Therefore, Jesus had both the authority to give His life as a sacrifice for sin and the authority to come back to life again – to come out of the grave in resurrection glory. Jesus was not forced to go to the Cross, but went voluntarily because of His love for us.

THE BENEFITS OF HIS SACRIFICE

Jesus' sacrifice resulted in several benefits for believers. One of them is found in Romans 5:

Romans 5:18-19
18 So then as through one transgression there resulted condemnation to all men, even so through one act of righteousness there resulted justification of life to all men.
19 For as through the one man's disobedience the many were made sinners, even so through the

55

obedience of the One the many will be made righteous.

Believers Are Justified

The ransom Jesus paid resulted in justification of life to all men. Justification is a legal act of God whereby He declares righteous all who trust in Jesus. Remember it was mentioned earlier that death is the penalty for sin. Since all have sinned, all are cut off from God; they are spiritually dead. Believers are restored to life and fellowship. When Jesus satisfied the righteous demands of the Law, God was able to restore fellowship with those of us who trusted in Jesus. Two things took place: 1) the legal requirement of the Law was satisfied because the penalty was paid and 2) since sins were taken away (Hebrews 10:11-12), eternal life was given to believers.

Jesus paid the entire penalty for sin, leaving the sinner debt free. The believer is received by God just as though he had never sinned at all. Again, it must be made perfectly clear that justification is received personally by trusting in Jesus Christ. His death and resurrection are solely and completely sufficient for your salvation. Paul wrote that Jesus *"was delivered over because of our transgressions* [the ransom], *and was raised because of our justification* [the result]" (Romans 4:25).

Peace with God

In addition to giving eternal life, justification brings peace. Romans goes on to say:

Romans 5:1-2
1 Therefore having been justified by faith, we have peace with God through our Lord Jesus Christ,
2 through whom also we have obtained our introduction by faith into this grace in which we stand; and we exult in hope of the glory of God.

56

Peace with God is needed by every troubled soul. To know that you are at peace with God and that He is at peace with you is great soul-satisfying knowledge. Because of Jesus, we have peace with God. The Scripture says, "*He Himself is our peace ... AND HE CAME AND PREACHED PEACE TO YOU WHO WERE FAR AWAY, AND PEACE TO THOSE WHO WERE NEAR*" (Ephesians 2:14, 17).

The Peace of God

Once we "lay down our weapons" and cease fighting against God, we come into fellowship with Him and enter into the peace of God. There is a world of difference between peace *with* God and the peace *of* God.

Philippians 4:6 says, "*Be anxious for nothing, but in everything by prayer and supplication with thanksgiving let your requests be made known to God.*" Of course, before we can let our requests be made known to God we have to come into a place of peace *with* God. Then verse seven goes on to say, "*And the peace of God, which surpasses all comprehension, will guard your hearts and your minds in Christ Jesus.*"

What a blessed thought that is – the peace *of* God. Imagine yourself in God's place. Imagine that nothing in the entire world can touch you. You have no needs; you can supply the need of every other being; you do not have to depend on anyone else. You have perfect peace. The peace you have just imagined – God's peace – can be yours. But that peace comes only by trusting in Jesus Christ and then submitting your life to Him.

Thus, according to Philippians 4:6, you can pray with thanksgiving because God has promised to answer prayer for those who come in Jesus' name, provided their lives and motives are right.

HIS RESURRECTION

Jesus moved from the humiliation of the Cross to the glory of the resurrection and ascension to God's right hand in heavenly places.

His Resurrection Was Physical

It is important to understand that Jesus Christ's actual physical body was raised from the grave after His crucifixion. With that resurrected body He proceeded into heaven where He now sits at the right hand of God. Some people believe that He was raised only in a spiritual sense, that is, His teachings and ideas continue to exist and influence people. The Bible, however, makes it plain Jesus was raised in a physical body. Luke 24 tells about the appearance of Jesus to His disciples gathered in Jerusalem after His resurrection:

> Luke 24:36-43
> *36 While they were telling these things, He Himself stood in their midst and said to them, "Peace be to you."*
> *37 But they were startled and frightened and thought that they were seeing a spirit.*
> *38 And He said to them, "Why are you troubled, and why do doubts arise in your hearts?*
> *39 "See My hands and My feet, that it is I Myself; touch Me and see, for a spirit does not have flesh and bones as you see that I have."*
> *40 And when He had said this, He showed them His hands and His feet.*
> *41 While they still could not believe it because of their joy and amazement, He said to them, "Have you anything here to eat?"*
> *42 They gave Him a piece of a broiled fish;*
> *43 and He took it and ate it before them.*

It is very clear from this passage that Jesus had a real physical body after His resurrection. Verse 37 says they *"thought"* they were seeing a spirit. They thought that because Jesus had been crucified and buried. But now, they saw Him standing before them! They had not counted on a physical resurrection even though Jesus had told them it would happen. They could not believe their eyes. Jesus stood before them, so they simply thought they were seeing His spirit. He quickly corrected them saying, *"See My hands and My feet ... touch Me and see."* He plainly indicated that His resurrection body was a physical body because it could be touched. He declared, *"a spirit does not have flesh and bones as you see that I have."*

Thus, His resurrection body was real flesh and bones. As further proof, He ate a piece of broiled fish in their presence. In this manner, the Bible establishes that the resurrection of Jesus was more than a spiritual resurrection – He was raised in a glorified, physical body that could be touched!

HIS ASCENSION

His Ascension Was Physical

Chapter one of the New Testament book of Acts tells about the physical ascension of Jesus Christ into heaven:

Acts 1:9-11
9 And after He had said these things, He was lifted up while they were looking on, and a cloud received Him out of their sight.
10 And as they were gazing intently into the sky while He was going, behold, two men in white clothing stood beside them.
11 They also said, "Men of Galilee, why do you stand looking into the sky? This Jesus, who has been taken up from you into heaven, will come in

just the same way as you have watched Him go into heaven."

He Ascended to God's Right Hand

According to the above Scripture, Jesus ascended to heaven in a physical body before their very eyes. Many passages tell us the exact location of Jesus Christ in heaven. He is exalted to the right hand of God. In Acts 2:33, Peter said, *"Therefore having been exalted to the right hand of God, and having received from the Father the promise of the Holy Spirit, He has poured forth this which you both see and hear."* The New Testament says that Jesus is at the right hand of God no fewer than 20 times. References are found in Matthew, Mark, Luke, Acts, Romans, Ephesians, Colossians, Hebrews, and 1 Peter.

The great number of references to this particular theme point up its extreme importance. The right hand of God is the place of power and authority over heaven and earth (Matthew 28:18-20). Notice what Jesus said before His ascension. He came up to the eleven disciples (Judas no longer among them) and said this, *"All authority has been given to Me in heaven and on earth"* (Matthew 28:18). Since all authority has been given to Him, there is no authority that He does not have. Satan and his demonic host are subject to Jesus, even though Satan is presently ruler over the world system (2 Corinthians 4:4; 1 John 5:19).

At the present time, Jesus is in heaven and is Lord of heaven and earth; God has given Him all authority over the entire creation. He presently chooses to exercise His authority in earthly affairs through the Church, which is His body. In Ephesians we are told that He is head over all things to the Church:

Ephesians 1:22-23
22 And He [God the Father] *put all things in subjection under His* [Christ's] *feet, and gave Him as head over all things to the church,*

60

*23 which is His body, the fulness of Him who fills
all in all.*

One reason we do not see an extensive influence for
Christ in many places is that the Church has lost sight of
this important truth. If believers would pray boldly and
work totally in submission to Christ, we could see many
more bad situations turned around to the glory of God.

† Jesus Christ – A Unique Ministry
WHAT IS HE DOING NOW?

We have seen that Jesus ascended into heaven and is
seated at God's right hand. Not only does He presently
exercise Lordship as Head of the Church, giving it direction
and guiding its conduct in the world, but He is also the
great High Priest of the Church. As High Priest He has
undertaken to do five things on behalf of those who believe
in Him. He has gone into heaven: 1) to prepare a place,
2) as a forerunner, 3) as an advocate, 4) as an intercessor,
and 5) as a mediator. For a fuller understanding of the
work Jesus is doing for us at this present time, we must
look at each of these five topics individually.

Preparing a Place for Us
One of the most precious promises of the Word of God
appears in the Gospel of John. Jesus was speaking to His
disciples when He said:

John 14:1-3
*1 "Do not let your heart be troubled; believe in
God, believe also in Me.
2 "In My Father's house are many dwelling
places; if it were not so, I would have told you; for
I go to prepare a place for you.*

3 "If I go and prepare a place for you, I will come again and receive you to Myself, that where I am, there you may be also."

Jesus spoke of preparing a place for believers in His Father's house. When that place is prepared, then He will come again and take us to Himself to be where He is.

When Paul was caught up to the third heaven, he heard words so wonderful that man is not allowed to speak them:

2 Corinthians 12:2-4
2   I know a man in Christ who fourteen years ago – whether in the body I do not know, or out of the body I do not know, God knows – such a man was caught up to the third heaven.
3   And I know how such a man – whether in the body or apart from the body I do not know, God knows –
4   was caught up into Paradise, and heard inexpressible words, which a man is not permitted to speak.

Paul speaks of the third heaven because the Scriptures tell us of three heavens. The biblical teaching is not like the doctrine of seven heavens that some teach. The Bible teaches there are only three heavens:

1)   The atmospheric heaven – the air around us.
2)   The starry heaven – the universe or outer space.
3)   The third heaven – the place of God's manifest presence.

It was this third heaven to which Paul was caught up and which he describes as being beyond human expression. Heaven is so wonderful that no human language can adequately describe it. Earlier in the same epistle, Paul wrote, "THINGS WHICH EYE HAS NOT SEEN AND EAR HAS NOT

HEARD, AND WHICH HAVE NOT ENTERED THE HEART OF MAN, ALL THAT GOD HAS PREPARED FOR THOSE WHO LOVE HIM" (1 Corinthians 2:9). Indeed the place which Jesus is preparing for us is good and beautiful beyond our imagination.

Not only is heaven a place of beautiful surroundings, it is a place of peace where we shall relax without pain or sorrow. The Apostle John wrote a wonderful description of the future new heaven and earth:

Revelation 21:1-5
1 Then I saw a new heaven and a new earth; for the first heaven and the first earth passed away, and there is no longer any sea.
2 And I saw the holy city, new Jerusalem, coming down out of heaven from God, made ready as a bride adorned for her husband.
3 And I heard a loud voice from the throne, saying, "Behold, the tabernacle of God is among men, and He will dwell among them, and they shall be His people, and God Himself will be among them,
4 and He will wipe away every tear from their eyes; and there will no longer be any death; there will no longer be any mourning, or crying, or pain; the first things have passed away."
5 And He who sits on the throne said, "Behold, I am making all things new." And He said, "Write, for these words are faithful and true."

This is a stunningly beautiful word picture John gives us of the new heaven and the new earth. It is certainly the place for which all the people of God are longing. It is a wonderful future we can look forward to with keen anticipation! We can rejoice and praise God in faith, knowing that all He is preparing will be ours to enjoy.

Going Before Us As a Forerunner

Not only did Jesus go to prepare a place for us, but we are told in the book of Hebrews that He went into heaven as a forerunner for us:

> Hebrews 6:19-20
> *19 This hope we have as an anchor of the soul, a hope both sure and steadfast and one which enters within the veil* [of the heavenly tabernacle],
> *20 where Jesus has entered as a forerunner for us, having become a high priest forever according to the order of Melchizedek.*

A forerunner goes to prepare the way for one who is coming later. John the Baptist was sent as a forerunner of Jesus, the Messiah. Isaiah, in figurative language, explains the job of John the Baptist as a forerunner of Christ.

> Isaiah 40:3-4
> *3 A voice is calling,*
> *"Clear the way for the LORD in the wilderness;*
> *Make smooth in the desert a highway for our God.*
> *4 "Let every valley be lifted up,*
> *And every mountain and hill be made low;*
> *And let the rough ground become a plain,*
> *And the rugged terrain a broad valley"*

Isaiah uses the picture of building a king's highway. The valleys were filled with dirt and the mountains were leveled to make a highway that could be traveled more easily. When Jesus went into heaven, He was our forerunner, making a highway into heaven itself for us. Figuratively speaking, every valley has been lifted up, every mountain and hill has been made low, the rough ground has become like a plain and the rugged terrain like a broad valley. We have easy access to the throne of God! In plain language the writer to the Hebrews says, *"Let us therefore draw near with confidence to the throne of grace, that we may receive mercy and may find grace to help in time of need"* (Hebrews 4:16). We can confidently draw near to the throne of grace because Jesus has entered there for us as our forerunner.

Acting as Our Advocate in Heaven

Acting as an advocate with the Father is part of Jesus' high priestly work. An advocate is a person who argues for a cause, that is, a supporter or defender – one who pleads in another's behalf. That is exactly what Jesus Christ does for those who trust in Him for salvation:

> 1 John 1:10; 2:1-2
> *10 If we say that we have not sinned, we make Him a liar, and His word is not in us.*
>
> *2:1 My little children, I am writing these things to you so that you may not sin. And **if anyone sins, we have an Advocate with the Father, Jesus Christ the righteous;***
> *2 and He Himself is the propitiation for our sins; and not for ours only, but also for those of the whole world.*

We should not sin, but when we do, we should not give up hope. According to 1 John 1:9, we must confess our sins to God and He will forgive us and cleanse us from all unrighteousness.

The word translated "advocate" in English is "paraclete." It means one called alongside to help. It is the same word used of the Holy Spirit in John's Gospel where Jesus said He and the Father would send us another Helper. Thus, we are helped here on earth by the Holy Spirit and we are helped in heaven by Jesus Christ. When we sin Jesus acts as a lawyer before the universal court of justice and declares that the penalty for our sin has been paid on the Cross. In human courts, once a case is tried and the penalty is paid it cannot be tried again. It is the same in heaven. God is eternally satisfied with the penalty Jesus paid for us. He does not require a second payment because Jesus points to His own settlement as sufficient and the case cannot be tried again. Because the penalty was paid, we are free from God's judgment and wrath.

Interestingly, the Apostle John, in speaking of Jesus as our Advocate, did not say, "Jesus Christ **who is** righteous," but *"Jesus Christ the righteous"* (1 John 2:1). Rather than expressing the conduct of Jesus Christ as righteous, it expresses His character as righteous. The very nature of Jesus Christ is righteous. He not only does what is right in His conduct, He Himself is righteous in His nature. We have a righteous Advocate with the Father. Praise God for one who is both faithful and righteous representing us before the throne of God.

Interceding for Us

Intercession in the spiritual realm is often associated with praying for another. Being an advocate and being an intercessor are two similar but different functions.

An advocate defends the accused in a court of law.
Jesus defends us before the Father in heaven.

An intercessor speaks with another on behalf of a person.
Jesus speaks to the Father on our behalf about our needs.

When Jesus sees us in need, in sin, or under the oppression of Satan, He intercedes with the Father on our behalf. He speaks to the Father for us asking that we may come through the situation, whatever it may be, in good spiritual condition.

Jesus told Peter that Satan desired to sift him as wheat. *"But,"* He continued, *"I have prayed for you, that your faith may not fail"* (Luke 22:32). Jesus prays for us as an intercessor before the Father. This scriptural truth is recorded in both Romans and in Hebrews:

Romans 8:33-34
*33 Who will bring a charge against God's elect? God is the one who justifies; 34 who is the one who condemns? Christ Jesus is He who died, yes, rather who was raised, who is at the right hand of God, **who also intercedes for us.***

Hebrews 7:25
*25 Therefore He is able also to save forever those who draw near to God through Him, since **He always lives to make intercession for them.***

In Hebrews 7:25 above, the eternal security believers enjoy in Jesus is tied to His intercession for us. Yes, it is a great blessing to have Jesus interceding for us.

Mediating for Us
A mediator brings together disputing parties so that the differences can be settled. Paul wrote to Timothy concerning the mediatorship of Jesus Christ:

1 Timothy 2:5-6
5 For there is one God, and one mediator also between God and men, the man Christ Jesus, 6 who gave Himself as a ransom for all, the testimony given at the proper time.

Jesus is the one who brings God and man together; He is the only mediator between the Father and us. Because of this we can go directly to God through Jesus. We need not go through any other person or other created being, living or dead. In fact, the Scripture says there is only *"one mediator also between God and men, the man Christ Jesus"* (1 Timothy 2:5). Since Jesus is the only mediator, then the others whom men have set up to be mediators cannot represent them before God. Jesus is God's only recognized mediator. Regardless of how holy others may have been, they cannot mediate between God and man. God Himself welcomes each of us directly to His throne when we pray because of the mediatorship of the Lord Jesus.

Awaiting for the Time of His Return
Hebrews 10:12-13
12 but He, having offered one sacrifice for sins for all time, SAT DOWN AT THE RIGHT HAND OF GOD,
*13 **waiting from that time onward** UNTIL HIS ENEMIES BE MADE A FOOTSTOOL FOR HIS FEET.*

Jesus is patiently waiting until the Father's predetermined time for His return to earth. No understanding about the unique person and mission of Jesus would be complete without some knowledge that He and His people have a great future ahead of them. Jesus will come to earth again to defeat the evil world system headed by the Antichrist. Satan will be bound in the abyss and Christ will establish a reign of righteousness for 1000 years before the final judgment of the ungodly and the creation of a new heaven and new earth. New earth will be a glorious place where God will dwell forever with His redeemed people. The earth will be illumined with the glory of God and His Son Jesus Christ. All these subjects are discussed in much more detail in chapters 11 through 13.

MAKE JESUS PERSONAL

We have seen that Jesus Christ is the Son of God and Son of Man who gave Himself a ransom for many. He died, but was resurrected and ascended to God's right hand where He is able to save all who come to God through Him. Speaking of Jesus, the Bible says, *"there is salvation in no one else; for there is no other name under heaven that has* been given among men by which we must be saved" (Acts 4:12). Because of Who He is and what He has done, we must pay closer attention to what He says than to anyone else. He said, *"I am the way, and the truth, and the life; no one comes to the Father but through Me"* (John 14:6). If we disregard His words, we will not escape being condemned on the day of judgment. Are you ready for that day? If you are not, then you must open your heart to Jesus Christ and trust Him to save you. He is not only *able* to cleanse you of sin and grant you eternal life, but He is completely *willing* to do it. Jesus Himself said, *"the one who comes to Me I will certainly not cast out"* (John 6:37).

Many people who know the truth fail to benefit from it because they do not personally receive Jesus Christ. You might ask, "How may I receive Him?" It is a very simple thing to do, yet very profound and life-changing. You may receive Him by: 1) trusting Him to save you because He died to pay for your sins, and 2) believing that God raised Him from the dead, showing that God was satisfied with His sacrifice on Calvary. Won't you trust Jesus to save you now?

John 1:12-13
12 But as many as received Him, to them He gave the right to become children of God, even to those who believe in His name,
13 who were born not of blood, nor of the will of the flesh, nor of the will of man, but of God.

69

Chapter 3

The Holy Spirit
† His Personality

A correct understanding of the biblical teaching about the Holy Spirit can revolutionize your life. Like other basic doctrines we have been studying, a good grasp of the personality and work of the Holy Spirit is essential for consistent Christian growth and living because it is through Him that we are empowered for Christian life and service. We need to know how this empowerment takes place in the lives of those who know and love Jesus.

In discussing the Holy Spirit, two basic teachings of Scripture will be studied: first, He is a person, just as God the Father and Jesus Christ are persons; and second, He is Himself deity, being part of the eternal Godhead. We start by seeing that the Holy Spirit is a distinct person.

MORE THAN AN INFLUENCE

The Holy Spirit Can Be Grieved

The Scripture teaches in many places and in many ways that the Holy Spirit is a person. For example, Ephesians 4:30 is an exhortation to Christians which says, *"Do not grieve the Holy Spirit of God, by whom you were sealed for the day of redemption."* This shows that the Holy Spirit has emotional feelings. He is grieved when we do things that are wrong. It is impossible to grieve a dead object – a mere force which flows from God. Only a person can be grieved, not a thing. When the Word of God says, *"Do not grieve the Holy Spirit of God,"* it gives us a definite understanding about the personality of the Holy Spirit.

Notice carefully the context of Ephesians 4 that speaks of the Holy Spirit being grieved. In this passage Paul tells us about some of the things that grieve Him.

Ephesians 4:25-32
25 Therefore, laying aside falsehood, SPEAK TRUTH EACH ONE of you WITH HIS NEIGHBOR, for we are members of one another.
26 BE ANGRY, AND yet DO NOT SIN; do not let the sun go down on your anger,
27 and do not give the devil an opportunity.
28 He who steals must steal no longer; but rather he must labor, performing with his own hands what is good, so that he will have something to share with one who has need.
29 Let no unwholesome word proceed from your mouth, but only such a word as is good for edification according to the need of the moment, so that it will give grace to those who hear.
30 Do not grieve the Holy Spirit of God, by whom you were sealed for the day of redemption.
31 Let all bitterness and wrath and anger and clamor and slander be put away from you, along with all malice.
32 Be kind to one another, tender-hearted, forgiving each other, just as God in Christ also has forgiven you.

Did you notice that the sins which grieve the Holy Spirit are not just corrupt language and the acts of overt violence and immorality? The more deceptive sins of heart attitude also bring grief to Him. Among those sins are bitterness, anger, and malice. Our wicked hearts grieve the Holy Spirit as much as overt sin.

The Holy Spirit Maintains Relationships with Mankind
　　He Fellowships with Us – Not only can the Holy Spirit be grieved, He also has personal dealings and relationships with other people. The Apostle's blessing in 2 Corinthians 13:14 says, *"The grace of the Lord Jesus Christ, and the love of God, and the fellowship of the Holy Spirit, be with you all."* The word "fellowship" implies a warm, personal relationship between individuals. It is individuals interacting with one another in a friendly atmosphere. Therefore, the Holy Spirit's fellowship with us is a proof of His personal being.

　　He Leads Us – Likewise, as a person, the Holy Spirit leads us to do good works, and shows us the best course of action to take. In the early Church a problem arose over circumcision and keeping the Law of Moses. Some taught that the Gentiles, in addition to having faith in Jesus, must be circumcised and keep the Law of Moses in order to be saved. A discussion in the first Church council recorded in Acts 15 came to a settled conclusion. A letter was written to Gentile believers stating in part:

> Acts 15:28-29
> *28 "For it seemed good to the Holy Spirit and to us to lay upon you no greater burden than these essentials:*
> *29 that you abstain from things sacrificed to idols and from blood and from things strangled and from fornication; if you keep yourselves free from such things, you will do well. Farewell."*

In this instance, the apostles acknowledged the leadership of the Holy Spirit in arriving at their conclusion. They knew they were in agreement with the Holy Spirit in making that exact declaration. *"It seemed good to the Holy Spirit,"* as well as to the apostles, to lay no greater burden on the Gentiles than the four essentials mentioned in the passage.

He Speaks to Us – In Acts 13 the Holy Spirit spoke to the church in Antioch. The Scripture says:

Acts 13:2-4
2 While they were ministering to the Lord and fasting, the Holy Spirit said, "Set apart for Me Barnabas and Saul for the work to which I have called them."
3 Then, when they had fasted and prayed and laid their hands on them, they sent them away.
4 So, being sent out by the Holy Spirit, they went down to Seleucia and from there they sailed to Cyprus.

It is obvious from the wording of this Scripture that the Holy Spirit is Himself a real person because He is able to communicate. He used the personal pronoun *"Me"* and said He was the one who called Barnabas and Saul to a particular work.

We saw that the Holy Spirit spoke to the churches in Acts 15 when He agreed with the apostles to send the letter. In Revelation 2 and 3 the Holy Spirit also speaks directly to the churches. For example, Revelation 2:7 says, *"He who has an ear, let him hear what the Spirit says to the churches."*

He Prays for Us – We learn much about the Holy Spirit from the Apostle Paul. He wrote in Romans, *"In the same way the Spirit also helps our weakness; for we do not know how to pray as we should, but the Spirit Himself intercedes for us with groanings too deep for words"* (Romans 8:26). The Holy Spirit prays on our behalf just as we saw in an earlier study that Jesus Christ prays on our behalf. It is important to note that He *"intercedes for us* *with groanings too deep for words."* Some say this means speaking in tongues. It should be pointed out that the Scripture says it is *"too deep for words,"* but speaking in tongues is indeed a use of words. Paul speaks of a groaning which is so deep, it is beyond any words our tongues can employ. The Holy Spirit is the one who intercedes for us in such a deep way with God.

The Holy Spirit Has a Mind

There are a number of other ways the Scripture indicates that we may see that the Holy Spirit is a person. For example, other personal characteristics are ascribed to Him. Paul taught that the Spirit has a mind to reason. He said, *"He who searches the hearts knows what the mind of the Spirit is, because He intercedes for the saints according to the will of God"* (Romans 8:27). Thus, God, who searches the hearts, knows what the mind of the Holy Spirit is. To put it plainly, the Holy Spirit thinks and reasons as no force can.

The Holy Spirit Has a Will

According to 1 Corinthians, the Holy Spirit distributes spiritual gifts *"just as He wills."* Paul wrote, *"But one and the same Spirit works all these things, distributing to each one individually just as He wills"* (1 Corinthians 12:11). The Holy Spirit knows what He wants and works according to His will in dispensing gifts to believers.

The Holy Spirit Can Be Insulted

Did you know that the Holy Spirit can be insulted? Have you ever insulted Him? The Bible says, *"How much severer punishment do you think he will deserve who has trampled under foot the Son of God, and has regarded as unclean the blood of the covenant by which he was sanctified, and has insulted the Spirit of grace?"* (Hebrews 10:29). People insult the Spirit of God when they reject His testimony to Jesus. What an awful thing it is to insult the Spirit of God. According to the verse above, it deserves severe punishment!

The Holy Spirit Can Be Told a Lie

Acts 5:1-11 teaches, through illustration, that a person can lie to the Holy Spirit. Ananias and Sapphira lied about the price they received for some property they sold. Peter asked Ananias, *"why has Satan filled your heart to lie to the Holy Spirit, and to keep back some of the price of the land?"* (Acts 5:3). Sapphira was in agreement with Ananias, conspiring with him to lie about the price of the land. As a result, both paid with their lives; they dropped dead in the assembly and had to be carried out.

Has the Holy Spirit ever convicted you of a sin and you denied it? It is certainly possible for a believer to lie to the Holy Spirit. Do not be guilty of such a terrible sin!

✝ The Holy Spirit – His Identity

The previous section discussed the characteristics that make it evident that the Holy Spirit is a person just as God the Father and Jesus are persons. The Bible ascribes the qualities of personality to the Spirit – He has feelings and emotions, He reasons and speaks – in short, He does everything that distinguishes a personal, living being from mere power, influence, or thing. The question is, however, "Does the fact that He is a personal being make Him equal with God the Father and God the Son as part of the Godhead?"

The Holy Spirit Is God

In chapter one we discussed the Trinity. We saw there is only one true and living God, yet existing simultaneously as God the Father, God the Son, and God the Holy Spirit. The Holy Spirit is God, equal in every way to the Father and the Son.

Just as it was essential to know that the Holy Spirit is a person, it is likewise essential to understand that He is fully

God. The Bible is as clear on His deity as it is that He is a person.

Divine Names of the Holy Spirit

He Is Called God – In the last section we learned that Ananias and Sapphira lied about their offering to God, and paid with their lives. Peter told Ananias he had lied to God and not to men. It is clear from the passage that Ananias and Sapphira had lied to the Holy Spirit whom Peter called God. Peter said:

Acts 5:3-4
3 ..."Ananias, why has Satan filled your heart to lie to the Holy Spirit, ...
4 "... You have not lied to men, but to God."

He Is Called Lord – Peter called the Holy Spirit God, but Paul also calls Him Lord:

2 Corinthians 3:17-18
17 Now the Lord is the Spirit; and where the Spirit of the Lord is, there is liberty.
18 But we all, with unveiled face, beholding as in a mirror the glory of the Lord, are being trans- formed into the same image from glory to glory, just as from **the Lord, the Spirit.**

In verse 17 above Paul wrote, *"Now the Lord is the Spirit."* At the time the New Testament was written, the term "lord" meant a deity or a god. In those days people worshiped many so-called gods in the Mediterranean area. Each city and village had its own god. When one referred to a lord, he was referring to the god of a particular city or village. When Paul ascribed lordship to Jesus Christ, he meant Jesus was more than a superior individual; he meant He was God Himself. The same is true when the Holy Spirit is called Lord. He is called *"the Lord"* and is thereby recognized as God Himself.

Divine Nature of the Holy Spirit

He Is Eternal – Another way to distinguish the deity of the Holy Spirit is to notice that He possesses the same divine qualities that God the Father possesses. For example, in Hebrews 9:14, He is called *"the eternal Spirit."* No one is eternal except God, because every created thing had a beginning point in time. Therefore, only God the Father, Son, and Holy Spirit are eternal. Existing eternally and having immortality are not the same thing. Immortality does not mean that one has always existed; it only means that one will not stop existing from now on. The word "eternal" means that one has existed forever without beginning and without end. We possess eternal life because we partake of the life that comes from God – His life – eternal life.

He Is Present Everywhere – Just as God the Father is present everywhere at one time, so is the Holy Spirit. Psalm 139 expresses it this way:

Psalm 139:7-10

7 *Where can I go from Your Spirit?*
   Or where can I flee from Your presence?
8 *If I ascend to heaven, You are there;*
   If I make my bed in Sheol [the grave],
   behold, You are there.
9 *If I take the wings of the dawn,*
   If I dwell in the remotest part of the sea,
10 *Even there Your hand will lead me,*
   And Your right hand will lay hold of me.

The Spirit of God is always present everywhere to help us in our time of need. We can rely upon Him to help us whenever we need Him on the basis of the finished work of Jesus Christ. All that we have and all the benefits of the Godhead toward us rest exclusively upon the finished work of Jesus and never upon our goodness or merit. If we think we can call upon God because we have lived a life pleasing to Him, we are wrong. No one is righteous in His sight:

> Romans 3:9-11
> *9   What then? Are we better than they? Not at all; for we have already charged that both Jews and Greeks are all under sin;*
> *10 as it is written,*
> *"THERE IS NONE RIGHTEOUS, NOT EVEN ONE;*
> *11 THERE IS NONE WHO UNDERSTANDS,*
> *THERE IS NONE WHO SEEKS FOR GOD."*

Only that which is done through the empowerment of the Spirit is acceptable to God.

He Is All-Powerful – The Old Testament prophet Zechariah wrote, *"'Not by might nor by power, but by My Spirit,' says the LORD of hosts"* (Zechariah 4:6). The Apostle John taught that *"greater is He who is in you than he who is in the world"* (1 John 4:4). The Holy Spirit is, of course, the One who is in us. Satan is the spirit working in the sons of disobedience (Ephesians 2:1). He is the one *"who is in the world."* The Holy Spirit working in us is greater than Satan working in the disobedient world!

He Knows Everything – Finally, the Bible teaches that the Holy Spirit knows even the deep things of God. Paul wrote to the church in Corinth:

> 1 Corinthians 2:10-11
> *10 ... for the Spirit searches all things, even the depths of God.*
> *11 For who among men knows the thoughts of a man except the spirit of the man, which is in him? Even so the thoughts of God no one knows except the Spirit of God.*

The Holy Spirit is the One who understands the very thoughts of God. Since He knows everything, He can teach and instruct us about the things of God.

The Holy Spirit Is Associated in Divine Works

Associated in Creation – Divine works are also ascribed to the Holy Spirit. In the second verse of the Bible, the Spirit of God takes part in creation. Genesis 1:2 says, *"The earth was formless and void, and darkness was over the surface of the deep; and the Spirit of God was moving over the surface of the waters."* The Spirit of God, right at the beginning of the Bible, is instrumental, with God the Father and God the Son, in the creation of the world.

It is amazing how God uses different passages from Scripture to lead people to Christ. "Unshackled," a famous radio program, portrayed the life of a man who was a drunkard. He picked up a Bible in a motel and read the second verse of Genesis. Because the Spirit of God was mentioned in that verse, he was so interested that he kept reading. He read until finally he came to faith in Jesus.

The book of Job also shows that the Holy Spirit has a part in creating and sustaining man.

Job 33:4, 34:14-15
4   *"The Spirit of God has made me,*
    And the breath of the Almighty gives me life."

14 *"If He should determine to do so,*
    If He should gather to Himself His spirit and
    His breath,
15 *All flesh would perish together,*
    And man would return to dust.

Associated in Regeneration – In the New Testament, while speaking with Nicodemus, Jesus ascribed to the Holy Spirit the power of regenerating lost men. He is the agent in the new birth. This is discussed in more detail elsewhere in this book. You cannot be born again without Jesus Christ, but neither can you be born again without the Holy

Spirit: *"He saved us, not on the basis of deeds which we have done in righteousness, but according to His mercy, by the washing of regeneration and renewing by the Holy Spirit"* (Titus 3:5).

Associated in Resurrection – He was involved in the resurrection of Jesus according to Romans: Jesus *"was declared the Son of God with power by the resurrection from the dead, according to the Spirit of holiness"* (Romans 1:4). This verse says clearly that the Spirit raised Jesus: *"But if the Spirit of Him who raised Jesus from the dead dwells in you, He who raised Christ Jesus from the dead will also give life to your mortal bodies through His Spirit who dwells in you"* (Romans 8:11).

The Holy Spirit Is Associated with the Father and Son
Finally, the deity of the Holy Spirit is shown by His association with God the Father and God the Son in several places in the New Testament.

At the Incarnation – He was active with the Father in the incarnation of Jesus Christ: *"And the angel answered and said to her* [Mary], *'The Holy Spirit will come upon you, and the power of the Most High* [God the Father] *will overshadow you; and for that reason the holy Child shall be called the Son of God'"* (Luke 1:35). The incarnation is the embodiment of God in the form of the Man, Jesus. The Holy Spirit, God the Father, and God the Son all appear in one verse in this account of the incarnation by Luke.

At the Baptism of Christ – The Spirit was also present at the baptism of Jesus Christ. At that time, the Holy Spirit descended upon Jesus in the form of a dove: *"After being baptized, Jesus came up immediately from the water; and behold, the heavens were opened, and he saw the Spirit of God descending as a dove, and lighting on Him"* (Matthew 3:16). Then, the Father spoke from heaven (Matthew 3:17), thereby associating the three members of the Godhead at the baptism of Jesus.

At the Great Commission – When Jesus gave the great commission He said, *"Go therefore and make disciples of all the nations, baptizing them in the name of the Father and the Son and the Holy Spirit"* (Matthew 28:19). There again the Holy Spirit is associated in one verse with God the Father and God the Son. Both the personality and the deity of the Holy Spirit are seen in Christ's words. As one writer noted, Jesus did not and could not say, "baptizing them in the name of the Father and the Son and the wind or force." That would have made no sense at all. It would have denied the personality of the Holy Spirit and His association with the Father and the Son.

At Pentecost – The Father and the Son were both involved in sending the Holy Spirit at Pentecost. Jesus was in Jerusalem at the time He said this:

John 7:38-39
38 "He who believes in Me, as the Scripture said, 'From his innermost being will flow rivers of living water.'"
39 But this He spoke of the Spirit, whom those who believed in Him were to receive; for the Spirit was not yet given, because Jesus was not yet glorified.

Jesus distinctly says that the Holy Spirit had not been given while He was ministering on earth because He had not been glorified. Later in John, Jesus promised:

John 14:16-17
16 "I will ask the Father, and He will give you another Helper, that He may be with you forever;
17 that is the Spirit of truth, ... "

That promise was fulfilled after He died on the Cross, was buried, raised from the dead, and then 40 days later ascended glorified to the right hand of God the Father.

Because He is glorified in heaven, the Father and the Son sent forth the Spirit into the world. The Holy Spirit came on the day of Pentecost and indwelt every believer who had faith in Jesus Christ.

† Holy Spirit – Names Reflecting His Nature

To learn more of the nature of the One who came at Pentecost, we need to study the names and the titles given to Him. It is one thing to know that He is a person and a member of the Godhead, but it is quite another thing to know what kind of person He is. In the first chapter we discussed the names of God. We saw, for example, that God provides a sacrifice, heals, and sanctifies us. In like manner, the names of the Holy Spirit also describe His nature and activities.

Spirit of God, Spirit of Christ
These two names of the Holy Spirit acknowledge His relationship to the Father and to the Son: *"However, you are not in the flesh but in the Spirit, if indeed the Spirit of God dwells in you. But if anyone does not have the Spirit of Christ, he does not belong to Him"* (Romans 8:9).

He has been given authority to act in the name of God the Father and in the name of Jesus Christ during this present age of grace. When we pray to the Father for a work of grace in our spiritual or physical lives, it is the Holy Spirit of God who acts as the agent of the Father and Son to perform that which we request for God's glory. We should be thankful that the Holy Spirit always acts in our behalf, for our good, and for the glory of God.

He Is the *HOLY* Spirit
The most prominent description of the Spirit is that He is holy. In fact, His holiness is so much a part of His being

that "Holy" is part of His name; He is known as the *Holy* Spirit of God. The words *"Holy Spirit"* appear 93 times in the NASB Bible, but only seven times in the KJV since it refers to Him as the *"Holy Ghost"* in the New Testament. That is far too many to study here; however, consider just one of them. In Luke, Jesus taught the disciples about prayer before Pentecost. He said:

> Luke 11:9-13
> *9 "So I say to you, ask, and it will be given to you; seek, and you will find; knock, and it will be opened to you.*
> *10 "For everyone who asks, receives; and he who seeks, finds; and to him who knocks, it will be opened.*
> *11 "Now suppose one of you fathers is asked by his son for a fish; he will not give him a snake instead of a fish, will he?*
> *12 "Or if he is asked for an egg, he will not give him a scorpion, will he?*
> *13 "If you then, being evil, know how to give good gifts to your children, how much more will your heavenly Father give the Holy Spirit to those who ask Him?"*

Luke makes an obvious contrast between evil and good. In verses 11 and 12 the words "snake" and "scorpion" represent the evil demonic world. Men are said to be evil in verse 13 because we are fallen creatures. But still, Jesus says, we give good gifts to our own children. That being the case, how much more will the heavenly Father give the Holy Spirit to those who ask Him. The contrast throughout the passage is between the evil of the satanic kingdom and the holiness and goodness of the Holy Spirit.

Keep in mind that Pentecost changed the Holy Spirit's relationship to believers. You do not have to ask God for the Holy Spirit since He came at Pentecost to indwell all believers. Jesus spoke the above for believers living before His glorification and the coming of the Holy Spirit in His new relationship to believers at Pentecost.

The Spirit of Holiness

In Romans 1:4 a similar name is given to the Holy Spirit by the Apostle Paul: He is called the *Spirit of holiness*. You may wonder, "What is holiness and how is it different from righteousness?" Holiness is an inherent part of the character – God is holy as a part of His being. The actual deeds of a holy character are righteous deeds. God is holy, therefore, all of His deeds are righteous. The Holy Spirit is absolutely holy with no taint of sin whatever.

As human beings, we can be holy only as we permit the Spirit of holiness to control our lives and reshape our characters into the moral image of God. Paul taught that you should:

> Ephesians 4:23-24
> *23 ... be renewed in the spirit of your mind,*
> *24 and put on the new self, which in the likeness of God has been created in righteousness and holiness of the truth.*

It is up to each of us to give God control of our lives in order that we may live pleasing to Him. Among the marks of a Spirit-filled life are integrity and holiness that reflect constant fellowship with God. The lack of integrity and holy living is a reflection of a poor spiritual condition.

Spirit of Truth

Jesus calls the Holy Spirit the Spirit of truth at least three times in the Gospel of John (14:17, 15:26, 16:13). He is the Spirit of truth in contrast to the spirit of error mentioned in 1 John 4:6. Men are born and grow up spiritually blind until the time the Holy Spirit illumines their minds to understand the truth of God.

Jesus used the term *"Spirit of truth"* when He told us that the Holy Spirit is called to our side to help us:

John 14:16-17
16 "I will ask the Father, and He will give you another Helper, that He may be with you forever;
17 that is the Spirit of truth, whom the world cannot receive, because it does not see Him or know Him, but you know Him because He abides with you, and will be in you.

He gives instruction, direction, and guidance according to the truth. If you want to know whether or not you are being led by the Spirit of God, examine the basis and result of your action. He will never lead you contrary to the truth revealed in the Bible. If the result of your action is not good, if it is troublesome, if it divides, if it leaves an unsettled feeling, then you may question whether or not the Spirit of truth is leading you. At times you may have to stand against error as Jesus did, but you must be sure you are being led by the Spirit of truth rather than a spirit of error. Jesus said to the Apostles:

John 16:13-14
13 "But when He, the Spirit of truth, comes, He will guide you into all the truth; for He will not speak on His own initiative, but whatever He hears, He will speak; and He will disclose to you what is to come.
14 "He will glorify Me; for He will take of Mine, and will disclose it to you."

Spirit of Life
Paul used the name *"Spirit of life"* when he wrote, *"For the law of the Spirit of life in Christ Jesus has set you free from the law of sin and of death"* (Romans 8:2). The Holy Spirit imparts life to the sinner who turns to Jesus. We have often heard the term "born again." Jesus explained what that means in John:

John 3:6-7
6 "That which is born of the flesh is flesh, and that which is born of the Spirit is spirit.
7 "Do not be amazed that I said to you, 'You must be born again.'"

When one receives Jesus Christ as his Savior, the Spirit of God gives him a new life in Christ. He is born of the Spirit. John's Gospel says that those who receive Jesus *"were born, not of blood nor of the will of the flesh nor of the will of man, but of God"* (John 1:13).

The implications of the name *"Spirit of life"* are far greater than we can cover in this study. For example, Paul wrote, *"But if the Spirit of Him who raised Jesus from the dead dwells in you, He who raised Christ Jesus from the dead will also give life to your mortal bodies through His Spirit who dwells in you"* (Romans 8:11). Notice the reference is to *"mortal bodies"* rather than immortal bodies. The Holy Spirit is the life-giving force who can restore the mortal body to health. Thousands of people through the ages have found healing through the name of Jesus, but the Holy Spirit is the agent who carries it out. If you have spiritual or physical needs, turn to Jesus Christ who will, through the Spirit of life, either heal you completely or grant you the grace you need for the situation. Romans 8:11 may also be a reference to the resurrection when *"this mortal must put on immortality"* (1 Corinthians 15:53).

✝ Holy Spirit – Names Reflecting His Activity

Just as some names reflect the nature of the Holy Spirit, others reflect His activity. Strictly speaking, some of His names reflect both His nature and His activity. The following name *"Spirit of grace"* is an example; He is both gracious in personality, but also ministers God's grace to believers.

The Spirit of Grace

The *"Spirit of grace"* is found in Hebrews 10:29 where the writer says, *"How much severer punishment do you think he will deserve who has trampled under foot the Son of God, and has regarded as unclean the blood of the covenant by which he was sanctified, and has insulted the Spirit of grace?"* Grace is God acting kindly toward us when we deserve the exact opposite. Our sin deserves the punishment of hell and eternal separation from God. There is no holiness in fallen man which makes him pleasing to God – none whatsoever! Only by His grace does God extend His love toward us. The Apostle Paul explains:

Ephesians 2:8-9
8 For by grace you have been saved through faith; and that not of yourselves, it is the gift of God;
9 not as a result of works, so that no one may boast.

Since grace is God acting in kindness toward us when we deserve the exact opposite, then the Spirit of grace works on our behalf to bring us into the full blessing of Christ in God when we do not deserve it. Even when our lives are against the purposes of God, the Spirit of grace convicts, and if necessary, disciplines us until we return to the path of truth.

Spirit of Promise

God promised to pour out the Spirit upon all flesh. Referring to the Holy Spirit, Jesus said that He would send the promise of the Father. Thus, the Holy Spirit is the Spirit of promise. In Acts 2:33, when Peter was preaching at Pentecost, he said, *"Therefore having been exalted to the right hand of God, and having received from the Father the promise of the Holy Spirit, He has poured forth this which you both see and hear."* The promise is repeated later in the same chapter of Acts:

Acts 2:38-39
38 ..."Repent, and let each of you be baptized in the name of Jesus Christ for the forgiveness of your sins; and you will receive the gift of the Holy Spirit.
39 "For the promise is for you and your children, and for all who are far off, as many as the Lord our God will call to Himself."

The Spirit of promise has been sent to us from God the Father and Jesus Christ His Son as a down payment on the inheritance He has prepared for us:

Ephesians 1:13-14
13 In Him, you also, after listening to the message of truth, the gospel of your salvation – having also believed, you were sealed in Him with **the Holy Spirit of promise,**
14 **who is given as a pledge of our inheritance,** *with a view to the redemption of God's own possession, to the praise of His glory.*

Spirit of Wisdom

From the Old Testament prophet Isaiah's pen came the words: *"The Spirit of the LORD will rest on Him, The spirit of wisdom"* (Isaiah 11:2). Paul prayed *"that the God of our Lord Jesus Christ, the Father of glory, may give to you a spirit of wisdom"* (Ephesians 1:17). When we face problems for which we have no human solution, the Spirit of wisdom will help us as we rely upon Him. In another place Paul wrote to the Corinthians *"by His* [God's] *doing you are in Christ Jesus, who became to us wisdom from God"* (1 Corinthians 1:30).

88

When you face a very difficult situation, turn to God and ask for wisdom. He will give it to you through His Spirit if you ask in faith: *"But he must ask in faith without any doubting, for the one who doubts is like the surf of the sea, driven and tossed by the wind"* (James 1:6).

Sometimes we are faced with a choice between two courses of action, both of which seem to be good. At those times, God gives wisdom to make the best choice in order to glorify His name.

Spirit of Knowledge

The Holy Spirit can guide and direct us according to His own knowledge, even though we ourselves may not know what to do. Since He is God, He has all knowledge. When we trust the Lord, He will guide us around many difficulties into which we would fall if we were not relying upon Him. One of my favorite prayers is in Ephesians where Paul prays that God *"may give to you a spirit of wisdom and of revelation in the knowledge of Him* [Jesus]*"* (Ephesians 1:17). Paul wants us to know much more about Jesus and have good judgment to use that knowledge to improve our lives for God's glory and our good.

Spirit of Glory

The Apostle Peter tells us about the *"Spirit of glory"* when he penned these words about persecution: *"If you are reviled for the name of Christ, you are blessed, because the Spirit of glory and of God rests on you"* (1 Peter 4:14). We are promised that if we suffer with Christ, we shall also be glorified with Him (Romans 8:17). The Spirit of glory rests upon those who suffer persecution for Jesus Christ as true saints of the living God.

Spirit of Judgment, Spirit of Burning

Fire is a symbol of judgment and purification from sin. The Old Testament prophet Isaiah mentions the Spirit of judgment and burning, showing by example what those names mean. He wrote:

Isaiah 4:4-5

4   When the Lord has washed away the filth of the daughters of Zion, and purged the bloodshed of Jerusalem from her midst, by the spirit of judgment and the spirit of burning,

5   then the Lord will create over the whole area of Mount Zion and over her assemblies a cloud by day, even smoke, and the brightness of a flaming fire by night; for over all the glory will be a canopy.

The Spirit of judgment and burning purges sin and rebellion from the hearts of those who come to God. He will not let one of God's children continue in sin without bringing strong conviction to his or her heart. John the Baptist, in speaking of Jesus Christ, said that *"He will baptize you with the Holy Spirit and fire"* (Matthew 3:11). The Spirit of God burns with judgment against the sin and evil we tolerate in our lives. However, it is comforting to know that He will also give us strength and help to overcome those very sins as we yield to Him for cleansing and strength.

✝ The Holy Spirit –
Moving the Unsaved toward Christ

The rest of our study about the Holy Spirit concerns His present-day activities in the world. His activities can be divided into four general areas which we will deal with in the following order:

1) His ministry of moving the unsaved toward Christ and imparting salvation upon repentance and faith;
2) His ministry of empowering the saved;
3) His ministry of perfecting the saved,
4) His ministry of bestowing gifts to the saved.

A misunderstanding of the ministry of the Holy Spirit has been a source of much heartache and division in both churches and families. It is important not to go beyond what is written: *"Anyone who goes too far and does not abide in the teaching of Christ, does not have God"* (2 John 9). To rely on experience is dangerous because experience is subjective and an unreliable guide to doctrine. Now, let us proceed to "Moving the Unsaved toward Christ."

CONVICTS AND CALLS TO CHRIST

The ministry of the Holy Spirit with regard to the unsaved is twofold. He causes them to realize they have sinned against God and He points to Jesus as the solution to their sin problem.

The Holy Spirit Convicts

Jesus taught us how the Holy Spirit accomplishes His ministry with people of the world who have not trusted Him:

John 16:8-11
8 "And He [the Spirit], *when He comes, will convict the world concerning sin and righteousness and judgment;*
9 concerning sin, because they do not believe in Me;
10 and concerning righteousness, because I go to the Father and you no longer see Me;
11 and concerning judgment, because the ruler of this world has been judged.

Conviction Concerning Sin – Jesus said distinctly that the Spirit would convict the world of sin *"because they do not believe in Me."* When the word "sin" is used in the singular, it usually refers to man's fallen nature, though not in every case. When it is used in the plural form, "sins," it refers to the acts of sin produced by the fallen nature. When the Gospel of Christ is preached and His own purity and holiness are emphasized, the Holy Spirit convicts men of their own innate sinfulness. But, unlike the feelings of guilt put on us by Satan, the Holy Spirit always points to Calvary as the way of forgiveness and freedom.

Conviction Concerning Righteousness – The Holy Spirit also convicts unsaved people about the need of being righteous. He points to Jesus Christ in all of His righteous perfection and purity. God cannot excuse sin. Only those who have had their sin removed will be permitted to live in His presence throughout eternity. The very fact that Jesus has gone into heaven to the Father and is seated at His right hand proves His complete sinlessness and utter righteousness. The Holy Spirit uses this to show a sinner his own sinfulness when he hears the Gospel. Then, Jesus Christ's righteousness stands out in bold contrast to his or her own unrighteousness. Jesus, who was sinless, died for our sin. He has been received into heaven itself, proving that God accepted both Him and His sacrificial work.

Conviction Concerning Judgment – Finally, Jesus said that the Spirit would convict the world concerning judgment *"because the ruler of this world has been judged."* Satan was judged and defeated at the Cross. Just as surely as Satan was defeated at the Cross of Jesus Christ, judgment will come upon all those who live in rebellion against the God of heaven. Again, the Holy Spirit always shows Jesus as the way to God when He brings conviction of sin, of righteousness, and of judgment to come. Only the Holy Spirit can convict men that they really need a Savior and Jesus is the Savior sent from God. This is the convicting ministry of the Holy Spirit.

The Holy Spirit Calls the Unsaved to Christ

The Holy Spirit works with the unsaved to bring them to faith in Christ. Hebrews 6:4 speaks *"of those who have once been enlightened and have tasted of the heavenly gift and have been made partakers of the Holy Spirit."* The

Holy Spirit reveals to sinners the reality and truth of the good news of salvation in Jesus Christ. He gives them a foretaste of what it is like to receive forgiveness of sins. In this way He creates in them a desire to come to Jesus for forgiveness. Those who respond are often referred to as *"the called"* (Romans 1:6, 1 Cor. 1:2, Gal. 1:6, and Jude 1).

THE MOMENT OF SALVATION

The Holy Spirit Regenerates – Imparts New Life

Another ministry of the Holy Spirit is with those who come to salvation. After He has convicted and called men to Christ, He gives them new life when they turn to Him. Jesus says, *"It is the Spirit who gives life"* (John 6:63). In talking with Nicodemus, He made it clear that the Spirit is the One who gives spiritual life:

John 3:4-7
4   Nicodemus said to Him, "How can a man be born when he is old? He cannot enter a second time into his mother's womb and be born, can he?"
*5   Jesus answered, "Truly, truly, I say to you, unless one is born of water **and the Spirit**, he cannot enter into the kingdom of God.*
*6   "That which is born of the flesh is flesh, and **that which is born of the Spirit is spirit.***
7   "Do not be amazed that I said to you, 'You must be born again.'"

There has been much controversy about Jesus' statement *"unless one is born of water and the Spirit."* Some people believe that "water" means water baptism; in that case it means unless one is baptized and born of the Spirit he cannot enter the kingdom of God. Others say that "water" is a symbol of regeneration and means, "unless you are regenerated and born of the Spirit, you cannot enter the kingdom of God." While the latter statement is true, it is not likely that is what Jesus means here. His meaning is very simple. A parallel helps explain:

born of water	=	born of the flesh is flesh
[born] of the Spirit	=	born of the Spirit is spirit

When a woman has a baby, the water around the fetus breaks before it is delivered. Human beings are born of water, that is, physical, natural birth. Once you have been born physically of water, then you can be born spiritually of the Spirit. Unless you have been born of the Spirit after your physical birth, you cannot see the kingdom of God. That is why you **must** be born again!

The Spirit gives life to those who trust in Jesus. This life-giving process is sometimes called "regeneration." Paul wrote of this: *"He saved us, not on the basis of deeds which we have done in righteousness, but according to His mercy, by the washing of regeneration and renewing by the Holy Spirit"* (Titus 3:5). Thus, the job of the Holy Spirit is to give new life to those who believe in Jesus.

The Holy Spirit Seals Believers in Christ
When the Holy Spirit puts the mark of God's owner-ship on believers, He seals them in Christ. Paul wrote to the Ephesians:

Ephesians 1:13-14
*13 In Him, you also, after listening to the message of truth, the gospel of your salvation – having also believed, **you were sealed in Him with the Holy Spirit** of promise,*
14 who is given as a pledge of our inheritance, with a view to the redemption of God's own possession, to the praise of His glory.

Eternal Security – Every believer is sealed as God's own property. Ephesians 4:30 likewise speaks of His

94

sealing work. It exhorts us, *"Do not grieve the Holy Spirit of God, by whom you were sealed for the day of redemption."* The sealing of the Holy Spirit guarantees our ultimate salvation. We are sealed *"for the day of redemption,"* that is, the day when Jesus comes again to resurrect those who die in Him. We are marked as God's own people from the time we trust Jesus until the resurrection. This is a strong argument for the absolute security of those who have put their faith in Him. True believers should not fear losing their salvation because the mark of God's ownership rests on them until Jesus comes again.

The Holy Spirit Indwells Every Believer

The Holy Spirit takes up permanent residence in every believer. Several verses clearly state this understanding. Paul wrote, *"if anyone does not have the Spirit of Christ, he does not belong to Him"* (Romans 8:9). If you are saved, you clearly must have the *"Spirit of Christ,"* i.e., the Holy Spirit. Other verses teach the same truth. For example: *"Do you not know that you are a temple of God, and that the Spirit of God dwells in you?"* (1 Corinthians 3:16). You do not have to be fearful that you may not have received the Spirit of God. If you have trusted Jesus, you already have the Spirit of God dwelling in you. It is simply a matter of stepping out by faith on what is written and conducting your life based on it.

✝ The Holy Spirit – Empowering the Saved

The baptism and filling of the Holy Spirit are perhaps the most widely discussed and controversial of the fundamental doctrines of Scripture. They are so controversial, in fact, that entire denominations have been built upon different understandings of the Bible's teaching on these subjects.

We must clearly understand what the Bible says lest we end up stumbling spiritually. Some go to emotional extremes and others miss out on much that God has for them.

THE BAPTISM OF THE HOLY SPIRIT

Two things are taught about the Christian's relationship to the Holy Spirit. First, as stated above, the Spirit of God dwells in the believer, and second, the believer is in the Spirit of God. Paul teaches this in Romans: *"However, you are not in the flesh but in the Spirit, if indeed the Spirit of God dwells in you."* (Romans 8:9). God is in us, and we are in God, in response to Jesus' prayer in the Gospel of John, *"that they may all be one; even as You, Father, are in Me and I in You, that they also may be in Us"* (John 17:21).

The words *"baptize in water"* (John 1:33) mean to be put under water or to immerse. Therefore, to be baptized in the Holy Spirit is to be put in Him or immersed in Him. It is the privilege of all of God's children to be indwelt and baptized in the Holy Spirit.

Some Christians teach that the baptism in the Holy Spirit comes after salvation. First one is saved and subsequently baptized in the Holy Spirit. They say it may happen immediately after being saved or sometime later. The Scripture teaches otherwise. For example, the Gospel of John teaches that salvation and baptism in the Holy Spirit are at the same time:

John 7:38-39
38 "He who believes in Me, as the Scripture said, 'From his innermost being will flow rivers of living water.'"
39 But this He spoke of the Spirit, whom those who believed in Him were to receive; for the Spirit

was not yet given, because Jesus was not yet glorified.

All who believe would receive the Holy Spirit after Jesus was glorified and the Holy Spirit would flow forth from their innermost being.

Furthermore, Paul taught this about the Holy Spirit: *"For by one Spirit we were all baptized into one body, whether Jews or Greeks, whether slaves or free, and we were all made to drink of one Spirit"* (1 Corinthians 12:13). When Paul said, *"we were all made to drink of one Spirit,"* apparently he was referring to what Jesus said in John 7:38 quoted above. When the Holy Spirit baptizes us into one body (of Christ), we are simultaneously made to drink (receive internally) the Spirit. One spiritual baptism accomplishes two purposes: 1) it places us in Christ and 2) the Holy Spirit takes up residence within us.

All believers are baptized into one body, by one Spirit. Notice the word *"all"* in 1 Corinthians 12:13. Paul is writing to the whole Corinthian church. When he wrote *"all baptized"* that included all believers regardless of how long they had been saved. They could have been mature believers saved for many years or immature believers just born-again a few minutes – the length of time makes no difference. He includes *every* Christian in this verse, for he says, *"For by one Spirit we were all baptized into one body."* It does not matter whether you are Jew or Gentile, slave or free, if you believe in Jesus, you were made to drink of the one Spirit and baptized into one body.

Compare the *"One Baptism"* of Ephesians

Now, by comparing the following verses, we find a very interesting fact:

Ephesians 4:3-6
3 being diligent to preserve the unity of the Spirit in the bond of peace.

97

4 There is one body and one Spirit, just as also you were called in one hope of your calling;
5 one Lord, one faith, one baptism,
6 one God and Father of all who is over all and through all and in all.

Paul says that we should be *"diligent to preserve the unity of the Spirit in the bond of peace."* Then he lists seven spiritual things in which we ought to maintain unity as Christians: one body, one Spirit, one hope, one Lord, one faith, one baptism, and one God and Father. As an example, there is one Spirit. If I taught there are two Holy Spirits, both of whom are God, you would forbid me to minister in your church. I cannot teach two Spirits, because there is only one Holy Spirit! The same is true of the six other spiritual unities. There is only one true Lord – not a lord Buddha **and** a Lord Jesus. Jesus is the one true Lord. Likewise, there is only one spiritual baptism.

Notice all these things are spiritual in nature, not physical. It is not reasonable for just one of them to refer to a physical event such as water baptism. Therefore, *"one baptism"* does not speak of water baptism; it speaks of spiritual baptism in this context.

It is clear, then, that if all believers are baptized into one body, and all made to drink of one Spirit, as Paul says in 1 Corinthians 12:13, there can be only one spiritual baptism. That baptism must, of necessity, occur the moment a person is saved and placed in the body of Christ since *all* believers are baptized. However, it is true that many believers do not live as though they are in the Holy Spirit and He is in them.

THE FILLING OF THE HOLY SPIRIT

In some cases the disagreement between Christians over the baptism and the filling of the Holy Spirit results simply from semantics, i.e., the meaning of words. While it is clear that all believers are indwelt by the Spirit and have been put in the Spirit, it is equally clear that not all Christians conduct themselves in the power of the Holy Spirit. Some believers are filled with the Holy Spirit and others are not. The words "filling" and "baptism" do not speak of the same thing. Baptism of the Holy Spirit takes place when a person is saved. Filling may happen then, or it may happen later, and one may be filled more than once in his or her Christian experience.

Filled with Him/Controlled by Him

What do we mean by the words "filled with the Holy Spirit"? The Bible explains it by contrasting a person who is filled with the Holy Spirit with one who is filled with wine and has become drunken:

Ephesians 5:17-18
17 So then do not be foolish, but understand what the will of the Lord is.
18 And do not get drunk with wine, for that is dissipation, but be filled with the Spirit.

The phrase *"so then do not be foolish"* can also be translated "do not act rashly." It is in keeping with the previous verse in which Paul wrote to be careful how you conduct your life. Here he says, "do not act rashly," that is, do not act without reason or understanding.

Paul continues with the words, *"understand what the will of the Lord is."* It is a wonderful thing that the Bible does not simply command us to understand the Lord's will without telling us what it is. Paul tells us exactly what His will is: *"do not get drunk with wine but be filled with the Spirit."* When one is drunk, he is under the influence of alcohol. Often a person who is very timid becomes bold and rash. On the other hand, one who is normally bold may become very shy and timid. Too much alcohol influences the way a person conducts himself. The same is true for

99

those who are filled with the Holy Spirit; He will influence the way they act. We are not to be under the influence of alcohol, but under the influence of the Holy Spirit. He will influence us for good, just as too much wine may influence a person for evil.

Be Being Filled – The phrase *"be filled with the Spirit"* gives us some very interesting insights also. It is given to us as a direct command from the Lord – it is not optional! If we obey the Lord, we will be filled with the Spirit of God. Not only is it a command, but it is written in a way that means we are to permit God to fill us rather than trying to fill ourselves. The filling or control of the Holy Spirit comes by His action within us. Our part is simply to allow Him to do so and submit our lives to His control.

The command is also continuous in meaning; the filling of the Spirit is not once for all time. It is a day by day, moment by moment filling. Another way of expressing the verse is "be being filled with the Holy Spirit." This says much to us about how to live a life pleasing to God. It does not teach us that we are to sit back and do nothing, waiting for God to do everything. But it does teach that we are to permit the Holy Spirit of God to have His way in our lives. We must not resist Him, but cooperate with Him at all times. We cannot fill ourselves with the Holy Spirit, but we should ask God to do it and permit Him to control us moment by moment.

How to Recognize the Filling of the Holy Spirit

How may one know if he has been filled with the Spirit? Ephesians 5:19-21 gives four marks of a Spirit-filled Christian. They will be seen in a Christian who walks with the Lord.

Joy – The first mark of being Spirit-filled is that of joy. Verse 19 is a manifestation of this characteristic: *"speaking to one another in psalms and hymns and spiritual* *songs. "* One does not often have psalms and hymns and spiritual songs on his lips unless he has a deep, abiding joy in his heart.

Notice another thing. It says the believers are speaking to one another. Where the Spirit of the Lord is in charge, there will be free and open communication with our fellow believers. If, because of pride, resentment, envy, or hurt you will not speak to a fellow believer, you are not filled with the Spirit of God. One cannot harbor these things in his heart and be filled with the Spirit of God at the same time. Resentment and bitterness cannot exist side by side with deep, abiding joy.

Praise – The second mark of a Spirit-filled Christian is found in the last half of verse 19, *"singing and making melody with your heart to the Lord."* This is praise. One filled with the Holy Spirit can sing and make melody with his heart to the Lord for all that God has done. Consider Psalm 103 in this connection where David wrote:

Psalm 103:1-2
1 Bless the LORD, O my soul;
   And all that is within me, bless His holy name.
2 Bless the LORD, O my soul,
   And forget none of His benefits;

Thanksgiving – The third mark of being filled with the Spirit is *"always giving thanks for all things in the name of our Lord Jesus Christ to God, even the Father"* (Ephesians 5:20). An attitude of thanksgiving to God is a sign that one is filled with the Spirit of God. The Holy Spirit enables us to give thanks for all things in the name of Jesus to the Father. Thanksgiving is related to the context in which we find this verse. God does not intend for us to give thanks for sinful acts, but we can give thanks for His grace to endure hardship and heartaches occasioned by sin, and to overcome sin.

Humble Submission – Voluntary submission to other Christians out of *"the fear of Christ"* is the final mark of a Spirit-filled Christian. Ephesians says, *"and be subject to one another in the fear of Christ"* (Ephesians 5:21). Fear in this case means reverence or respect. Being submissive is commonly called humility. It takes great humility to be subject to other people in the Lord, but this is exactly what the Spirit of God will work in our lives if we will permit it.

Humility that allows submission does not mean that one does not stand for his principles or that he lets other people run over him. Moses was very humble (Numbers 12:3) and yet he was a strong leader of Israel in the wilderness. He withstood opponents and was victorious because his cause was righteous. But he also submitted himself to God and to His divine order.

Do you manifest any of the four marks of a Spirit-filled Christian – joy, praise, thanksgiving, or humble submission?

† The Holy Spirit – Perfecting the Saved

The Holy Spirit ministers in the believer to do two things: 1) to bring him to maturity in Christ, and 2) to work through him to help other people. In this section we will discuss the Holy Spirit's work of perfecting believers to be like Christ, that is, bringing them to spiritual maturity. To get that result He does a number of different works in the life of a Christian believer yielded to Him. This involves His ministries of filling, anointing, sanctifying, illuminating, and interceding.

The Holy Spirit Fills
In the previous section, the filling of the Holy Spirit was discussed. We learned that the Bible is clear that every Christian has the Holy Spirit living within him. But it is

equally clear that some Christians are filled with the Holy Spirit and some are not. If every Christian were filled with Him, then there would be no reason for the Bible to command us to be filled.

The filling of the Holy Spirit is an act of the Spirit of God by which He controls the life of an individual who yields voluntarily to Him. It is so natural in expression that sometimes a person does not know that he is filled by the Holy Spirit. At other times, it is a very dramatic experience which varies from person to person. Through the filling of the Spirit, God works to bring believers to maturity in Christ and then to make them productive in His kingdom.

On the day of Pentecost, all believers in the house where they were gathered were filled with the Holy Spirit (Acts 2). They came under His gracious power and began to carry out the will of God. Prior to Pentecost they had been frightened, hiding behind locked doors. Remember that Jesus had just been crucified and certainly many of the rulers and people did not want to hear any more about Him. But the moment the apostles and disciples were filled with the Holy Spirit, they exhibited great boldness and began witnessing with power to the resurrection of Jesus Christ.

Proper Motivation to Seek Filling – There are a number of reasons for desiring the fulness of the Spirit. Simon wanted power to bestow the Holy Spirit by laying his hands on people – apparently to make a name for himself (Acts 8). That was not a worthy motive. It is the same today. Some desire to be filled with the Holy Spirit in order to experience some spectacular or miraculous gift. That is not a worthy motive for seeking Him.

The Bible indicates three reasons why one should desire to be filled with the Holy Spirit:

1) To produce the fruit of the Spirit in order to live a life pleasing to God (Galatians 5:22-23).

2) To be enabled to exercise the gifts of the Spirit, not for personal pleasure or pride, but for the building up of the body of Christ (Ephesians 4:11-12).

3) To have power for witnessing (Acts 1:8).

If you desire to be filled with the Holy Spirit for these reasons and have never asked to be filled, you may pray something like this:

"Heavenly Father, Your Word commands me to be filled with the Holy Spirit. I offer myself to You completely. Please fill me with your Spirit so that I may live my life in a way pleasing to you. I want to exercise the gifts that the Holy Spirit has given me for the glory of Jesus Christ and the good of His Church. Please enable me to be a powerful witness for Jesus wherever I go. Thank you, Father, for the gift of Your Spirit and His filling. In the name of the Lord Jesus. Amen."

If you ask that in simple faith, God will answer you. Don't always expect some explosive experience. Accept by faith that God will answer your prayer because He commands His children to be filled with the Spirit (Ephesians 5:18).

The Holy Spirit Anoints

An anointing is a special power or ability given by the Holy Spirit for a particular task. Jesus told those in His hometown, *"THE SPIRIT OF THE LORD IS UPON ME, BECAUSE HE ANOINTED ME TO PREACH THE GOSPEL TO THE POOR. HE HAS SENT ME TO PROCLAIM RELEASE TO THE CAPTIVES, AND RECOVERY OF SIGHT TO THE BLIND, TO SET FREE THOSE WHO ARE OPPRESSED"* (Luke 4:18). Jesus specifically claimed the anointing of the Holy Spirit for the power to fulfill the ministry which God had given Him. Luke, the physician, later in Acts 10:38 states, *"You know of Jesus of Nazareth, how God anointed*

Him with the Holy Spirit and with power, and how He went about doing good, and healing all who were oppressed by the devil, for God was with Him."

Christians are anointed by the Spirit of God to understand the truth. His anointing is especially important when it comes to understanding the truth or error of what is being taught about the Word of God. The Apostle John told us:

1 John 2:20-21
20 But you have an anointing from the Holy One, and you all know.
21 I have not written to you because you do not know the truth, but because you do know it, and because no lie is of the truth.

Thus, the Holy Spirit gives us the ability to distinguish truth from error as we hear men teach different doctrines. Many people still follow false doctrine either willfully or because they are out of fellowship with the Lord. In that condition, they do not recognize error when it is being taught.

The Holy Spirit Sanctifies

The word "sanctify" means "to be set apart unto God." Like many other spiritual benefits, it has two aspects: positional standing before God and progressive state of life.

Positional Sanctification – Everyone who has faith in Jesus has already been permanently sanctified: *"By this will* [God's] *we **have been sanctified** through the offering of the body of Jesus Christ **once for all"*** (Hebrews 10:10). Notice the past tense there. Those who are so sanctified are also perfected for all time: *"For by one offering He has perfected for all time those who are sanctified"* (Hebrews 10:14). Verse 29 warns us, *"How much severer punishment do you think he will deserve who has trampled under foot the Son of God, and has regarded as unclean the blood of the covenant by which he was sanctified, and has insulted*

105

the Spirit of grace?" Thus, there is a sense in which every believer is fully, completely, and permanently sanctified once for all time. It is a gift of grace to all those who trust in the Lord Jesus. This is called positional sanctification.

Progressive Sanctification – However, the working out of positional sanctification in experience is something else again. The Holy Spirit, through His sanctifying work, enables us to have in our daily experience that which Jesus purchased for us by His blood. He continues to show us our sin, enabling us to confess it and repent so that we become more like Him. God is interested in purifying the saints and He is doing that by the sanctifying work of the Holy Spirit. Christians are chosen *"according to the foreknowledge of God the Father, by the sanctifying work of the Spirit"* (1 Peter 1:2). Read more about sanctification beginning on page 210.

The Holy Spirit Illuminates
He also perfects believers through teaching and revealing the truth of God to them that they could not otherwise learn. This process is called illumination. Paul teaches this concept in 1 Corinthians:

1 Corinthians 2:9-10
9   ... "THINGS WHICH EYE HAS NOT SEEN AND EAR HAS
    NOT HEARD,
    AND which HAVE NOT ENTERED THE HEART OF MAN,
    ALL THAT GOD HAS PREPARED FOR THOSE WHO LOVE
    HIM."
10 **For to us God revealed them through the Spirit;** *for the Spirit searches all things, even the depths of God.*

The Spirit of God uses the Bible to reveal to us the glory of God and the glory of the age to come which we will share when Jesus Christ returns. Few other things give us as good a reason to live for the Lord as this one does. Paul prayed for the Christians in Ephesus that God would give to them *"a spirit of wisdom and of revelation in the knowledge of"* Jesus Christ (Ephesians 1:17). We also ought to pray that God would open our eyes to the truth through the Holy Spirit.

The Holy Spirit Intercedes

Prayer is another way by which the Spirit of God perfects the people of God. Ephesians 2:18 teaches that we have access through Jesus to the Father by one Spirit. The throne of God is as close to us as the Holy Spirit who actually lives within us. Not only does He give us access to the Father, but He also prays for us Himself. Paul teaches in a familiar Romans passage, *"the Spirit also helps our weakness; for we do not know how to pray as we should, but the Spirit Himself intercedes for us with groanings too deep for words"* (Romans 8:26). This subject is discussed in more detail under the heading, "He Prays for Us," on page 73.

In addition to the Holy Spirit interceding for us, we are taught to pray in the Holy Spirit for other believers. Paul commands us to pray *"in the Spirit"* for others in view of spiritual warfare. He writes, *"With all prayer and petition pray at all times in the Spirit, and with this in view* [spiritual warfare], *be on the alert with all perseverance and petition for all the saints"* (Ephesians 6:18). Thus, we are to cooperate with Him to intercede for others.

† The Holy Spirit –
Bestowing Gifts, Ministries, and Effects

Gifts of the Holy Spirit are given to us to serve people in the church for the common good of the body. Gifts are another of those much studied and much discussed topics.

Each of the gifts has been discussed in detail in this author's book, <u>A Fresh Look at the Holy Spirit</u>. However, because of the nature of this book, we must be brief here. We will look at three passages about gifts that God has given to His Church: Romans 12, 1 Corinthians 12, and Ephesians 4. We will start in 1 Corinthians to establish a biblical basis for our discussion:

> 1 Corinthians 12:4-6
> *4 Now there are varieties of **gifts**, but the same Spirit.*
> *5 And there are varieties of **ministries**, and the same Lord.*
> *6 There are varieties of **effects**, but the same God who works all things in all persons.*

Three different things are mentioned in this passage: gifts, ministries, and effects. Notice also that the entire Trinity – Father, Son, and Holy Spirit – is involved in spiritual gifts. Gifts from the Father are discussed in detail in Romans 12, the effects or manifestations of the Holy Spirit are discussed in 1 Corinthians 12, and Ephesians 4 discusses the ministries carried on by ministers given to the Church by the Lord Jesus Christ for *"the equipping of the saints for the work of service"* (Ephesians 4:12).

Gifts from the Father

First, consider the gifts of the Father to the Church in Romans 12:

> Romans 12:6-8
> *6 ... we have gifts that differ according to the grace given to us, let each exercise them accordingly: if **prophecy**, according to the proportion of his faith;*
> *7 if **service**, in his serving; or he who **teaches**, in his teaching;*

> *8   or he who **exhorts**, in his exhortation; he who*
> *gives, with liberality; he who **leads**, with diligence;*
> *he who shows **mercy**, with cheerfulness.*

This passage lists seven gifts of God the Father to the Church of Jesus Christ. Each person who believes has at least one gift. They are, with a brief explanation:

(1) **Prophecy** – is the inspired preaching of the Word of God with a pointed message to those who hear. On occasion, it may be a warning of some problem or danger close at hand. An example of this is in Acts 21:9-14 where a prophet named Agabus warned Paul about the bonds that awaited him in Jerusalem.

(2) **Service** – comes from the same root word as "deacon ." It is the gift to perform tasks that glorify God and build up believers, such as distributing food to those in need (Acts 6:1-3).

(3) **Teaching** – is enlightening, explaining, comparing, and clarifying the Word of God in a way that makes difficult subjects easy to understand.

(4) **Exhortation** – is the God-given ability to move other believers to proper conduct or action. It contains the idea of comfort, and includes correcting someone else with meekness.

(5) **Giving** – is the desire and enablement to give above and beyond normal giving to meet the needs of others or to extend the work of the Church of the Lord Jesus Christ on earth. This gift is not restricted to those who are wealthy.

(6) **Leading** – is the ability to preside, to rule, and to maintain order within a group. It is the ability to lead the Church in the right path for the glory of God.

(7) **Showing mercy** – is the ability to exercise compassion by word and deed beyond the ordinary call of duty. It

enables one to show practical love for the sake of Christ to those whom he would not ordinarily love.

It is apparent that Christians exercise these gifts in varying degrees. For example, all Christians should show mercy and all should give. However, God endows certain believers with special abilities to exercise these gifts above and beyond the others. God gives these gifts for the benefit of the whole Church. You should be diligent in the use of the gifts God has given you so there will be no lack in your church.

Ministries from Jesus Christ

Jesus is said to give ministers to the Church in Ephesians chapter 4. The Apostle Paul wrote these words:

Ephesians 4:11-12
11 And He [Jesus Christ] *gave some as **apostles**, and some as **prophets**, and some as **evangelists**, and some as **pastors and teachers**,*
12 for the equipping of the saints for the work of service, to the building up of the body of Christ;

(1) **Apostles** – are men who carried special authority in the early church. Their position is generally believed to have ceased with the passing of the first century apostles. However, in the sense that apostle means "sent one," this ministry is performed now by missionaries who found churches. No one has the same authority today as the original apostles. However, there are those who are sent out to preach the Gospel and plant churches throughout the world.

(2) **Prophets** – are those whom God has gifted to preach His Word with great power. God uses His prophets in such a way that you know that He has spoken when they speak.

(3) **Evangelists** – are those people who are especially gifted in persuading others to receive Jesus Christ as

110

personal Lord and Savior. However, this does not relieve those who are not so gifted from witnessing.

(4) **Pastors and teachers** – seems to be a single office. Some divide this ministry into two different offices; others believe it is one office because the word *"teachers"* does not have a definite article in the original language. In the latter case, the pastor/teacher is one gifted person who shepherds a local church. Such men are gifted more along the lines of teaching than evangelization, though they may do the work of an evangelist, as Paul told Timothy to do (2 Timothy 4:5).

Effects or Manifestations of the Holy Spirit

Nine manifestations of the Holy Spirit are listed by Paul:

1 Corinthians 12:7-10
7 But to each one is given the manifestation of the Spirit for the common good.
*8 For to one is given the **word of wisdom** through the Spirit, and to another the **word of knowledge** according to the same Spirit;*
*9 to another **faith** by the same Spirit, and to another **gifts of healing** by the one Spirit,*
*10 and to another the **effecting of miracles**, and to another **prophecy**, and to another the **distinguishing of spirits**, to another various **kinds of tongues**, and to another the **interpretation of tongues.***

The question of the gifts and manifestations of the Holy Spirit is, perhaps, the issue that divides Christians today more than any other. Entire books have been written on the subject. However, it is outside the purpose of this book to have a lengthy discussion of the issues. Let us look at gifts and manifestations as they are given in the New Testament and as they appear to have been used at that time.

(1) **The word of wisdom** – is a special wisdom that God gives when a need arises for direction or understanding. Often a few individuals will be recognized as possessing wisdom greater than others; however, this gift goes beyond that to meeting needs for wisdom in specific circumstances.

(2) **The word of knowledge** – consists of specific facts or situations revealed by the Holy Spirit for the advancement of the Gospel or for the good of the body of Christ.

(3) **Faith** – is a gift of faith beyond the kind necessary for salvation. Every true believer has the kind of faith necessary to be saved. This gift is the faith to see God do great and mighty things.

(4) **Gifts of healing[s]** – are both plural words in the original language, meaning God gives healing as a gift to the person He wishes to heal. A permanent "gift of healing" to an individual for the purpose of healing others is not taught in Scripture.

(5) **Miracles** – are works of power that occur in cases of special need. An example is the healing of the lame man in Acts 3:1-10. Note that while several miracles are recorded in the book of Acts, they were done over a period of 30 years. They were fewer and farther between than one might think before studying the subject. Apparently, extraordinary miracles were not the ordinary daily occurrence in the life of the early church.

(6) **Prophecy** – was explained earlier in this chapter. It is an important gift because it is mentioned in all three passages we are studying. Keep in mind that prophecy in the Bible is not foretelling in the sense of personal fortunetelling.

112

(7) **Distinguishing of spirits** – is the ability to know whether particular words or actions originate in God or in the satanic kingdom.

(8) **Kinds of tongues** – is the ability given through the Spirit of God to speak in a language not previously known or studied.

(9) **Interpretation of tongues** – is the ability to interpret such languages.

Regardless of your position on the use and nature of these gifts, the most important thing to remember is their specific purpose. According to 1 Corinthians 12:7, gifts are given for the common good of the body of Christ. Paul makes a very important point:

1 Corinthians 12:24-25
24 ... God has so composed the body, giving more abundant honor to that member which lacked,
25 so that there may be no division in the body, but that the members may have the same care for one another.

It is very carefully noted that the purpose of the gifts is the building up of the Church; genuine gifts unite the body of Christ rather than divide it. Anything that is genuinely produced by the Spirit of God should not divide the body of Christ. Much of what happens in a local church can be measured by that standard. If arguments and splits arise over a gift, then it should be very carefully and prayerfully examined in the light of God's Word and put away if it is not of His Spirit.

MAKE THE HOLY SPIRIT PERSONAL

The importance of recognizing that the Holy Spirit is a person can hardly be overstated. Once we realize that the Spirit of God is a person, it should make us careful not to grieve Him through our sin, or insult Him by refusing His ministry of grace in our lives. When the Holy Spirit convicts of sin through God's Word, we must listen with an open heart. His conviction is clear and gentle, always pointing us to Jesus and Calvary for forgiveness and cleansing.

It is only as we cooperate with the Holy Spirit that we come to experience the full blessing that God intends for us. Before Jesus was crucified and ascended, the Holy Spirit could not be given (John 7:39). His coming had to await the ascension and glorification of Jesus Christ. Once Jesus paid for our sin and was glorified, the Holy Spirit came to live in the innermost being of those who believe.

If you already trust Jesus for the forgiveness of your sins, but do not realize that God has put His Spirit within you, you should take a moment now to thank God for His gift. Invite the Holy Spirit to take control of your life for the glory of the Lord Jesus Christ. You will find a great difference as He gives you power over sin and power to witness about Jesus.

If you do not trust Jesus, then you are missing the most blessed relationship you could ever have with another person. The Holy Spirit is waiting for you to trust Jesus. When you do, you will also have His help and fellowship day by day. I urge you to trust Jesus Christ right now for the forgiveness of your sins.

John 15:26
"When the Helper comes, whom I [Jesus] will send to you from the Father, that is the Spirit of truth who proceeds from the Father, He will testify about Me,

Ephesians 5:17-21
17 So then do not be foolish, but understand what the will of the Lord is.

18   And do not get drunk with wine, for that is dissipation, **but be filled with the Spirit,**
19   speaking to one another in psalms and hymns and spiritual songs, singing and making melody with your heart to the Lord;
20   always giving thanks for all things in the name of our Lord Jesus Christ to God, even the Father;
21   and be subject to one another in the fear of Christ.

Chapter 4

The Bible
† God's Word to Man

The Bible is the Word of God revealed to mankind. It is the only authoritative and reliable source of precise knowledge about God and His relationship to creation and humanity. All that man can arrive at apart from Scripture is merely speculation.

ACCURATE KNOWLEDGE ABOUT GOD

As discussed in chapter one, a person may come to know about God in two ways. One way is through the created world in which he lives. The Bible makes it clear that a thinking person can easily see the hand of an intelligent Being behind the detailed design of the world. It takes far more faith to believe that the process of evolution brought about the beauty and intricate design in nature than it does to believe that a Being of superior intelligence made it all work together.

Paul wrote about God: *"For since the creation of the world His invisible attributes, His eternal power and divine nature, have been clearly seen, being understood through what has been made, so that they are without excuse"* (Romans 1:20). A simple reading of this verse shows that the created world gives a person with an open mind an understanding of the eternal power and divine nature of the Godhead.

The Scripture is also clear, however, that one can search for God through creation and never arrive at a personal relationship with Him. It is absolutely necessary for God to reveal Himself in order for mankind to know Him as a person. Therefore, the only way to come to know Him personally is through the revelation which He has given about Himself in the Scriptures. That is why the Bible is of such great importance in human life and history.

IS THE BIBLE THE WORD OF GOD?

The Old Testament Declares Itself to Be

Someone may ask, "What makes you think the Bible is God's word to man?" There are several good reasons to believe in the divine inspiration of the Scriptures. First of all, the Bible declares itself to be the Word of God. The Old Testament affirms time and again that its message comes directly from God.

Here are just two passages out of many, one from the Law and one from the Prophets, which come directly from the mouth of God. Deuteronomy 4:2 says, *"You shall not add to the word which I am commanding you, nor take away from it, that you may keep the commandments of the LORD your God which I command you."* Later, Jeremiah the prophet wrote:

Jeremiah 1:7-9
7 *But the LORD said to me,*
  "Do not say, 'I am a youth,'
  Because everywhere I send you, you shall go,
  And all that I command you, you shall speak.
8 *"Do not be afraid of them,*

117

> *For I am with you to deliver you," declares the*
> LORD.
> *9 Then the* LORD *stretched out His hand and*
> *touched my mouth, and the* LORD *said to me,*
> **"Behold, I have put My words in your mouth."**

William Evans mentioned in his book, <u>The Great
Doctrines of the Bible</u>, that Genesis 1 has the words *"God
said"* ten times. Others have said that the Old Testament
contains phrases like *"the* LORD *said," "the* LORD *spoke,"*
and *"the word of the* LORD *came,"* some 3,808 times.
Certainly the Old Testament writers thought of themselves
as the revealers of the will of God, and often began their
messages with the words, *"Thus says the* LORD*."* Clearly,
the Old Testament is a book which declares itself to be
from God.

The New Testament Declares Itself to Be
The New Testament writers also claim divine inspiration for themselves and for each other, as well as for Old
Testament writers. An example of the latter is found in
2 Peter, where the Apostle Peter writes:

> 2 Peter 1:20-21
> *20 But know this first of all, that no prophecy of
> Scripture is a matter of one's own interpretation,
> 21 for no prophecy was ever made by an act of
> human will,* **but men moved by the Holy Spirit
> spoke from God.**

Several passages in the New Testament show that the
writers understood that they were being used by God to
give us His message. Paul said: *"which things we also
speak, not in words taught by human wisdom, but in those
taught by the Spirit"* (1 Corinthians 2:13). He likewise
wrote, *"If anyone thinks he is a prophet or spiritual, let him
recognize that* **the things which I write to you are the
Lord's commandment"** (1 Corinthians 14:37).

Peter Recognizes Paul's Writings as Scripture

It is a remarkable thing that the Apostle Peter declares Paul's writings to be Scripture. It is remarkable because, in the book of Galatians, Paul rebuked Peter in front of other people in Antioch. He told him that the thing he was doing was wrong. And even though this happened to him, Peter later wrote that Paul's letters were on the same level as the rest of Scripture. This is what he said:

> 2 Peter 3:15-16
> *15 ... regard the patience of our Lord as salvation; just as also our beloved brother Paul, according to the wisdom given him, wrote to you,*
> *16 as also in all his letters, speaking in them of these things, in which are some things hard to understand, which the untaught and unstable distort, as they do also **the rest of the Scriptures,** to their own destruction.*

Notice that Peter says, *"the rest of the Scriptures,"* thus making Paul's writings the very Word of God.

Jesus Pre-Validated the New Testament

Jesus speaks of the New Testament as being inspired in John's Gospel. Just before He was crucified He told the apostles that they had many things yet to learn. However, the Holy Spirit would show them those things after His departure:

> John 16:12-13
> *12 I have many more things to say to you, but you cannot bear them now.*
> *13 But when He, the Spirit of truth, comes, **He will guide you into all the truth;** for He will not speak on His own initiative, but whatever He hears, He will speak; and He will disclose to you what is to come.*

Through these words, Jesus said the Holy Spirit would lead the apostles into areas of truth they had not yet learned.

Both the Old and New Testaments state in no uncertain terms that they are truly the Word of God.

The Bible Has Proven to Be God's Word

Miracles – Some people question the validity of the Bible's self-declaration to be the Word of God. It is one thing to state something, but quite another thing to prove it. Through the centuries the Bible has proven to be the Word of God. When the Law was given about 1400 B.C., miracles took place to show the people that God was in it. Israel could not deny the presence of God because of the evidence. Moses' face shone so brightly when he came down from the presence of God that he had to wear a veil so the people could look at him. Paul compared the ministry of the Law of Moses with that of the Spirit:

> 2 Corinthians 3:7-8
> 7 *But if the ministry of death, in letters engraved on stones, came with glory, so that the sons of Israel could not look intently at the face of Moses because of the glory of his face, fading as it was,*
> 8 *how will the ministry of the Spirit fail to be even more with glory?*

Israel not only heard the thunder and lightning on Mount Sinai, but they saw the face of Moses shining so brightly they could not look upon him without a veil covering his glory and brilliance.

On the day of Pentecost, God manifested His presence in a mighty way. Fourteen different language groups were represented in Jerusalem on that day. Each of those language groups heard the good news about the mighty deeds of God preached to them in their own tongue by uneducated fishermen (Acts 2:11). When needed, miracles have been performed when the Gospel is preached. God never does a miracle to satisfy human curiosity or desire – there must always be a real need. Jesus refused to perform a miracle while on trial as a means to save His own life; but He did many to meet the needs of other people.

Fulfilled prophecy – another strong argument for the validity of the Bible as the Word of God is fulfilled prophecy. Just one specific prophecy, out of hundreds of fulfilled prophecies, is the naming of Cyrus who was to rule Persia and influence the Jews. Isaiah called Him by name some 150 years before he was born! (Isaiah 44:28).

Ever since it was written, the Bible has proven to be God's Word by every test one can imagine. It has been hated, spoken against, burned, and declared illegal. Yet it is still with us, not only on the printed page, but in the hearts and minds of millions of people. Those who have received Jesus Christ as Savior know the truth of its origin in God.

† The Bible – Background and Content

We have seen that both the Old and New Testaments declare themselves, and have proven themselves, to be the Word of God in the face of all opposition through the ages. The unusual background lends more credible evidence to the divine nature and origin of the Scriptures.

THE BIBLE'S BACKGROUND AND INFLUENCE

The Bible is considered by many to be the greatest book ever written. No other book has such an unusual background. It is made up of 66 books of varying lengths, written by approximately forty authors over a period of some 1600 years, from about 1500 B.C. to 100 A.D. Among the authors were kings, priests, lawyers, shepherds, fishermen, and tax-gatherers. They represented all parts of the old world – from the wilderness of Sinai in southern Israel, to the cliffs of Arabia; from small towns in Palestine, to large capital cities, like Babylon, on the Euphrates River; from the courts of temples to prisons in the land of exile. What a variety of places from which the Scriptures were written! What a variety of people doing the writing! Free men, slaves, prisoners, and kings were all involved in writing the Scripture.

The Bible's Unity

And yet, with such a difference of time, authors, and circumstances, the entire 66 books have one central theme; that is incredible! That theme is the separation of man from God through sin and God's provision to bring man back to Himself. The testimony throughout is uniform and clear that salvation is never by works but always by grace through faith in God and His plan of salvation. The Bible begins with the fall of man and ends with believers completely restored to perfect fellowship with God.

The Bible's Prophecy

Another reason for believing that the Bible is the Word of God is the control which it has exercised over human history. Thousands of years ago the Bible made predictions about the nations near the end of this age. It has proven to be correct and demonstrates the control of God over history even though men are, for the most part, acting in rebellion against Him. Even recent events in Europe and the Middle East have a bearing on the end times. Many believe these things are happening to the nations in order to set the stage for the return of Jesus Christ.

The Bible's Influence for Good

The fact is, that wherever the Bible has been preached and taught clearly and simply, men have been freed and women have been raised to their proper, God-given place.

Unbelievers often accuse Christianity of keeping men and women in bondage. However, in areas not under its influence, people are in bondage to fear, poverty, famine, and disease. The Word of God has the power to break all bondage in the name of Jesus Christ (John 8:32).

THE BIBLE'S CONTENT

The Bible's Accuracy

The amazing accuracy of the Bible is a good reason for believing it to be the Word of God. It was never intended to be a book of science, but where it speaks on scientific matters it has proven to be reliable. One example comes from Job, the oldest book of the Bible, written some 1,500 years before Jesus Christ. It spoke about the cycle of rain long before scientists discovered it – it evaporates, ascends, cools, and falls as rain. Job says that God is responsible for the rain cycle:

Job 36:26-29
26 *"Behold, God is exalted, and we do not know Him;*
    The number of His years is unsearchable.
27 *"For He draws up the drops of water,*
    They distill rain from the mist,
28 *Which the clouds pour down,*
    They drip upon man abundantly.
29 *"Can anyone understand the spreading of the clouds,*
    The thundering of His pavilion?"

Another example of Job's scientific accuracy well ahead of its time is the statement, *"He stretches out the north over empty space, And hangs the earth on nothing"* (Job 26:7). Job points out that the earth is hung in space on nothing. How much truer to actual science than the idea of

123

the earth resting on the back of an elephant, or the Greek god Atlas, condemned to support the heavens on his shoulders! Remember, even though Job is the oldest book of the Bible, it contains truth, not fantasy!

Long before science determined that the earth is not flat, as people used to believe, the book of Job referred to its shape as being like a circle. He wrote, *"He has inscribed a circle on the surface of the waters At the boundary of light and darkness"* (Job 26:10). This verse also refers to the division between night and day caused by the earth turning in relation to the sun. These facts are common knowledge today. Therefore, it is not surprising to read them in the Bible. But, if you had lived 500 years ago, you would have thought such information absolutely unbelievable. And yet, it was written in Job 3,000 years before that! These are only a few of the many scientifically correct statements that were made thousands of years before their discovery by science.

The Bible's Great Wisdom

Not only is the Bible filled with facts, it also contains more wisdom than all other books in the world combined. Proverbs alone contains wonderful advice for living a good life with oneself and with one's fellowman. Here are a few of the common sense rules for living from among more than thirty chapters of wisdom. The book of Proverbs tells us about living at peace with a neighbor:

Proverbs 3:29-30
29 *Do not devise harm against your neighbor,*
   While he lives securely beside you.
30 *Do not contend with a man without cause,*
   If he has done you no harm.

It also speaks about not being lazy:

Proverbs 6:6-11

  6 *Go to the ant, O sluggard,*
     Observe her ways and be wise,
  7 *Which, having no chief,*
     Officer or ruler,
  8 *Prepares her food in the summer*
     And gathers her provision in the harvest.
  9 *How long will you lie down, O sluggard?*
     When will you arise from your sleep?
 10 *"A little sleep, a little slumber,*
     A little folding of the hands to rest" –
 11 *Your poverty will come in like a vagabond*
     And your need like an armed man.

A little later in the same chapter of Proverbs, we find the Scriptures speaking of seven things that God hates.

Proverbs 6:16-19

 16 *There are six things which the LORD hates,*
     Yes, seven which are an abomination to Him:
 17 *Haughty eyes, a lying tongue,*
     And hands that shed innocent blood,
 18 *A heart that devises wicked plans,*
     Feet that run rapidly to evil,
 19 *A false witness who utters lies,*
     And one who spreads strife among brothers.

And finally, Proverbs 15:1 gives good advice about how to handle people who become angry with us. It says, *"A gentle answer turns away wrath, But a harsh word stirs up anger."*

Near the Bible's Middle

If you have a Bible including the Old and New Testaments but without study notes and concordances, you will find that Psalm 119 is the approximate middle of it. It is interesting that this Psalm at the middle of God's Word deals with the wonderful value of His Word. It is made up of 176 verses based on the Hebrew alphabet.

Psalm 119:9 gives a young man advice about how to live a good and satisfying life: *"How can a young man keep his way pure? By keeping it according to Your word."* When ones life is lived according to the Word of God, he is blessed with inner peace and satisfaction.

The Psalmist also tells us how God's Word works to keep us from sin. It has to do with memorizing the Word so that it is easily recalled in moments of temptation. He wrote: *"Your word I have treasured in my heart, That I may not sin against You"* (Psalm 119:11).

He believed in the enduring truth of God's Word: *"The sum of Your word is truth, And every one of Your righteous ordinances is everlasting"* (Psalm 119:160). Because God's Word is true, he expected God to keep His Word. Reverence for the Lord is tied to the fulfillment of His Word. The Psalmist expressed his thought on this subject this way: *"Establish Your word to Your servant, As that which produces reverence for You"* (Psalm 119:38).

This Psalm emphasizes the individual's relationship to the Word and its effect on life and his relationship to God. Verse 58 expresses the longing of the writer to have God's favor on his life: *"I sought Your favor with all my heart; Be gracious to me according to Your word."* He knew that knowledge of right and wrong is gained from understanding God's Word: *"From Your precepts I get understanding; Therefore I hate every false way"* (Psalm 119:104). He likewise knew that the truth of the Word could keep him free: *"Establish my footsteps in Your word, And do not let any iniquity have dominion over me"* (Psalm 119:133).

The Psalmist certainly appreciated the Word of God. Be sure to take time to read the entire Psalm for yourself from the Bible.

MAKE THE BIBLE PERSONAL

No other book, whether it is religious or secular, has such an unusual background and content. It is literally amazing that some forty authors wrote over a period of 1600 years, in such a variety of places, yet all bear the same message and all give the same testimony to the living God. The Scripture records, *"Forever, O LORD, Your word is settled in heaven."* (Psalm 119:89).

Since the Bible is the Word of God, we should heed its words, *"See to it that you do not refuse Him who is speaking. For if those did not escape when they refused him who warned them on earth, much less will we escape who turn away from Him who warns from heaven"* (Hebrews 12:25).

The purpose of the Bible is to bring men back into the place of blessing under God's love. Paul wrote Timothy some words of great importance:

2 Timothy 3:16-17
16 All Scripture is inspired by God and profitable for teaching, for reproof, for correction, for training in righteousness;
17 so that the man of God may be adequate, equipped for every good work.

If you desire to serve God and be useful to Him and His kingdom, then by all means learn as much of the Scriptures as you possibly can. For then the Lord will use you in His Kingdom as you apply His Word to your own life. May God grant you the desire to serve Him in such a way.

The Bible is likewise a testimony to God's Son:

1 John 5:11
11 And the testimony is this, that God has given us eternal life, and this life is in His Son.
12 He who has the Son has the life; he who does not have the Son of God does not have the life.

127

Paul wrote to the Romans:

Romans 5:6-8
6 For while we were still helpless, at the right time Christ died for the ungodly.
7 For one will hardly die for a righteous man; though perhaps for the good man someone would dare even to die.
8 But God demonstrates His own love toward us, in that while we were yet sinners, Christ died for us.

Do not spurn the love God demonstrated through Christ on the Cross. Trust the resurrected Christ today as your own Lord and Savior.

Chapter 5

God's Creation
† The Creator

The Gospel of John tells us that: *"God is spirit, and those who worship Him must worship in spirit and truth"* (John 4:24). God is invisible to the natural human eye. John 1:18 says, *"No one has seen God at any time."* Paul described God in these words: *"Now to the King eternal, immortal, invisible, the only God, be honor and glory forever and ever. Amen"* (1 Timothy 1:17). God, who is spirit, is likewise eternal, immortal, and invisible.

GOD THE FATHER – ACTIVE IN CREATION

God Is Creator
Those who believe in the only true God, believe in a spirit being by whom everything else came into being. Some philosophers teach that spirit is good and material is bad. But that idea is wrong. John wrote in Revelation about both worlds where an angel: *"swore by Him who lives forever and ever, WHO CREATED HEAVEN AND THE THINGS IN IT, AND THE EARTH AND THE THINGS IN IT, AND THE SEA AND THE THINGS IN IT ... "* (Revelation 10:6). *"God saw all that He had made, and behold, it was very good"* (Genesis 1:31) – even the material world.

God Is Praised for Creating – The final book of the Bible, Revelation, depicts the events of the end of this age.

Chapters four and five record a scene set in the throne room of heaven. Chapter four has a description of the One who sits on the throne and the created spirit beings who are in His presence. Four living creatures, who are the seraphim described in Isaiah 6, fly around God's throne day and night worshiping Him, saying, *"HOLY, HOLY, HOLY, IS THE LORD GOD, THE ALMIGHTY, WHO WAS AND WHO IS AND WHO IS TO COME"* (Revelation 4:8). Then the Apostle John writes:

> Revelation 4:10-11
> *10 the twenty-four elders will fall down before Him who sits on the throne, and will worship Him who lives forever and ever, and will cast their crowns before the throne, saying,*
> *11 "Worthy are You, our Lord and our God, to receive glory and honor and power; for You created all things, and because of Your will they existed, and were created."*

This scene illustrates the very basis for the praise of God by the host in heaven. He is Creator and all things exist because He willed it so. Both men and angels owe their very life and breath to the Creator. Concerning man's dependence upon God, Job says:

> Job 34:14-15
> *14 "If He should determine to do so,*
> *If He should gather to Himself His spirit and His breath,*
> *15 All flesh would perish together,*
> *And man would return to dust."*

Thus, God is not only the Creator of the universe and all who are in it, but He is the Sustainer of that universe.

When God responded to the complaints of Job and the charges of his friends, He began by showing His power and ultimate sovereignty in creation. God answered:

Job 38:4-7

*4 "Where were you when I laid the foundation of the
   earth?*
   Tell Me, if you have understanding,
5 Who set its measurements? Since you know.
   Or who stretched the line on it?
6 "On what were its bases sunk?
   Or who laid its cornerstone,
7 When the morning stars sang together,
   And all the sons of God shouted for joy?"

Throughout that chapter of Job and the next, God speaks about various aspects of His creation and the things He has done that no one else can do.

THE SON OF GOD – ACTIVE IN CREATION

Revelation 4:11, quoted earlier in this chapter, ascribed glory to the Lord God Almighty because He created all things. However, many people do not realize that Jesus also had a significant role in creation before His birth in Bethlehem. John wrote about this in his Gospel:

John 1:1-3 and 14

*1 In the beginning was the Word, and the Word
was with God, and the Word was God.*
2 He was in the beginning with God.
**3 All things came into being through Him, and
apart from Him nothing came into being that has
come into being.**

*14 And the Word became flesh, and dwelt among
us, and we saw His glory, glory as of the only
begotten from the Father, full of grace and truth.*

Thus, it is clear from these verses that Jesus Christ, here called *"the Word,"* had an active part in creation prior to His incarnation.

Paul agrees. He said about Jesus, *"For by Him all things were created, both in the heavens and on earth, visible and invisible, whether thrones or dominions or rulers or authorities – all things have been created through Him and for Him"* (Colossians 1:16). Each of these two very clear passages state that Jesus Christ was an active agent in the creation of both the visible and the invisible worlds, including the angelic host.

THE HOLY SPIRIT – ACTIVE IN CREATION

The Spirit of God was likewise an active agent in creation. The second verse in the Bible speaks of the Spirit of God early in creation history, *"The earth was formless and void, and darkness was over the surface of the deep; and **the Spirit of God was moving** over the surface of the waters"* (Genesis 1:2).

The Spirit of God participated in the creation of heaven and earth; He also participated in the creation of man. The book of Job ascribes man's being and life to the Spirit of God: *"The Spirit of God has made me, And the breath of the Almighty gives me life"* (Job 33:4). Thus, all three members of the Trinity were active in creation: Father, Son, and Holy Spirit.

The Purpose of Creation

One of the principal reasons for creation is to bring praise to God. Psalm 19 contains some often repeated words:

Psalm 19:1-4
1 *The heavens are telling of the glory of God;*
   And their expanse is declaring the work of His hands.
2 *Day to day pours forth speech,*
   And night to night reveals knowledge.
3 *There is no speech, nor are there words;*

132

Their voice is not heard.
4 *Their line has gone out through all the earth,*
  And their utterances to the end of the world. ...

Those who have a biblical faith in God have no difficulty in praising Him because He is the Creator.

† God's Creation – The Spirit World

Creation is made up of two parts: 1) the spirit world which God created first, and 2) the physical or visible world, which He created second.

There are three classes of spiritual beings. *"God is spirit"* according to John 4:24. As the Creator and Supreme Sovereign Being, He is in a class by Himself. He is the Creator of the two other classes of spiritual beings, angels and mankind.

THE EXISTENCE OF ANGELS

The Bible has many references to angels. Many writers affirm the existence of angels and their involvement in the affairs of men. So many references abound that we cannot deal with all of them, but here are a few.

Jesus Affirms the Existence of Angels

Jesus taught about angels many times. For example, He taught that children are guarded by holy angels who have access to God the Father in heaven: *"See that you do not despise one of these little ones, for I say to you that their angels in heaven continually see the face of My Father who is in heaven"* (Matthew 18:10). Christian parents should commit their children to the care of the Lord who assigns His guardian angels to watch over them. But you must never put your trust in angels instead of God.

133

According to Jesus, God the Father could have put more than 12 legions of angels at His disposal, if He had asked. Seventy-two thousand angels would have rushed to His side to save Him from arrest and crucifixion! However, He chose not to call for help in order that the Scriptures might be fulfilled (Matthew 26:54).

Angels will accompany Jesus at His second coming. He said, *"The Son of Man will send forth His angels, and they will gather out of His kingdom all stumbling blocks, and those who commit lawlessness"* (Matthew 13:41). And again He said, *"For whoever is ashamed of Me and My words in this adulterous and sinful generation, the Son of Man will also be ashamed of him when He comes in the glory of His Father with the holy angels"* (Mark 8:38).

For one who knows Jesus, it is enough that He affirmed the existence of angels. However, the Bible's account does not stop there. Other New Testament writers also affirm their existence.

Paul and John Affirm the Existence of Angels
Paul mentions angels and the spirit world in several places, among which are Colossians 2:18 and 2 Thessalonians 1:7. The Apostle John speaks of angels throughout the book of Revelation. According to John, there will apparently be a marked increase in the activity of angels **and** demons, at the end of this age.

Peter and Jude Affirm the Existence of Angels
Peter says very clearly that Jesus is now in heaven at the right hand of God *"after angels and authorities and powers had been subjected to Him"* (1 Peter 3:22). Even Jude, though it has only one chapter, refers both to Satan and the archangel Michael in verse nine. These are only a few of many references to the spirit world throughout Scripture.

THE ANGELIC CREATION

God created the angelic beings before He created man. This fact is clear from the book of Job:

Job 38:4-7
4 *"Where were you **when I laid the foundation of the earth?** Tell Me, if you have understanding,*
5 *Who set its measurements? Since you know. Or who stretched the line on it?*
6 *"On what were its bases sunk? Or who laid its cornerstone,*
7 *When the morning stars sang together And all the **sons of God shouted for joy?"***

"Sons of God" is an Old Testament reference to angels as a creation of God. They were present when God laid the foundation of the earth, i.e., before man was created. The fact that angels are spirits is confirmed by the author to the Hebrews where he said about them: *"Are they not all ministering spirits, sent out to render service for the sake of those who will inherit salvation?"* (Hebrews 1:14).

This author wrote in his book, <u>Christ and the Occult,</u> "Several names in Scripture suggest ranks or levels of command among angels. These ranks are difficult to put in precise order." Even so, some theologians in the Middle Ages believed there were nine orders of angels which were subdivided even further. (See "orders of angels" on the Internet). Here are the angelic groups named in the Bible:

Seraph/Seraphim are mentioned in Isaiah 6:1-6. Verse two of that passage says: *"Seraphim stood above Him, each having six wings: with two he covered his face, and with two he covered his feet, and with two he flew."* These six-winged creatures who serve around the throne of God are literally "the burning ones." Revelation 4:6-9 speaks of four *"living creatures"* that have the same characteristics as the Seraphim in Isaiah 6; both have six wings, whereas Cherubim have only four wings (Ezekiel 1:6).

135

Cherub/Cherubim – Cherubim are a class of angels whom God has assigned a special relationship to earth and man (Ezekiel 10:7, 28:11-19). We find them in Genesis 3:24, *"So He drove the man out; and at the east of the garden of Eden He stationed the cherubim and the flaming sword which turned every direction to guard the way to the tree of life."* The archenemy of our souls, Satan, is called both a cherub and an angel: *"You were **the anointed cherub** who covers ..."* (Ezekiel 28:14). *"They have as **king over them, the angel** of the abyss; ... in Greek he has the name Apollyon"* (Revelation 9:11). *Apollyon,* according to Strong's Concordance, is "a destroyer (i.e., Satan)." Since Satan is both an angel and a cherub, the indication is that "cherub" is the name given to a special group of high ranking angels.

Thrones – *"For by Him* [Jesus] *all things were created, both in the heavens and on earth, visible and invisible, whether **thrones** or **dominions** or **rulers** or **authorities** – all things have been created through Him and for Him"* (Colossians 1:16). The word *"throne"* refers to a seat of a ruler or potentate. Satan's throne was in Pergamos when Revelation was written (Rev. 2:12-13). In Revelation 4:4 the twenty-four elders, whom some believe to be angelic beings, are seen seated upon thrones in heaven.

Dominion is found in Ephesians 1:21 – *"far above all rule and authority and power and **dominion**, and every name that is named, not only in this age but also in the one to come."* Some angelic beings are assigned to specific political areas; dominion is sometimes translated *"government"* in the King James Version (Colossians 1:16).

Powers/authorities (see Ephesians 1:21 above). With reference to our subject, the Greek word *exousia* is translated *"power"* or *"authority"* in the KJV. On one occasion *"powers"* is the translation of *"dunamis"* (1 Peter 3:22) from which we get our word "dynamite." Paul says that Jesus is the creator of all these in Colossians 1:16.

Rulers (Principalities in KJV) (see Ephesians 1:21 above) – Political divisions called "principalities" also exist among men (Example, The Principality of Monaco). Principalities are ruled over by a prince, like *"the prince of the kingdom of Persia"* (Daniel 10:13). Both good and evil supernatural spiritual powers have divisions known as principalities (Ephesians 1:21, 6:12, 3:10; etc.).

Archangel means "chief or first angel." *"But Michael the archangel, when he disputed with the devil and argued about the body of Moses, did not dare pronounce against him a railing judgment, but said, 'The Lord rebuke you!'"* (Jude 9). Michael is the only angel designated an archangel in the Bible.

Authorities (Ephesians 1:21, 3:10; Colossians 1:16). *"Who is at the right hand of God, having gone into heaven, after angels and **authorities** and powers had been subjected to Him"* (1 Peter 3:22). "Authorities" is a translation of the Greek word, *exousia*. It is often translated *"powers"* in the King James Version. See "Powers/authorities" above.

Might (*dunamis* in Ephesians 1:21) – The Greek *"dunamis,"* is translated *"power"* or *"might."* Perhaps this division of angels is known for their superior strength.

It does not seem possible to make a hard and fast classification in terms of rank from the Scriptures. Therefore, the above nine groups may not be in the proper order of their authority and some groups may overlap. Only enough is given to indicate that there are clearly different groups.

The Nature of Angels

Angels are individually created spirits. Contrary to popular belief, angels are not spirits of people who have died. Each one was individually created by God before the creation of the earth and man. At times they become visible and look like men. This can be seen in Daniel 9:21 and other places. Christians are exhorted, *"Do not neglect to show hospitality to strangers, for by this some have entertained angels without knowing it"* (Hebrews 13:2). The only way to entertain an angel without knowing it, is for the angel to look human. Abraham and Sarah, as well as others in the Bible, were visited by angels.

There are both holy and fallen angels. Jesus spoke of *"holy angels"* who will come with Him on His return to earth (Mark 8:38). Thus, heavenly angels are sinless because they are holy. However, some angels rebelled with Satan. Thus, they fell into sin and became fallen angels.

Angels are intelligent spirit beings (Ezekiel 28:12-16; Matthew 24:36). Peter alludes to their intelligence when he said they have a desire to look into, and presumably understand, the Gospel: *"... those who preached **the gospel to you by the Holy Spirit sent from heaven – things into which angels long to look"*** (1 Peter 1:12).

Angels are powerful according to the Apostle Peter (2 Peter 2:11). David, the sweet psalmist of Israel, referred to their great power when he wrote, *"Bless the LORD, you His angels, **Mighty in strength**, who perform His word, Obeying the voice of His word"* (Psalm 103:20).

Angels are quick in their movements and sometimes look like men. Both of these facts are brought out by Daniel the prophet: *"Yes, while I was speaking in prayer, the man Gabriel, whom I had seen in the vision at the beginning, **being caused to fly swiftly**, reached me about the time of the evening offering"* (Daniel 9:21 NKJV). Satan also roams to and fro and up and down in the earth, which seems to indicate rapid movement (Job 1:7).

Angels are extremely numerous (Revelation 5:11; Job 25:3). The writer to the Hebrews expresses the truth in this way: *"But you have come to mount Zion, and to the city of the living God, the heavenly Jerusalem, and to myriads of angels"* (Hebrews 12:22 KJV). The word *"myriads"* means too many to count.

Mankind is strictly forbidden to worship angels or any other being than the Lord God (Exodus 20:3, Revelation 19:10). While an angel may be sent to communicate a message to someone (Luke 1:11-20), it is dangerous to seek out angels as a source of knowledge or help because Satan and his ministers masquerade as angels of light and righteousness in order to deceive people (2 Corinthians 11:14-15).

The Activity of Angels
Now that we have seen the nature of angels and how they may be organized, let us see how they spend their time. What do they do?

Angels serve and worship God according to Isaiah 6:1-8 and Revelation 4 and 5. They were sent to minister to Christ after the temptation and they delivered special messages from God to men and women in both the Old and New Testaments. An example of this is the appearance of the angel Gabriel to Mary to announce the birth of Jesus (Luke 1:26-27).

Angels serve the people of God. They protected Daniel in the lions' den (Daniel 6:22) and delivered the Apostle Peter from prison (Acts 12:7). They acted as guides to Israel during the exodus from Egypt (Exodus 14:19) and to Philip when he was directed to the chariot of the Ethiopian eunuch to share the Gospel of Jesus Christ (Acts 8:26).

They have an important part in God's government over mankind. They took part in the revelation of the Word of God to man (Acts 7:53, Galatians 3:19, Hebrews 2:2). They also observe the activities of local churches (1 Corinthians 4:9, 11:10, 1 Timothy 5:21).

Since angels are intelligent and powerful beings, the Apostle Peter says that it is foolish to treat them lightly. He spoke of some unwise men who are:

> 2 Peter 2:10-11
> *10 ... Daring, self-willed, they do not tremble when they revile angelic majesties,*
> *11 whereas angels who are greater in might and power do not bring a reviling judgment against them before the Lord.*

† God's Creation – The Physical World

Did God create heaven and earth and all that is in them, or are they the product of selective evolution? Did God create the "big bang" and then go off to let it develop on its own? If there is no God, where did the materials come from to initiate the "big bang?" These questions are the focal point of the conflict between many scientists and biblical creationists. However, keep in mind there are creditable scientists who also believe in creation. In this section we will be looking at the biblical teaching about creation of the physical world.

Creation of the Heavens and Earth

Genesis, the book of beginnings, records this summary statement of the physical creation: *"In the beginning God created the heavens and the earth"* (Genesis 1:1). That same first chapter goes on to tell us about the six days of creation in which God created on successive days: light (1:3-5), the expanse or atmospheric heavens (1:6-8), dry land, vegetation, plants, and trees (1:11-13), the sun, moon, and stars appointed for light on earth (1:14-19), birds of the air, fish, and sea animals (1:20-23), wild and domesticated animals, and mankind in God's own image last of all (1:24-29).

Creation and Fall of Man Is Essential

The Genesis account of mankind's creation and fall into sin is absolutely essential for a right view of the problem of sin. Everyone knows that man is not perfect. But why is he not perfect and is he able to improve his nature through education, training, and hard work?

The book of Romans teaches that man is a sinner because the first man Adam sinned and damaged his whole being. His sinful nature was passed on to the entire human race. If the teaching of evolution were correct, mankind would not have come from a single pair at the beginning. Likely, there would be more than one line of human beings. In that case some men might have been sinners while others might not have been. However, it is quite clear biblically that all men are sinners because they descended from Adam. Romans 5:12 says, *"Therefore, just as through one man sin entered into the world, and death through sin, and so death spread to all men, because all sinned."* The proof that all have sinned is that all die. Romans 6:23 says, *"For the wages of sin is death, but the free gift of God is eternal life in Christ Jesus our Lord."*

Creation Is a Matter of Faith

In Acts, Paul had this to say about God as Creator in his message in Athens:

Acts 17:24, 29-31
24 "The God who made the world and all things in it, since He is Lord of heaven and earth, does not dwell in temples made with hands;

29 "Being then the children of God, we ought not to think that the Divine Nature is like gold or silver or stone, an image formed by the art and thought of man.
30 "Therefore having overlooked the times of ignorance, God is now declaring to men that all people everywhere should repent,

141

31 because He has fixed a day in which He will judge the world in righteousness through a Man whom He has appointed, having furnished proof to all men by raising Him from the dead."

We can see that God is Creator through the things He made, but it is still a matter of faith. Hebrews 11:3 says, *"By faith we understand that the worlds were prepared by the word of God, so that what is seen was not made out of things which are visible."* Some people strongly resist believing in a Creator, because if it is admitted, responsibility to Him must also be admitted; they must give an account to Him for their actions. The problem is all have sinned and fall short of the standard God has laid out for them.

Earlier, the fact was mentioned that death spread to all men because all sinned. The scientific and medical community are doing all they can to extend the life span of man, and that is good. We ought to do all we can to help people. But, while the average life span has been extended, the present death rate for all mankind is still 100 percent! Because of sin, the Bible says, *"it is appointed for men to die once and after this comes judgment"* (Hebrews 9:27). Since that is the case, we cannot afford to ignore our personal accountability to God.

THE INTERACTION OF
SPIRITUAL AND PHYSICAL BEINGS

Understanding the interaction between the spiritual and physical worlds gives some insight into many of the problems we face in modern society. This area of teaching is often ignored or else taken to the extreme. In either case, one may stumble spiritually. Again, it is important to go to the Bible, the only authoritative source of knowledge on this subject.

142

Satan and Angels Are Spirits

The Bible reveals that God is not the only spirit being. Angels are spirit beings created by God as seen in Colossians 1:16 quoted earlier. The Bible teaches that Satan, the enemy of God and man, is a spirit being of indescribable evil. He is referred to in Ephesians 2:2 as *"the prince of the power of the air, of the spirit that is now working in the sons of disobedience."* He is the fallen cherub described in Ezekiel 28:11-19 and Isaiah 14:12-17, which we will examine later.

Man Is Also Spirit

The Bible teaches that man is spirit, soul, and body. Notice that order – **spirit**, soul, and body. We normally refer to man as body, soul, and spirit. But God says that man is spirit, soul, and body, thus emphasizing the spiritual nature of man. Man is more than a soul and body: *"Now may the God of peace Himself sanctify you entirely; and* **may your spirit and soul and body** *be preserved complete, without blame at the coming of our Lord Jesus Christ"* (1 Thessalonians 5:23). Hebrews 4:12 agrees when it says, *"the word of God is living and active and sharper than any two-edged sword, and piercing as far as the division of soul and spirit."* There is a distinct difference between the soul and spirit of a human being.

Man's contact with God is through the human spirit. This makes us far superior to animals. The Apostle Paul wrote:

1 Corinthians 2:11, 14
11 For who among men knows the thoughts of a man except the spirit of the man which is in him? Even so the thoughts of God no one knows except the Spirit of God.

14 But a natural man does not accept the things of the Spirit of God, for they are foolishness to

143

him; and he cannot understand them, because they are spiritually appraised.

Since man is capable of communication and fellowship with God, he can also communicate with spiritual beings who are in rebellion against God. Mind reading, sorcery, witchcraft, and other occult practices may work under certain conditions. Therefore, caution needs to be exercised in dealing with the supernatural world. When help is needed, seek it from God, not from angels, the occult, or the paranormal. God may use his angels to help (Hebrews 1:14), but it should be at His direction, not ours. Do not fall prey to talking directly to angels. Keep your prayer directly with the Father and Son through the Spirit.

MAKE THE CREATOR PERSONAL

God is Creator of both the physical and spiritual worlds. Even if you refuse to acknowledge God in this life, you will give an account to Him afterward *"because He has fixed a day in which He will judge the world in righteousness through a Man whom He has appointed, having furnished proof to all men by raising Him from the dead"* (Acts 17:31). That Man, of course, is Jesus Christ. Then, an account will be given for the life you lived as a creature of God whether or not you acknowledge Him as God and Creator now.

It matters to the point of urgency that each one realize that he or she is a creature responsible to the Creator. The time has come when repentance and faith in the death and resurrection of God's Son for salvation is vital. Jesus did not sacrifice His life without good reason. He did it that He might deliver you from the guilt and bondage of your sin. May God your Creator grant you the repentance and faith which leads to eternal life.

Genesis 1:27

27 God created man in His own image, in the image of God He created him; male and female He created them.

Chapter 6

The Adversary
† Satan's Fall into Sin

The spirit world is as real as our physical world. The Bible tells us that the Supreme Being, God Himself, is spirit. Angels, both good and bad, are likewise spirit beings created by God. When creating man in His own image, God gave him a spirit as well.

In this chapter we will look at the fascinating subject of the introduction of sin into the universe by an angel named Lucifer, who became known as Satan the Adversary. Two passages deal with his fall into sin; both are in the Old Testament prophetic books. We will begin with the prophet Ezekiel's account of Satan's fall, and then, we will study Satan's purpose in the world according to Isaiah.

Before Satan's Fall

The fall of Satan is described in some detail in Ezekiel 28:11-23. Some people do not believe that this passage is addressed to Satan because it says *"take up a lamentation over the king of Tyre."* But, if you will look at the verses preceding these, you will find that Ezekiel 28:2 addresses this person as the leader of Tyre or the prince of Tyre. Later the title changes from prince of Tyre to the king of Tyre. As you read the following verses, you will see that the things that are said about this person cannot apply to a mere man. For example, *"You were in Eden, the garden of God"* and *"On the day that you were created they were prepared. You were the anointed cherub who covers."* Therefore, many teachers believe these verses actually speak to and about the power behind the throne, i.e., Satan. Starting at Ezekiel 28:11 is the teaching about the power that drove the king of Tyre:

Ezekiel 28:11-12
11 Again the word of the LORD came to me saying,
12 "Son of man, take up a lamentation over the king of Tyre and say to him, 'Thus says the LORD GOD,
'You had the seal of perfection,
Full of wisdom and perfect in beauty.'"

Once again, it is evident that this passage speaks of one who is more than a mere man. It speaks of Satan, who was the evil, spiritual power behind the throne of Tyre. No human being, other than Jesus Christ, ever had the seal of perfection, except perhaps Adam and Eve before they sinned.

Satan is also full of wisdom. The book of James speaks of two kinds of wisdom: one that is earthly, natural, and demonic; and the other that comes from above. The first produces jealousy, selfish ambition, disorder, and every evil thing. The second is peaceable, gentle, reasonable, full of mercy and good fruits, unwavering, and without hypocrisy (James 3:13-17). Satan was full of wisdom which became corrupt when he fell. He has since used that corrupt wisdom to produce all sorts of evil.

According to Ezekiel, Satan was in the garden of God before he fell into sin:

Ezekiel 28:13
13 "You were in Eden, the garden of God;
Every precious stone was your covering:
The ruby, the topaz, and the diamond;
The beryl, the onyx and the jasper;

> *The lapis lazuli, the turquoise and the*
> *   emerald;*
> *And the gold, the workmanship of your settings*
> *   and sockets,*
> *Was in you.*
> *On the day that you were created*
> *They were prepared."*

Adam and Eve were the only human beings in the garden of Eden. They were cast out after they sinned. This creature, however, is said to have been in Eden, the garden of God. Furthermore, verse 13 says, *"Every precious stone was your covering"* and proceeds to list nine precious stones. Interestingly, those nine stones were among the twelve precious stones found on the breastplate of the Old Testament high priest who served in the tabernacle. More will be said about this later.

Ezekiel 28:13 goes on to say, *"On the day that you were created they were prepared."* Note that this being was created directly by God, not procreated as all people have been, with the exception of Adam and Eve.

Ezekiel 28:14
14 "You were the anointed cherub who covers,
*   And I placed you there.*
*   You were on the holy mountain of God;*
*   You walked in the midst of the stones of fire."*

"The anointed cherub" is a high order of angelic being. Cherubim serve God in some relationship to the great tribes of the earth. They are described elsewhere as having four faces – a lion, an ox, a man, and an eagle – all facing in different directions. These faces represent the earthly creation: the lion stands for wild animals, the ox for tame animals, man for humanity, and the eagle for the birds of the air. This relationship with the earth may partially explain Satan's interest in earth and those who live here.

148

Satan's Fall

Following his creation, Satan was on the holy mountain serving God. He was created in perfection directly from the hand of God without sin:

Ezekiel 28:15-16
15 "You were blameless in your ways
From the day you were created
Until unrighteousness was found in you.
16 "By the abundance of your trade
You were internally filled with violence,
And you sinned;
Therefore I have cast you as profane
From the mountain of God.
And I have destroyed you, O covering cherub,
From the midst of the stones of fire. "

In order to have creatures who could love Him without being forced, God created both angels and man as free moral agents. Of necessity that made it possible for His creatures to make both right and wrong moral choices. If that were not so, neither angels nor men would be free, but would rather function as robots, able to follow only one predetermined course. If that were the case, then God could not hold either angels or men responsible for their actions. But, He does hold us responsible for what we do!

However, something tragic happened. There came a time when Satan's heart turned against God. As a result, he was filled with violence just as others who live in sin. They have inner turmoil, finding no rest for their souls. Because sin entered through this cherub, God declared, *"I have destroyed you, O covering cherub, from the midst of the stones of fire."* Satan lost his place of service to God and was removed from his important ministry.

WHY SATAN FELL

Pride Over Beauty

It is clear that pride was Satan's motivation for falling into sin. Pride is, therefore, the original sin. Ezekiel 28:17 begins, *"Your heart was lifted up because of your beauty; You corrupted your wisdom by reason of your splendor."* He saw that he was beautiful and took the credit for himself rather than giving God the glory.

This is a good lesson for those who desire to serve the Lord. God gives us gifts and talents to use in His service. How often do we fall into pride because of God's gifts to us? We should not boast over His gifts. They are ours only because God gives them. If God makes you a good teacher or preacher or if He gives you some other gift to serve Him, do not let your heart be filled with pride. Satan took credit for God's gift and work in creating him and that produced pride rather than worship of the Lord.

Pride Over Position

Because of the Ezekiel 28 passage, many believe that Satan led the angels in the worship of God. He had a covering of precious stones (verse 13). A comparison of those stones with the twelve stones of the High Priest of Israel shows that Satan's were the same as those worn on the high priest's breastplate. The difference is the High Priest had twelve stones rather than nine, because he represented the twelve tribes of Israel. It is interesting that both the High Priest and Satan had these stones as a covering.

Satan is also called the *"anointed cherub who covers."* Two cherubim were carved on the Ark of the Covenant in the Old Testament tabernacle holy of holies. The cherubim covered the mercy seat and symbolically looked on where the blood of atonement was sprinkled once a year by the high priest.

150

Satan also had great musical ability. Tambourines and flutes (Ezekiel 28:13, marginal reading) were created within his very being. Music is used in worship in heaven (Revelation 5). This is also an indication that he was involved with leading heaven's worship of God.

The first part of Ezekiel 18:18 adds to the understanding that Satan led heaven's worship of God:

Ezekiel 28:18a
18a "By the multitude of your iniquities,
 In the unrighteousness of your trade
 You profaned your sanctuaries.

A sanctuary is a place of worship. Putting these things together, it is not unreasonable to believe that Satan led the angels in worship of God until he decided to divert worship to himself because of his beauty and splendor. That decision defiled his place of worship and caused his fall.

The Results of Satan's Fall
Verse 17b through verse 19 describe some results of his fall.

Ezekiel 28:17b
17b I cast you to the ground;
 I put you before kings,
 That they may see you.

Both in Ezekiel and in Isaiah, the results of his fall reach through time to the fall of the Antichrist who will rule the world at the end of this age. Ezekiel 28:18-19 describe in graphic poetic language the humiliation of Satan and his man, Antichrist, at the return of the Lord Jesus Christ. Paul describes for us the dethronement of Antichrist:

2 Thessalonians 2:8-9
8   Then that lawless one will be revealed whom the Lord will slay with the breath of His mouth and bring to an end by the appearance of His coming;

*9   that is, the one whose coming is in accord with
the activity of Satan, with all power and signs and
false wonders.*

The passage from Ezekiel continues with a description
of what happened as a result of Satan's fall, and looks on
into the future to Satan's imprisonment when he *"will
cease to be forever"* upon the earth to torture and harass.

Ezekiel 28:18-19
*18   "By the multitude of your iniquities,
     In the unrighteousness of your trade
     You profaned your sanctuaries.
     "Therefore I have brought fire from the midst
     of you;
     It has consumed you,
     And I have turned you to ashes on the earth
     In the eyes of all who see you.
19   "All who know you among the peoples
     Are appalled at you;
     You have become terrified,
     And you will cease to be forever."*

Old Testament prophecies reach to the very end of this
age and beyond into the eternal state. The final destiny of
Satan is everlasting torment in the Lake of Fire and he
"will cease to be forever," insofar as terrifying the earth is
concerned. Those who choose to follow him, whether they
be angelic or human, will be with him forever in the place
created for him (Matthew 25:41).

† The Adversary — Satan's Purpose

Much has been learned about Satan's character, his
work, and his position before he fell into sin. In this
section we will study the prophecy of Isaiah to see what
Satan's purpose is since he fell into sin.

SATAN STATES HIS INTENTIONS

Isaiah 14:12-15

12 "How you have fallen from heaven,
O star of the morning, son of the dawn!
You have been cut down to the earth,
You who have weakened the nations!
13 "But you said in your heart,
'I will ascend to heaven;
I will raise my throne above the stars of God,
And I will sit on the mount of assembly
In the recesses of the north.
14 'I will ascend above the heights of the clouds;
I will make myself like the Most High.'
15 "Nevertheless you will be thrust down to Sheol,
To the recesses of the pit."

To Take God's Place

The Word of God says, *"But you said in your heart, 'I will ascend to heaven.'"* Some people believe that the earth was under the dominion of angelic beings prior to the creation of Adam and Eve. Then Satan's rebellion led to a terrible judgment which made the earth a waste place. Genesis 1:1 says, *"In the beginning God created the heavens and the earth."* Those who hold this position say, "When God creates something, He does it right." It was a perfect creation from His hand. Genesis 1:2 goes on to say, *"The earth was formless and void."* According to students of Hebrew, the verse may also be translated, "the earth **became** formless and void." When Satan exalted himself, trying to take God's place, judgment fell upon him and resulted in the earth becoming formless and void. Whether this was the actual scenario or not, it makes for interesting study! Wherever Satan was when he lifted up his heart against God, judgment fell.

To Rule as Sovereign of Heaven

The second willful statement Satan made was, *"I will raise my throne above the stars of God."* Revelation 1:20 shows that the term *"stars,"* when used symbolically, can refer to angels or to pastors, both of whom are messengers. Thus, Satan's meaning seems to be, "I will exalt my throne above the angels of heaven." To put it another way, he wanted to rule over the angels of heaven. He intended to move God from His position of sovereignty and take it for himself.

To Sit in the Angelic Assembly

The third instance of Satan's exercise of his will against God's will is found in the statement, *"I will sit on the mount of assembly in the recesses of the north."* The mount of assembly is mentioned in Psalm 89. It shows us something about Satan's meaning when he said he wanted to sit on the mount of assembly or mount of the congregation. A congregation or assembly of holy ones, meaning angels, meets in heaven and is described in these words:

Psalm 89:5-7
5 *The heavens will praise Your wonders, O LORD;*
   Your faithfulness also in **the assembly of the**
   holy ones.
6 *For who in the skies is comparable to the*
   LORD?
   Who among the sons of the mighty is like the
   LORD,
7 *A God greatly feared in* **the council of the holy**
   ones,
   And awesome above all those who are around
   Him?

The council of the holy ones in heaven is apparently a kind of governing body. Satan's objective was to sit in that assembly and to rule over it, since he had the desire to take God's place.

To Be Higher than God

The fourth *"I will"* which Satan expressed was, *"I will ascend above the heights of the clouds."* Clouds are associated with the presence of God in many places in Scripture. A thick cloud covered Mount Sinai at the giving of the Law. A pillar of cloud by day and a pillar of fire by night stood over the tabernacle during the years of Israel's wanderings in the wilderness. When the Lord Jesus Christ ascended into heaven after His resurrection, He ascended in the clouds. Moreover, He will come back to earth in like manner. Revelation 1:7 says, *"BEHOLD, HE IS COMING WITH THE CLOUDS, and every eye will see Him."* Satan's desire to ascend above the height of the clouds indicates his desire to place himself above the level of God Almighty.

Rather than having to bow down before the Lord, Satan wants God to bow down before him. Satan expressed this desire in the temptation of Jesus. Jesus was led by the Spirit of God into the wilderness to be tempted by Satan. In one of those temptations, Jesus was shown the entire wealth, glory, and honor of the kingdoms of the world in a moment of time. Satan said to Him, *"All these things I will give You, if You fall down and worship me"* (Matthew 4:9). If Jesus, who is God in the flesh, had yielded to that temptation, Satan's greatest dream would have come true! God Himself would have been worshiping at his feet. Thank God that Jesus did not yield for a moment, but rather was victorious for us all.

To Possess Heaven and Earth

Finally, Satan said, *"I will make myself like the Most High."* There are several names for God in the Bible. When Satan chose to exalt himself against God, he wanted to be like "El Elyon," the Most High God. "El Elyon" first appears in Genesis where Abraham met the priest Melchizedek, King of Salem. The record of the meeting between them reads:

155

Genesis 14:18-19
18 And Melchizedek king of Salem brought out bread and wine; now he was a priest of God Most High.
19 He blessed him and said,
"Blessed be Abram of God Most High,
Possessor of heaven and earth."

As we saw earlier in this book, the name "El Elyon," in this context, shows that God possesses both heaven and earth. Satan desires to possess them himself. God allows him limited control over sinful men and over earth because Adam submitted to Satan's temptation in the Garden of Eden. However, Jesus regained control of the earth for mankind because, as a man, He defeated Satan.

God still permits Satan to control sinful men today in a limited way. According to Scripture, God has everything under control, though it appears outwardly that Satan is winning. History, however, is moving precisely toward an end which God has fixed and written in Scripture. That being the case, Jesus, not Satan, is Lord of heaven and earth. Satan does have a great influence over mankind, but God still rules over all things to bring about His desired goals. Consequently, even though Satan would like to be possessor of heaven and earth, he is not. As a matter of fact, he is still under the sovereignty of God and must obtain His permission to touch anything that belongs to Him, including God's children.

Summary of Satan's Purpose
To clarify Satan's rebellious statements in Isaiah, the probable meaning is given below. Keep in mind that this is an interpretation, though I believe it correctly represents Satan's intent.

I will occupy heaven,
I will rule over the angels of heaven,

I will put my throne in place of God's throne,
I will exalt myself above God's presence,
I will possess both heaven and earth.

When Satan set his will against God's will, he fell into terrible sin. The wrath of God rests upon him and his end in the Lake of Fire is fixed. He will be in everlasting torment in the lake created for him and his angels. The Lord Jesus spoke about the place called the Lake of Fire, commonly known as hell. He said, *"Then He will also say to those on His left, 'Depart from Me, accursed ones, into the eternal fire which has been prepared for the devil and his angels'"* (Matthew 25:41). Please notice that Jesus said that the eternal fire was prepared for the devil and his angels. It was not made primarily for fallen mankind.

MAKE THIS LESSON PERSONAL

Only Two Ways – Ultimately, there are only two spirit beings to follow. One is the true and living God; the other one is Satan. Either you choose to follow God's Son for eternal life or to follow Satan for eternal damnation. If you follow Satan, you will go to the place prepared for him – the Lake of Fire (Revelation 20:10-15). If you follow Jesus, you will go to the place that He has prepared for you in God's eternal Kingdom (John 14:1-3, Revelation 21:3).

God Offers Salvation – Salvation comes by the way of the Cross, i.e., the way of Jesus, the way that includes His blood shed for our sins. He offers salvation to us as a free gift. If we refuse His gift of eternal life – if we do not accept what God has done for us through Jesus Christ – there remains no more sacrifice for sin. Hebrews put it this way:

Hebrews 10:26-27
26 For if we go on sinning willfully after receiving the knowledge of the truth, there no longer remains a sacrifice for sins,

27 but a certain terrifying expectation of judgment, and THE FURY OF A FIRE WHICH WILL CONSUME THE ADVERSARIES.

If you have been following in the footsteps of Satan in his rebellion against God, remember that Jesus died for your sins. Today is the day of salvation. Today is the only day you have been promised. Turn now to Jesus and trust Him to save you from the enemy of your soul.

Colossians 1:13
13 For He rescued us from the domain of darkness, and transferred us to the kingdom of His beloved Son.

Chapter 7

Man and God's Law
† Man's Sin and Lost Dominion

Many of the world's philosophers have looked at the problems of mankind – war, sickness, disease, misery, and poverty – and tried to work out an acceptable explanation of the way things are. Christians have a valid explanation. The Bible describes events which caused the world to be in its present state of corruption and decay.

Genesis 2 records the detailed account of the creation of man. Moses wrote, *"Then the LORD God formed man of dust from the ground, and breathed into his nostrils the breath of life; and man became a living being"* (Genesis 2:7). Consequently, man is a partaker of two kinds of life. He is formed of the dust of the ground, which is part of the physical creation. But he is more than simply physical – he partakes of the spiritual also. God breathed into him the breath or spirit of life. Thus, man became a living soul.

Man's Duty – Obedience to God
After his creation, Adam was put in the Garden of Eden and given a command:

Genesis 2:16-17
16 The LORD God commanded the man, saying, "From any tree of the garden you may eat freely;
17 but from the tree of the knowledge of good and evil you shall not eat, for in the day that you eat from it you shall surely die."

God is absolutely perfect and requires, as well as deserves, perfect obedience from His creatures. He cannot be brought down to the level of man, nor can man be raised to the level of God. While man is created in the image of God, there still remains a great difference between the two. It can only be described as the difference between the finite and the infinite. Man, the finite, should always be perfectly obedient to God, the infinite.

Man's Fall through Disobedience

Genesis records the fall of mankind when Adam and Eve chose to do what God said they should not do. Apparently, Satan tempted Eve to sin soon after her creation. At first, the serpent did not openly contradict God, but he did cast doubt on His goodness and kind intentions. He implied to Eve that God had taken cruel delight in forbidding them to eat from **any** tree of the garden. Satan said to her:

> Genesis 3:1-3
> *1 ..."Indeed, has God said, 'You shall not eat from any tree of the garden'?"*
> *2 The woman said to the serpent, "From the fruit of the trees of the garden we may eat;*
> *3 but from the fruit of the tree which is in the middle of the garden, God has said, 'You shall not eat from it or touch it, or you will die.'"*

Eve fell for Satan's attack against God's character. While she may have thought that she stated the truth, she actually added to God's Word saying that they should not "touch" the fruit. Then the serpent, seeing Eve fall into his trap, in effect directly said that God had lied. He flatly contradicted God saying, *"You surely will not die!"* (Genesis 3:4). Then two short verses describe Adam and Eve's acts of disobedience and the consequences of their sin:

Genesis 3:6-7

6   When the woman saw that the tree was good
for food, and that it was a delight to the eyes, and
that the tree was desirable to make one wise, she
took from its fruit and ate; and she gave also to
her husband with her, and he ate.
7   Then the eyes of both of them were opened, and
they knew that they were naked; and they sewed
fig leaves together and made themselves loin
coverings.

Disobedience Results in Death

Because of their disobedience, Adam and Eve were
immediately out of fellowship with their Creator. The very
next verse shows that they were afraid of God because they
had sinned. They heard the LORD God walking in the
garden and hid themselves from Him (Genesis 3:8). Their
disobedience caused the world of mankind to be in its
present terrible state.

The LORD God had said to Adam, *"for in the day that*
you eat from it [the tree of the knowledge of good and evil],
you will surely die" (Genesis 2:17). Those who misunderstand the real nature of death misunderstand what God said
to Adam here. Death is **not** the end of activity or existence.
It is a separation from the source of life. When Adam
sinned, he died spiritually – he was separated from God, the
source of all life. The New Testament speaks of being
"dead in your trespasses and sins" (Ephesians 2:1). Thus,
it is obvious that death has both physical and spiritual
aspects.

Lost Dominion and Fallen Nature

Adam's sin not only separated man from God, but man
lost his dominion over the earth to Satan. In addition,
because he could not be trusted, he no longer trusted others.
A distinct inclination toward evil took place in his soul

when he sinned. And he passed that change on to his descendants; everyone has a natural inclination toward evil. This explains the widespread problems of mankind throughout the centuries, and throughout the whole earth.

In Romans 5:12-21, the Apostle Paul explained what happened when Adam sinned. He said in 5:12, *"Therefore, just as through one man [Adam] sin entered into the world, and death through sin, and so death spread to all men, because all sinned."* Paul makes his point from a fact we all see: all men die. Death is not the natural state of man. It is the result of sin. The proof that everyone sins is that everyone dies.

Paul then contrasts sin and death in Adam with grace and life in Jesus. He wrote:

Romans 5:15-16
15 But the free gift is not like the transgression. For if by the transgression of the one the many died, much more did the grace of God and the gift by the grace of the one Man, Jesus Christ, abound to the many.
16 The gift is not like that which came through the one who sinned; for on the one hand the judgment arose from one transgression resulting in condemnation, but on the other hand the free gift arose from many transgressions resulting in justification.

Then Paul brings his whole argument to its main point:

Romans 5:17-19
17 For if by the transgression of the one, death reigned through the one, much more those who receive the abundance of grace and of the gift of righteousness will reign in life through the One, Jesus Christ.

18 So then as through one transgression there resulted condemnation to all men, even so through one act of righteousness there resulted justification of life to all men.
19 For as through the one man's disobedience the many were made sinners, even so through the obedience of the One the many will be made righteous.

The main point is that death came through Adam, but life came through Jesus Christ. The question is, "How does man obtain that life?" Look back at verse 17 again. It says, *"much more **those who receive** the abundance of grace and of the gift of righteousness will reign in life through the One, Jesus Christ."* To obtain eternal life one **must receive** the abundance of grace and the gift of righteousness from Him. Those who do, receive eternal life and can live triumphantly through Jesus.

The Gospel of John says this about receiving Jesus:

John 1:11-12
11 He [Jesus] came to His own, and those who were His own did not receive Him.
12 But as many as received Him, to them He gave the right to become children of God, even to those who believe in His name.

There are many people who have heard the Gospel and understood it with their mind. But they never receive Jesus Christ as their own *personal* Savior. Remember, you must receive Him in order to have eternal life. If you have not received Jesus Christ, you are still without the life of God.

You should pray to Him, confess your sin, and believe Jesus died in your place to give you eternal life. You are not promised a life of ease. Indeed, the life of a Christian is sometimes harder than that of others. However, Jesus offers something that is impossible to have without Him.

163

He offers peace with God, peace with oneself, and the ability to live in peace with those around you, so far as it depends on you. This truly is a treasure of great price – you can lay down your head at night and immediately go to sleep because you are right with God and men.

If you do not know Jesus, confess to God that you are a sinner, and trust Him to forgive your sins and cleanse you. Your life can be turned into a story of victory and glory in Christ Jesus our Lord.

† Man & God's Law – Using God's Law Today

In this section we will discuss the Law of God as it was given in the Old Testament and as it applies now.

God's Law Is Good

First, it should be noted that God's Law is good. Many people look upon it as a burden. However, the Apostle John says that *"His commandments are not burdensome"* (1 John 5:3). The Bible also says the Law is good, but that it must be used in a lawful way. Paul, when writing to Timothy, said:

1 Timothy 1:8-11
8   But we know that the Law is good, if one uses it lawfully,
9   realizing the fact that law is not made for a righteous person, but for those who are lawless and rebellious, for the ungodly and sinners, for the unholy and profane, for those who kill their fathers or mothers, for murderers
10   and immoral men and homosexuals and kidnappers and liars and perjurers, and whatever else is contrary to sound teaching,

*11 according to the glorious gospel of the blessed
God, with which I have been entrusted.*

Paul wrote to the Romans, *"So then, the Law is holy, and
the commandment is holy and righteous and good"* (Romans
7:12). He continued in verse 14, saying, *"we know that the
Law is spiritual."* However, the author of Hebrews wrote
that the old covenant of Law has a problem. But, he said,
the problem was not with the covenant itself; rather, it was
with the people to whom it was given:

Hebrews 8:7-8
*7 For if that first covenant had been faultless,
there would have been no occasion sought for a
second.*
8 For finding fault with them, He says,
"BEHOLD, DAYS ARE COMING, SAYS THE LORD,
WHEN I WILL EFFECT A NEW COVENANT
WITH THE HOUSE OF ISRAEL AND WITH THE HOUSE OF
JUDAH."

Notice verse eight faults *"them,"* not the Law. So, the New
Testament covenant of grace bears abundant testimony to
the fact that the Old Testament covenant of Law was good.

The Commandments of God
Just what is the Law of God? Many people who have
not read the Bible do not know that God gave laws to
regulate the affairs of mankind. Those rules govern conduct
between people, and between God and man.

Exodus records the Ten Commandments of God which
form the basic moral law from which other laws are taken.
There are more than 600 laws in the Old Testament, but
they mainly have to do with the detailed application of the
basic Ten Commandments. Here are the Ten Commandments that God gave to Moses:

Exodus 20:3-4, 7-8, 12-17

3   "You shall have no other gods before Me.

4   "You shall not make for yourself an idol, or any likeness of what is in heaven above or on the earth beneath or in the water under the earth.

7   "You shall not take the name of the LORD your God in vain ...

8   "Remember the sabbath day, to keep it holy.

12   "Honor your father and your mother ...

13   "You shall not murder.

14   "You shall not commit adultery.

15   "You shall not steal.

16   "You shall not bear false witness against your neighbor.

17   "You shall not covet your neighbor's house; you shall not covet your neighbor's wife or his male servant or his female servant or his ox or his donkey or anything that belongs to your neighbor."

God's Purpose for Giving the Law

The problem is that no one can keep the Law all the time. However, the problem lies with us, not with the Law. The question then is, even though the Law is good, if we **cannot** keep it, why did God give it? What was the purpose of the Law which God gave? The purpose was twofold. First, God's laws were given to prove to man that he is a sinner in need of a Savior. Paul wrote:

Romans 3:19-20

19   Now we know that whatever the Law says, it speaks to those who are under the Law, so that every mouth may be closed and all the world may become accountable to God;

20   because by the works of the Law no flesh will be justified in His sight; for through the Law comes the knowledge of sin.

166

When the time comes for each person to stand before God in judgment, no one will be able to say that he lived an acceptable life, nor can he say that he did not know right from wrong. Every mouth will be shut. No one will have a word to say in self-defense because the Word of God is very clear as to what is right and what is wrong. Furthermore, Romans says that through the Law no person will be justified in God's sight because through the Law comes the knowledge of sin. As you can see, the first purpose of the Law is to show man that he is a sinner who has broken specific laws and is, therefore, guilty before the Lord God of heaven and earth.

But that is not the only purpose of the Law. If it were, we would have no hope and no place to turn. But there is hope! Paul wrote this about the Law to the Galatians:

Galatians 3:23-24
23 But before faith came, we were kept in custody under the law, being shut up to the faith which was later to be revealed.
24 Therefore the Law has become our tutor to lead us to Christ, so that we may be justified by faith.

The second purpose for the Law is made clear. Its purpose is to lead people to Jesus in order that they may be justified by faith. The picture is of a child under the direction of a tutor until he reaches adult age. The Law was a tutor given to lead us to Christ.

The two purposes of the Law work together. First, it shows us that we are unable to be justified by keeping the commandments. Therefore, we need another way – a way of grace. When the Ten Commandments were given in the Old Testament, the laws of sacrifice for salvation by grace were also given as an example of the grace that was to come through Jesus Christ. Thus, the second purpose of

167

the Law was to give us hope by leading us to Jesus Christ that we may be justified by faith.

Using the Law Today

We began by saying that the Law is good if one uses it lawfully. The question then is what is a lawful use of the Law? Today it can still be used to show men that they are guilty before God and need a Savior. A correct use of the Law is to preach God's requirements very clearly as a standard by which men will be judged. Men need to realize there is a judgment to come.

We do not preach that one can be saved by the Law, for by it no one will be justified. We do point to the broken Law as the sign of condemnation and judgment. Then, at the same time, we point to Jesus Christ as the One who perfectly fulfilled the Law for us. He gave His life on Calvary as an atonement for those who have broken the Law and sinned against God. So, our use of the Law today still fulfills its twofold purpose revealed in the Scriptures.

Charles Finney, a well-known evangelist of past years, said that you cannot get men saved until you first get them lost. There is a great deal of truth in that. While it is true that all men are lost without Jesus Christ, it is equally true that many do not know they are lost because they have not heard the preaching of the Law. Jesus said, *"For I did not come to call the righteous, but sinners, to repentance"* (Matthew 9:13 NKJV). He also said that healthy people do not need a physician, but the sick do. Jesus came to give help to those who are sick and know it, and to those who are sinners and know it. We can use the commandments of God as a starting point for the Holy Spirit to bring the conviction of sin to the hearts of those who hear the message preached.

✝ Man and God's Law – God's Law, Good But Broken

The New Testament uniformly proclaims that the Law given in the Old Testament is good, holy, and spiritual. The reason for a new covenant is based on the inability of the people to keep the Law rather than in a defect in the Law itself. In this section we continue to look at the Law from a New Testament point of view. We will see that while it was not defective, it did have a built-in weakness.

The Ten Commandments

But before we do that, look at the Ten Commandments again. The Ten Commandments are so important that God gave them twice in the Old Testament. In the last section we quoted from Exodus; this time, we will quote from Deuteronomy:

> Deuteronomy 5:7-8, 11-12, 16-21
> *7 'You shall have no other gods before Me.*
> *8 'You shall not make for yourself an idol, or any likeness of what is in heaven above or on the earth beneath or in the water under the earth.*
>
> *11 'You shall not take the name of the LORD your God in vain, for the LORD will not leave him unpunished who takes His name in vain.*
> *12 'Observe the sabbath day to keep it holy, as the LORD your God commanded you.*
>
> *16 'Honor your father and your mother ...*
> *17 'You shall not murder.*
> *18 'You shall not commit adultery.*
> *19 'You shall not steal.*
> *20 'You shall not bear false witness against your neighbor.*

21 'You shall not covet your neighbor's wife, and you shall not desire your neighbor's house, his field or his male servant or his female servant, his ox or his donkey or anything that belongs to your neighbor.'

This restatement of the Law in the book of Deuteronomy was given by Moses to the Children of Israel just before they were to go into the promise land.

Why was the Law restated? You may remember that everyone 20 years old or older when Moses first sent spies into the land died in the wilderness for their rebellion against God, except Joshua and Caleb. The Israelites heeded the evil report of ten of the twelve spies who surveyed the land before their invasion. Only Joshua and Caleb stood by their faith in the ability of God to take them into the land and give them victory over the giants they had seen there. Seven nations occupied the land before they went into it. Consequently, the new generation of people had to hear the Law for themselves. That necessitated its repetition in Deuteronomy.

The Unity of the Law

Earlier, it was mentioned that the Law had a built-in weakness. That weakness will be discussed, but first, consider the book of James for a moment. He has some important things to say about the Law. He taught us about the unity of the Law:

James 2:8-11
8 If, however, you are fulfilling the royal law according to the Scripture, "YOU SHALL LOVE YOUR NEIGHBOR AS YOURSELF," you are doing well.
9 But if you show partiality, you are committing sin and are convicted by the law as transgressors.
10 For whoever keeps the whole law and yet stumbles in one point, he has become guilty of all.

11 For He who said, "DO NOT COMMIT ADULTERY," also said, "DO NOT COMMIT MURDER." Now if you do not commit adultery, but do commit murder, you have become a transgressor of the law.

The Law is a unit – that is, a complete whole. It has been compared to a chain with many links. It does not matter which link one breaks in a chain; the chain is broken if any link is broken. The Law is the same. A man may go all his life and not commit adultery, but if he covets his neighbor's wife, he has broken the Law. It does not matter which law is broken, because to break one law is to be guilty before God.

Coveting is a good example. It is a sin for which men generally do not have a bad conscience. Coveting is a strong desire to have what belongs to someone else and then plot to get it. For example, it is a sin to strongly desire the spouse of another person and do things to get the attention of that spouse. It is sin to covet another person's spouse or possessions, for that breaks the tenth commandment of God: *"You shall not covet your neighbor's wife ... or anything that belongs to your neighbor"* (Exodus 20:17). God requires absolute perfection to enter heaven. If you have broken even one commandment at any time in your life, you cannot get to heaven without a mighty Savior. Jesus Christ is that Savior!

Weakness of the Law

God has given a holy, righteous, and spiritual Law. However, it does have one weakness. It cannot give life to the sinner: *"Is the Law then contrary to the promises of God? May it never be! For **if a law had been given which was able to impart life**, then righteousness would indeed have been based on law"* (Galatians 3:21). That means if one could keep the commandments from birth until death, he still would not qualify for heaven because of the sin nature. The sin nature is spiritually dead, i.e., cut off from the life of God. The problem is not so much that we commit individual sins, though that is bad in itself. The problem is that we are innately sinners and are spiritually dead in sins (Ephesians 2:1). We need spiritual life! No law has ever been given by which a person can obtain life. That is why Jesus Christ had to die on Calvary. He did it to give us life. The Apostle John wrote:

> 1 John 5:11-12
> *11 And the testimony is this, that God has given us eternal life, and this life is in His Son.*
> *12 He who has the Son has the life; he who does not have the Son of God does not have the life.*

It is through Jesus' death and resurrection that the Holy Spirit is able to impart eternal life. He gives it to us as the Law never could and never will be able to do.

No doubt you have heard the expression "born again." If you are to receive a new, fresh life from God, you must be born, not only physically into this world through your mother, but also spiritually by the Spirit of God. Without this second birth, you cannot see the kingdom of God. Jesus explained it to Nicodemus in John's Gospel in this way:

> John 3:3-8
> *3 Jesus answered and said to him, "Truly, truly, I say to you, unless one is born again he cannot see the kingdom of God."*
> *4 Nicodemus said to Him, "How can a man be born when he is old? He cannot enter a second time into his mother's womb and be born, can he?"*
> *5 Jesus answered, "Truly, truly, I say to you, unless one is born of water and the Spirit he cannot enter into the kingdom of God.*
> *6 "That which is born of the flesh is flesh, and that which is born of the Spirit is spirit.*

7 "Do not be amazed that I said to you, 'You must be born again.'
8 "The wind blows where it wishes and you hear the sound of it, but do not know where it comes from and where it is going; so is everyone who is born of the Spirit."

The experience of being born again can never come through keeping the Law. But the Lord Jesus can and does give eternal life to those who receive Him as Savior. Therefore, the Law was given to lead us to Jesus that we may be given life by faith in Him.

If you have been struggling to please God by keeping the Law, or trying to live a life pleasing to Him in order to get to heaven, you can forget that once and for all. The only way you will ever get to heaven is to forsake your own way of trying to get there and accept the way God gives through Jesus (John 14:6).

MAKE GOD'S LAW PERSONAL

Only the Lord Jesus has been able to keep God's Law perfectly. It is a Law no other man can keep! Therefore, it condemns all men. Apart from the mercy and the grace of God no one could ever be saved.

Furthermore, the Law's own weakness keeps it from being able to provide salvation for mankind. People are spiritually dead and the Law cannot give life. It only serves to show a person his sinful condition. Once a person understands that he is a sinner and turns to Jesus Christ, he is saved in response to his faith. Eternal life comes as a free gift from God. One who has trusted Christ has the Holy Spirit within him to supply the power to fulfill the Law of Christ.

The Scripture says that once you are born again through faith in Jesus, you are God's *"workmanship, created in Christ Jesus for good works, which God prepared beforehand so that we would walk in them"* (Ephesians 2:10). We are to love the Lord our God with all our heart, soul, mind, and might, and our neighbor as ourself. That can only be done through the Holy Spirit and thus fulfill the royal law of love which James speaks about in his epistle: *"If, however, you are fulfilling the royal law according to the Scripture, 'YOU SHALL LOVE YOUR NEIGHBOR AS YOURSELF,' you are doing well"* (James 2:8).

If you have been striving to keep God's Law, either to get to heaven or to live the Christian life, then you must give up that fruitless approach. Turn to Jesus in full faith, expecting Him to both save you and enable you to live so that the royal law may be fulfilled in you without the striving and bondage brought by trying to keep the Law.

Romans 10:4
4   For Christ is the end of the law for righteousness to everyone who believes.

Chapter 8

Salvation
† By Grace, Not by Works

Does a person contribute to his or her own salvation, or is salvation a free gift for which God expects no payment by good works? In this section we will study whether salvation is by works or by grace, or a combination of works and grace.

GOD'S PLAN OF SALVATION

God has established a plan of salvation to bring man back to Himself. He has made a way for those who will trust in Jesus to come back into fellowship with Him through the salvation He provided. His plan includes the following essentials.

All People Are Born Naturally Sinful

We must first see that natural man cannot live a godly life. The person who tries to keep the Law and do good works in order to be saved will soon find himself in the spiritual condition Paul describes:

Romans 7:14-17
14 For we know that the Law is spiritual, but I am of flesh, sold into bondage to sin.
15 For what I am doing, I do not understand; for I am not practicing what I would like to do, but I am doing the very thing I hate.

16 But if I do the very thing I do not want to do, I agree with the Law, confessing that the Law is good.
17 So now, no longer am I the one doing it, but sin which dwells in me.

A person finds himself in this condition when he tries to keep the Law. He soon discovers that his fallen nature simply will not cooperate either in keeping the Law of God or in living by the spirit of the Law. Paul found himself doing things he did not want to do and not doing things he knew he should do. This is the common experience of mankind. Paul concluded that sin was present within him; he could not keep the Law as he wanted to do.

Then, in Romans 7:18-21, Paul states the principle that evil dwells in him, even though with his mind he wishes to do good and live for God. The problem is that he is unable to do so. Paul finishes the chapter like this:

Romans 7:22-25
22 For I joyfully concur with the law of God in the inner man,
23 but I see a different law in the members of my body, waging war against the law of my mind and making me a prisoner of the law of sin which is in my members.
24 Wretched man that I am! Who will set me free from the body of this death?
25 Thanks be to God through Jesus Christ our Lord! So then, on the one hand I myself with my mind am serving the law of God, but on the other, with my flesh the law of sin.

Paul concluded that he needed to be set *"free from the body of this death."* But freedom does not come by human striving to keep the Law. It is a gift of God through Jesus Christ our Lord (Romans 6:23). The freedom which we have in Jesus Christ is not a result of our work; it is a result of the grace of God.

Paul's experience related in the above passage was probably after his conversion, else he would not have joyfully agreed with the Law of God in his inner being. Romans 6 is about the experience of those who have passed from death into life through union with Jesus Christ. Chapter seven speaks of the same person who tries his best to live pleasing to God, but finds himself unable to do so.

However, our subject now is not the Christian life, but the matter of whether salvation is by works or by grace. Then you might ask, "If Romans 7 speaks of a Christian being unable to please God without God's help, then why use it in a study about salvation?" The reason is this: if one who is already saved cannot live pleasing to God through his own effort, how much more is it true of one who is lost? Romans 7 serves as an illustration of the impossibility of pleasing God through self-effort, whether one is saved or whether one is unsaved.

God Requires Perfection to Enter Heaven
Your very first sin excluded you from heaven. Someone may argue, "But if I do enough good works, will that not pay for the sin which I committed?" Never! Why? Because according to Romans 6:23, the penalty of sin is death. And the penalty placed upon man for his sin is eternal death. Therefore, good works will never pay for your sin because the sacrifice of death is required. Jesus paid that sacrifice on the Cross by shedding His own blood for you and me. Actually, it is an insult to God to offer Him good works in place of His only begotten Son's death and resurrection.

Furthermore, even if good works could suffice, you could never be sure that you've done enough, because good works are required all the time. You can never do more good works than is required because perfection is always required. Thus, nothing is ever left over to pay for previous wrongs. All the good works that you can do will never pay for the sin which you have already committed. Another way of salvation must be provided if you are to make it into heaven. That way of salvation, as already mentioned, is the death of Jesus Christ on the Cross, His burial, and His resurrection on your behalf.

Heaven Cannot Be Gained by Good Works

Old Testament Israel made a big mistake about how to get into heaven. Paul argues with great wisdom in Romans 9 through 11 that their big mistake was trying to keep the Law of God for salvation rather than accepting God's mercy in grace. They had been given the sacrifices of the Old Testament tabernacle system to demonstrate God's grace. Later, His grace was demonstrated in actual fact by their Messiah, the Lord Jesus Christ. Speaking about Israel, Paul says:

> Romans 9:30-32
> *30 What shall we say then? That Gentiles, who did not pursue righteousness, attained righteousness, even the righteousness which is by faith;*
> *31 but Israel, pursuing a law of righteousness, did not arrive at that law.*
> *32 Why? Because they did not pursue it by faith, but as though it were by works. They stumbled over the stumbling stone,*

Israel did not attain the righteousness necessary to get into heaven because they pursued it by law rather than by faith. They looked at righteousness as something to be attained by good works rather than something to be obtained from God as a gift of His love.

178

The Law Was Not Given for Mankind to Earn Salvation

Since salvation does not come by keeping the Law, then why was the Law given and what is Christ's relationship to the Law? Paul says, *"Christ is the end of the law for righteousness to everyone who believes"* (Romans 10:4). He does not mean that Christ did away with the Law, but rather that Christ has fulfilled the Law on behalf of those who believe. In that verse, the word "end" can also be translated "goal." Then the sentence would read, "Christ is the goal of the Law for righteousness." Rather than making the Law void, He reached the goal intended by the Law for righteousness. To put it another way, Christ lived a perfect, sinless life and fulfilled the Law for righteousness. Now, God transfers the righteousness of Jesus to the account of the one who has faith in Him. Thus, Christ is the goal or *"the end of the law for righteousness to everyone who believes."*

Salvation Comes Only by Trusting God and His Son

Grace means that God freely gives salvation to mankind when we deserve judgment. He requires nothing from us in the form of good works to earn salvation. Paul explains this idea very clearly:

Ephesians 2:8-9
8 For by grace you have been saved through faith; and that not of yourselves, it is the gift of God; 9 not as a result of works, so that no one may boast

In Romans, he explains that salvation is by faith in the Lord Jesus Christ. He says:

Romans 10:9-10
9 ... if you confess with your mouth Jesus as Lord, and believe in your heart that God raised Him from the dead, you will be saved;

179

10 for with the heart a person believes, resulting in righteousness, and with the mouth he confesses, resulting in salvation.

Paul makes it clear there are two parts to believing the Gospel of salvation by grace: 1) confessing that Jesus Christ is Lord, and 2) believing that God raised Him from the dead. There are, of course, other teachings which one will hold as he learns more of the truth.

Confessing – It is obvious that many people have been saved who did not, at the moment they believed, also make a verbal confession that Jesus is the Lord. That was my personal experience, and that is especially true of children. As a matter of fact, few people are well schooled in theology when they first come to Jesus. However, even little children understand that God gave His Son to pay for their sins, as adults do. As true believers grow in the knowledge of Jesus, they will confess Him as the Lord He really is.

Believing – All who come to Jesus have some understanding, however basic, that He is alive and able to forgive. The resurrection of Jesus was one of the key elements in the preaching of the apostles, and must remain so today in any reliable testimony of the Gospel. Acts 4:33 says about the apostles: *"And with great power the apostles were giving testimony to the resurrection of the Lord Jesus, and abundant grace was upon them all."*

Getting Right with God Apart from Law

Paul explains the difference between the grace of God and the Law of God in Romans 3. The purpose of the Law is to bring men to acknowledge their sin and guilt before God. But, thank God that He did not leave us condemned under the Law; He provided a way of salvation without keeping the Law. Paul explains this in Romans:

Romans 3:21-24
21 But now apart from the Law the righteousness of God has been manifested, being witnessed by the Law and the Prophets,
22 even the righteousness of God through faith in Jesus Christ for all those who believe; for there is no distinction;
23 for all have sinned and fall short of the glory of God,
24 being justified as a gift by His grace through the redemption which is in Christ Jesus;

What is Paul saying in these few verses? He explains that the righteousness God requires to get to heaven has now been provided apart from the Old Testament Law. It has nothing to do with keeping the Law. But even though it is obtained without keeping the Law, the Law itself, and the Old Testament prophets, tell of the righteousness of God which one obtains by faith. Isaiah the prophet wrote these words about Jesus:

Isaiah 53:4-6
4 Surely our griefs He Himself bore,
And our sorrows He carried;
Yet we ourselves esteemed Him stricken,
Smitten of God, and afflicted.
5 But He was pierced through for our transgres-
sions,
He was crushed for our iniquities;
The chastening for our well-being fell upon
Him,
And by His scourging we are healed.
6 All of us like sheep have gone astray,
Each of us has turned to his own way;
But the LORD has caused the iniquity of us all
To fall on Him.

Isaiah 53:11 sums it up, saying, *"... By His knowledge the Righteous One, My Servant, will justify the many, As He will bear their iniquities."* Jesus bore our sins on the Cross and, as a result of bearing those sins, He is able to justify us. He can impart to us the righteousness of God through faith in His work on the Cross.

Jesus did two things on the Cross: 1) He completely paid for our sin, and 2) He provided a positive righteousness for us. There was nothing positive whatever in our lives to make us pleasing to God. Before we had faith in Jesus it was impossible to please Him (Hebrews 11:6). However, God takes the righteousness of Jesus Christ and places it to the account of those who have faith. Rather than being a moral neutral, we now have a positive righteousness before God. God, through Christ, provided for us the righteousness we need for heaven.

† Salvation — Repentance

We looked closely at the question of whether salvation comes by doing good works or simply and purely by the grace of God as a free gift. Upon examination of the Scripture, we determined that salvation is a gift of God and cannot be earned by good works. Since salvation cannot be earned, the question is, "What is man's part in salvation, if he has any at all?" A person who genuinely trusts in Christ will have both repentance and faith, neither of which is a "work." In this section we will examine repentance, and in a later one we will look at faith.

Genuine Repentance Changes Life

Repentance produces change. In some places much emphasis is put on faith in Jesus to be saved, without teaching that a change in attitude and action should follow ones salvation. However, the truth of the book of James is very important to the whole question of salvation. James argues forcefully in chapter two that one may have faith, but if he has no resulting change of life, then his faith is not genuine – it is vain and useless:

James 2:14-20
14 What use is it, my brethren, if someone says he has faith but he has no works? Can that faith save him?
15 If a brother or sister is without clothing and in need of daily food,
16 and one of you says to them, "Go in peace, be warmed and be filled," and yet you do not give them what is necessary for their body, what use is that?
17 Even so faith, if it has no works, is dead, being by itself.
18 But someone may well say, "You have faith and I have works; show me your faith without the works, and I will show you my faith by my works."
19 You believe that God is one. You do well; the demons also believe, and shudder.
20 But are you willing to recognize, you foolish fellow, that faith without works is useless?

James is not arguing that one must do good works in order to be saved. His teaching is that genuine faith will produce repentance that brings forth good works.

Some have imagined Paul and James were opposed to each other on this subject. However, when it is seen that James teaches that faith will produce good works, it is in perfect agreement with what Paul teaches in his letters. For example, Paul wrote:

Ephesians 2:8-10
8 For by grace you have been saved through faith; and that not of yourselves, it is the gift of God;

183

*9 not as a result of works, so that no one may
boast.
10 For we are His workmanship, created in Christ
Jesus for good works, which God prepared beforehand so that we would walk in them.*

Paul says the same thing here that James does in his letter.
He makes both faith <u>and</u> works a part of Christian experience. The important point is that works cannot in any way
purchase or contribute to salvation. Good works are merely
the result of godly faith and repentance. Neither faith nor
repentance is a "work." Both involve proper heart attitudes
and actions toward God, Jesus Christ, sin, and self. Paul
stated that he taught ...

Acts 20:20-21
*20 "... publicly and from house to house,
21 solemnly testifying to both Jews and Greeks of
repentance toward God and faith in our Lord Jesus
Christ."*

What Is Repentance?
Having determined that good works do not earn us
salvation, the next question must be, "What is repentance
and how does it fit in with faith and good works?" When
John the Baptist came as the forerunner of Jesus Christ, *"he
came into all the district around the Jordan, preaching a
baptism of repentance for the forgiveness of sins"* (Luke 3:3).
Luke continued his report with these words:

Luke 3:7-8
*7 So he began saying to the crowds who were
going out to be baptized by him, "You brood of
vipers, who warned you to flee from the wrath to
come?
8 "Therefore bear fruits in keeping with repentance, and do not begin to say to yourselves, 'We*

have Abraham for our father,' for I say to you that
from these stones God is able to raise up children
to Abraham."

They were told to let their lives reflect their professed repentance rather than rely on their religious heritage.

Repentance is not simply feeling sorry for sin. There is a sorrow which leads to death rather than to repentance. Judas Iscariot is an example of the sorrow that leads to death. He was sorry when he saw that Jesus was condemned because he betrayed Him; he went out and hanged himself. His sorrow did not produce repentance toward God; it produced pity for himself. The Word of God teaches us, *"the sorrow that is according to the will of God produces a repentance without regret, leading to salvation, but the sorrow of the world produces death"* (2 Corinthians 7:10). Therefore, repentance is not simply feeling sorry for your sin.

Repentance is having a change of heart, attitude, and action toward God and toward sin. One who truly repents comes to trust God and His Word. Therefore, he desires to change his actions to conform to God's known will. Paul said of the Thessalonians that they turned from idols to God. That is a good illustration of what repentance is. When they came to God, they turned their backs on their idols. When we come to God, we turn our backs on our sin. That is a good definition of repentance. It is turning completely in the opposite direction – from loving and serving sin, to loving and serving God in righteousness. It is a change in attitude toward God, Christ, sin, and self. Repentance does not mean one will never sin again, but it does mean that his attitude toward sin is changed. Genuine faith *"produces a repentance without regret, leading to salvation"* (2 Corinthians 7:10).

185

Repentance Illustrated

After John preached repentance, the multitude questioned him concerning what they should do in view of his message. Luke 3:11 gives the response: *"And he would answer and say to them, 'The man who has two tunics is to share with him who has none; and he who has food is to do likewise.'"* That sounds very similar to what we just read in James about the kind of faith that helps people who are in need. One who has turned to God should no longer be cruel, but rather he should be kind as God is kind.

Next, those who collected taxes came to John and asked him what they should do. *"And he said to them, 'Collect no more than what you have been ordered to'"* (Luke 3:13). They were to become honest in their business dealings. They were to stop collecting more taxes than was really owed. They were not to cheat anyone of what rightfully belonged to them.

Following the tax men, some soldiers were questioning him, saying in Luke 3:14, *"'And what about us, what shall we do?' And he said to them, 'Do not take money from anyone by force, or accuse anyone falsely, and be content with your wages.'"* This is repentance in action – to stop robbing and stealing, lying and falsely accusing other people, and being content with a proper wage. In those days, soldiers were among the best paid people in the Roman Empire. John did not tell them to be content with less than a livable wage. He told them to be content with their wages because they were well paid. Thus, we see from these questions and answers that repentance involves a change in attitude that changes the way one lives.

Repentance: A New Testament Message

Following John the Baptist, the message of repentance continued to be preached by Jesus and His apostles. Peter's message at Pentecost concluded with the words, *"Therefore let all the house of Israel know for certain that God has made Him both Lord and Christ – this Jesus whom you crucified"* (Acts 2:36). Many who heard him were pierced to their hearts and they said to Peter and the rest of the apostles:

Acts 2:37-38
37 ..."Brethren, what shall we do?"
38 Peter said to them, "Repent, and each of you be baptized in the name of Jesus Christ for the forgiveness of your sins; and you will receive the gift of the Holy Spirit."

The message of Peter to the multitude on the day of Pentecost was repent! Later he exhorted his listeners to, *"Therefore repent and return, so that your sins may be wiped away, in order that times of refreshing may come from the presence of the Lord"* (Acts 3:19).

Paul explained his own ministry to the Ephesian elders.

Acts 20:20-21
20 ... I did not shrink from declaring to you anything that was profitable, and teaching you publicly and from house to house,
*21 solemnly testifying to both Jews and Greeks of **repentance toward God** and faith in our Lord Jesus Christ.*

Paul preached both repentance and faith. It is like a coin with two heads – on one side repentance, on the other side, faith. You cannot spend the coin without spending both repentance and faith. You cannot enter the kingdom of Heaven without repenting and you cannot enter it without faith in our Lord Jesus Christ. It takes both: *"repentance toward God and faith in our Lord Jesus Christ."* Without genuine repentance there can be no salvation.

187

† Salvation — By Grace through Faith

In the last section an example was used comparing faith and repentance to a coin with repentance on one side and faith on the other. The doctrine of faith alone for salvation is closely associated with repentance. They are so closely related to salvation that neither will- be found without the other. In this section the "other side of the coin," faith, will be considered.

Faith Is Essential to Please God

Repentance is only a part of turning to God for salvation. Faith toward our Lord Jesus Christ is also necessary for salvation. Hebrews 11:6 says, *"without faith it is impossible to please Him, for he who comes to God must believe that He is and that He is a rewarder of those who seek Him."*

Notice that faith in God in this verse includes two things. First, God is — that is, He exists. Certainly if you are an agnostic or an atheist, and remain so, you will never turn to God. If you are an atheist, you do not believe there is a God, so how could you possibly turn to Him? If you are an agnostic, you believe there may or may not be a God, but there is no way to know for sure. If you do not know there is a God, how will you ever turn to Him? Therefore, the first essential for having faith in God is to believe that He exists.

The second essential is a belief that God is good. The Scripture says, *"He is a rewarder of those who seek Him."* When you come to God He will not turn you away. He will not condemn you to hell. He will not do any of those things if you turn to Him in faith because He is a rewarder of those who seek Him.

The French have a saying, "Le Bon Dieu," — the good God. This is often used in a context that does not honor

God, but there is a lot of truth in the phrase. God is good! He is the good God, and those who come to Him must believe that He is a rewarder of those who seek Him. No matter how good a life one tries to live, he cannot please God without believing Him.

The word *"believe"* is often used for faith. It is used 98 times in the Gospel of John alone. It means more than just an intellectual acceptance of facts. It means to trust oneself completely to the facts or to the promise involved. In the case of the Gospel, it means to trust Jesus Christ and God's Word. For example, Paul said in Acts 27:25, *"I believe God that it will turn out exactly as I have been told."* When God tells you something, you can believe it! God never lies and if He says it is so, it is so. Therefore, Paul believed God completely, just as you and I should believe Him.

Abraham Illustrates Faith

The idea of belief occurs very early in the Bible. Genesis 15:6 says of Abraham, *"Then he believed in the LORD; and He reckoned it to him as righteousness."* Someone pointed out that belief in God's promises can be reckoned or counted as righteousness because it is the right thing to do. This verse about Abraham's faith from Genesis is quoted three times in New Testament passages talking about faith, and for good reason. Abraham is a good example of one who had real faith in the promises of God. Paul says of Abraham:

Romans 4:18-22
18 In hope against hope he believed, so that he might become a father of many nations according to that which had been spoken, "SO SHALL YOUR DESCENDANTS BE."
19 Without becoming weak in faith he contemplated his own body, now as good as dead since he

was about a hundred years old, and the deadness of Sarah's womb;
20 yet, with respect to the promise of God, he did not waver in unbelief but grew strong in faith, giving glory to God,
21 and being fully assured that what God had promised, He was able also to perform.
22 Therefore IT WAS ALSO CREDITED TO HIM AS RIGHT-EOUSNESS.

Abraham persisted in believing God when natural circumstances were against it. Even when everything else seems to the contrary, we must always receive God's promises as absolute truth. The original sin was disbelieving what God had said and thereby calling Him a liar. The requirement for salvation is simply for each person to reverse that original sin for himself. Rather than calling God a liar, one must believe God and affirm that every word of His is absolute truth.

Faith in God's Witness
The Apostle John speaks about God's witness to the human race in his first epistle:

1 John 5:9-12
9 If we receive the testimony of men, the testimony of God is greater; for the testimony of God is this, that He has testified concerning His Son.
10 The one who believes in the Son of God has the testimony in himself; the one who does not believe God has made Him a liar, because he has not believed in the testimony that God has given concerning His Son.
11 And the testimony is this, that God has given us eternal life, and this life is in His Son.
12 He who has the Son has the life; he who does not have the Son of God does not have the life.

We have defined faith as "believing God." Faith for salvation is not valid unless the object is God and His Son. It is often said that any religion is good and will lead to God if the person is sincere and has faith. That is not so! The object of faith must be the only true God of heaven and earth as He has revealed Himself. The faith that saves believes the record God gave about His Son.

Faith Is All Embracing

Genuine faith affects the entire man – intellect, emotions, and will. Many people know the facts of the good news about Jesus Christ. And it is necessary to hear the truth in order to believe it, for as Paul wrote to the Romans *"So then faith cometh by hearing, and hearing by the word of God."* (Romans 10:17 KJV). But simply understanding the facts is not enough. A person must realize his or her own need and respond to God's offer of salvation by a definite decision to receive Jesus as personal Savior.

Faith in Jesus Essential

Those who have their faith centered in God receive His witness concerning His Son. They receive Jesus Christ as Savior, believing what He has done for them. The Apostle John testified about Jesus, *"He who has the Son has the life; he who does not have the Son of God does not have the life"* (1 John 5:12). Therefore, to have the salvation which God offers, one must have the Son He offers as Savior. God's Son is the only Savior recognized by God the Father. As Jesus said, *"No one comes to the Father but through Me"* (John 14:6).

No matter what you do, you cannot get to heaven without eternal life. And you cannot have eternal life without having Jesus Christ. The question then is, "How do you receive Jesus Christ?" The Word of God puts it simply in John 1:12 where it says, *"But as many as received Him [Jesus], to them He gave the right to become children of God, even to those who believe in His name."*

191

To receive Jesus, you must acknowledge that He is the Son of God who died on the Cross in payment for your sin. He is offering forgiveness and the gift of eternal life. Will you receive that free gift today? As a personal statement, you might say: "Because I know the truth and I realize my need, I do receive God's Son Jesus as my Savior and trust Him to save me."

† Salvation — Justification by Faith

Justification by faith is explained at some length in Paul's letter to the Romans. In fact, it is the major theme of that important New Testament book.

What Is Justification?

Justification is an act of God by which He declares righteous, in a legal sense, a person who has faith in Jesus. It does not mean the person has not sinned; it means the penalty for his sin has been paid by Christ. Jesus died in the sinners place to pay the righteous penalty of death required by the Law.

The penalty for sin is the death of the one who commits sin or a legally recognized substitute. God set the penalty before the first man ever committed a sin. God said to Adam, *"from the tree of the knowledge of good and evil you shall not eat, for in the day that you eat from it you will surely die"* (Genesis 2:17). It came to pass exactly as God said it would. The day that Adam and Eve sinned they died spiritually and they began to die physically. Both spiritual and physical death result from sin.

Justification by Blood Sacrifice

Later, in Leviticus 17:11, God made it plain why blood had to be shed for the forgiveness of sin. He said, *"the life of the flesh is in the blood, and I have given it to you on the altar to make atonement for your souls; for it is the blood by reason of the life that makes atonement.*" Because death is the penalty for sin and shedding blood results in death, God made shedding of blood the requirement for forgiving sins. The just penalty of the law had to be paid to uphold moral justice in the universe. The writer of Hebrews said, *"without shedding of blood there is no forgiveness"* (Hebrews 9:22). Therefore, justification comes to us only because our legally appointed substitute, the Lord Jesus Christ, paid the penalty for our sins. We are *"justified by His blood"* (Romans 5:9).

The sinner who trusts in Jesus is freed from the penalty of sin and stands before God just as though he had never sinned. Those who have faith in Christ are granted, for Christ's sake, forgiveness of sins and the taking away of the guilt and punishment which sin requires. The eternal court of legal justice has been satisfied by the death of Jesus Christ on behalf of sinners.

Elements of Justification

You can see from the definition and explanation just given above that justification involves at least three things: 1) forgiveness of sins, 2) legal acquittal, and 3) restoration to divine favor. In Acts, Paul preached in the synagogue at Pisidian Antioch:

Acts 13:38-39 (KJV)
38 Be it known unto you therefore, men and brethren, that through this man is preached unto you the forgiveness of sins:
39 And by him all that believe are justified from all things, from which ye could not be justified by the law of Moses.

Paul made it clear that faith in Jesus provides justification from all things, even from things which the Old Testament

Law of Moses could not. Justification covers every sin we have ever committed. We are not only forgiven, but we are legally acquitted before the court of heaven.

Since the penalty is paid and the sin is removed, we are restored to a place of divine favor. God grants us exactly the same standing before Him that Jesus has. We are literally blessed of God forever. Paul wrote to the Ephesians that God *"has blessed us with every spiritual blessing in the heavenly places in Christ"* (Ephesians 1:3).

Justification by Faith

It is impossible to be acquitted of past sins by present good works. This is a fact that has been repeated time and again in these studies. Romans 3:20 says, *"by the works of the Law no flesh will be justified in His sight."* In verse 28 of the same chapter Paul writes, *"For we maintain that a man is justified by faith apart from works of the Law."* The faith the Scriptures speak of in that verse is faith in the sacrifice which Jesus made on the Cross for our sins. It is not that God overlooks sin or that He freely forgives sin without requiring justice. Justice is as much a part of the nature of God as love and mercy. Jesus paid the penalty, satisfying the righteous demands of the Law, to free us from God's wrath. The Bible says that Jesus Christ:

> Romans 4:25-5:1
> *4:25 ... was delivered over because of our transgressions, and was raised because of our justification.*
>
> *5:1 Therefore having been justified by faith, we have peace with God through our Lord Jesus Christ.*

In Romans 5:9 Paul says, *"Much more then, having now been justified by His blood, we shall be saved from the wrath of God through Him."*

Justification through Jesus

Just as the other benefits of salvation come to the believer through the death, burial, resurrection, and glorification of Jesus Christ, so justification comes to the believer in the same way. Romans 5:9, quoted above, says that we are justified by His blood, which involves His death. And Romans 4:25 says that He was raised for our justification. Thus, the entire historical event of Christ's death and resurrection was for our justification, just as it was for the other benefits of our salvation.

The fact that faith in the Gospel of Christ is necessary for justification is illustrated by Paul in his epistle to the Romans, chapter 4. First, he uses Abraham to show that men were justified by faith before the Law of Moses was given. Then, he uses David to point out that men were justified by faith in God during the time of the Mosaic Law. Therefore, believing God has always been His requirement to be justified from sin. Once one believes in the Gospel of Christ and is legally acquitted before the court of heaven, he can never stand trial again.

Once again, justification is the legal declaration by God that the sinner who has faith in Jesus Christ is released from the guilt and penalty of the sins which he has committed. Thus, the believer can rest in Christ without being concerned about the security of his salvation. It is secured by Jesus who said, *"Truly, truly, I say to you, he who hears My word, and believes Him who sent Me, has eternal life, and does not come into judgment, but has passed out of death into life"* (John 5:24). This is truly a remarkable statement, considering how much some people fear the judgment to come.

God's judgment is coming upon the godless and the sinners. However, Jesus promised that those who trust in Him do not come into judgment. While it is true that the believer will stand before God to answer for deeds done during his life, it is an examination for degree of reward, not judgment for eternal destiny. We will not have to come into judgment and hear the word "guilty" because we have already been acquitted. God made justification available to all men who would believe when Jesus died on Calvary (Romans 5:18). Believers are justified the moment they receive the Lord Jesus Christ as their personal Savior.

† Salvation — Regeneration

Not long ago people were using, or we should say misusing, the biblical term "born again." Anytime someone got a fresh start at their job, they were "born again." If a stalled project was revitalized, it was likewise "born again." It was almost as if there were a concerted effort to sow confusion over the real meaning of the term Jesus used to describe regeneration.

What Is Regeneration?
When Jesus said, *"You must be born again,"* what did He mean? He meant you must have a second birth – a spiritual birth. The second birth is a spiritual "re-genera-tion" from the Holy Spirit. He imparts new spiritual life to those who trust in Christ.

Regeneration is a very important doctrine, though the word itself is used only once in the New Testament when referring to personal spiritual rebirth. Paul wrote to Titus:

Titus 3:4-5
4   But when the kindness of God our Savior and His love for mankind appeared,

196

*5 He saved us, not on the basis of deeds which
we have done in righteousness, but according to
His mercy, by the washing of **regeneration** and
renewing by the Holy Spirit.*

Paul adds to the understanding of regeneration an
element of cleansing – *"washing of regeneration."* One
reason babies are so attractive is their newborn innocence.
They are still clean from premeditated sin. Perhaps that is
why the Bible refers to new believers as newborn babes
(1 Peter 2:2). They are newly born by the washing of
regeneration.

WHY REGENERATION IS NECESSARY

To Partake of the New Race

Men born in the sinful line of Adam and Eve have a
fallen nature and stand under the condemnation of God.
However, because we had no choice about being born into
the human race, God in His mercy provided a way out of
the problem. If we receive the gift of life in Jesus Christ, a
new birth takes place. God takes us out of the condemned
sinful line of Adam and puts us into a new regenerated
group of mankind with Jesus Christ as its Head: *"For He
rescued us from the domain of darkness, and transferred us
to the kingdom of His beloved Son"* (Colossians 1:13). As
Adam is head of a fallen race, so Jesus Christ is Head of an
unfallen spiritual race. *"For as in Adam all die, so also in
Christ all will be made alive"* (1 Corinthians 15:22).

To Receive Spiritual Life

Perhaps the most important reason that regeneration is
necessary is because men without Jesus are spiritually dead.
Notice that each of these reasons has to do with the necessity of having life. Ephesians speaks of the transition
between spiritual death and spiritual life:

Ephesians 2:1, 4-5
*1 And **you were dead** in your trespasses and
sins,*

4   But God, being rich in mercy, because of His great love with which He loved us,
5   even when we were dead in our transgressions, made us alive together with Christ (by grace you have been saved).

The difference between spiritual death and spiritual life is the difference between not knowing the true God and knowing Him and His Son Jesus Christ. If you are without Jesus, what you need is the eternal life He alone can give – nothing short of that is sufficient or satisfying.

To Be in the Book of Life

Another reason why regeneration is necessary is you must have your name written in the Lamb's book of life to be saved. All who are born again are recorded therein; those who are spiritually dead are not. Therefore, you need life to have your name recorded in the Lamb's book of life.

To Enter the Kingdom of God

Finally, regeneration is necessary because one cannot see the kingdom of God without it. Jesus made this fact clear to a seeker named Nicodemus. Jesus compared regeneration to physical birth in His conversation with Nicodemus in John 3. You may remember the story – Nicodemus came to Jesus one night and Jesus said to him, *"Truly, truly, I say to you, unless one is born again he cannot see the kingdom of God"* (John 3:3).

To be *"born again"* is the same thing as being regenerated or having a new birth. Immediately Nicodemus related it to his first birth through his mother's womb. In John 3:4, *"Nicodemus said to Him, 'How can a man be born when he is old? He cannot enter a second time into his mother's womb and be born, can he?'"* In verse five, *"Jesus answered, 'Truly, truly, I say to you, unless one is born of water and the Spirit he cannot enter into the kingdom of God.'"*

For further discussion of the term "born again" see the section "The Holy Spirit – Convicts, Regenerates, Seals, and Indwells" in chapter three under the left heading "He Regenerates – Imparts New Life" on page 93.

AGENTS IN REGENERATION

The Word of God and the Spirit of God

The idea of regeneration appears in 1 Peter 1:23 where the Word of God says, *"for you have been born again not of seed which is perishable but imperishable, that is, through the living and enduring word of God."* The seed of regeneration is the Word of God, which is truth. The Holy Spirit, the agent in regeneration, acts upon the seed of truth to cause it to spring up into life. Therefore, two things are present in the process of regeneration. One is the Word of God and the other is the Spirit of God.

The Holy Spirit applies the Word of truth to the heart and mind of an individual. When the Spirit uses the Word in a person's heart, he receives the truth of God, resulting in the new birth. Therefore, it follows that one cannot be born again without first hearing and believing the truth. Paul said virtually the same thing: *"So then faith cometh by hearing, and hearing by the word of God"* (Romans 10:17 KJV). Furthermore, one cannot believe without the Spirit's work in his life. Once he trusts Christ, he receives new life through the power of God. Eternal life is imperishable because the seed is imperishable. It lives and abides forever.

EVIDENCES OF REGENERATION

How can one know that he has been regenerated? Or, put in another way, "How may I know I have been born again?" Two basic ways to know are: 1) a new awareness of the reality and presence of God, and 2) a new love for God and His people shed abroad in your heart.

199

New Awareness of God

The Holy Spirit comes to take up permanent residence in the believer's heart and gives him assurance of belonging to God. The Bible says in 1 John 3:24, *"We know by this that He abides in us, by the Spirit whom He has given us."* We have fellowship with the Godhead, Father, Son (1 John 1:3) and Holy Spirit (2 Corinthians 13:14). God no longer seems remote and unapproachable in a far off heaven, but He is now close at hand.

A Love for God and His People

The Holy Spirit also gives the true believer a new love for God and for His people. You can know that you are born again when you begin to love other Christian people. According to Romans 5:5, *"the love of God has been poured out within our hearts through the Holy Spirit who was given to us."* There is a new desire to serve and please God because we love Him rather than because we fear Him. John, the Apostle of love, wrote:

1 John 2:3-6
3   By this we know that we have come to know Him, if we keep His commandments.
4   The one who says, "I have come to know Him," and does not keep His commandments, is a liar, and the truth is not in him;
5   but whoever keeps His word, in him the love of God has truly been perfected. By this we know that we are in Him:
6   the one who says he abides in Him ought himself to walk in the same manner as He walked.

The word *"walk,"* in a context like this, means to conduct one's life in a certain way. The one who says he abides in Jesus, ought to conduct his life in the same way as Jesus conducted His life. We must behave ourselves and do what is right.

We have by no means exhausted the ways one may know that he has been born again of the Spirit of God. But,

200

we have said enough to give you assurance if you really want to know. However, keep in mind that 1 John 2:4 above does not mean that a true believer will keep God's commandments without fail. In fact, just a few verses before this, he made it clear that a Christian may sin from time to time. One who belongs to God will respect God's commandments and will determine to obey them. When he fails to keep them, he comes to God, confesses his sin, and asks for cleansing and forgiveness.

† Salvation – Adoption as Adult Sons

The subject of the adoption of the believer into the family of God is not discussed very often, but it is a very important part of salvation. Therefore, we are dealing with it in this section.

Adoption Defined

What does adoption mean? Adoption literally means "to be placed as a son" or to take another parent's child willingly as your own child. We have already learned that those who trust Jesus have been spiritually born again, resulting in their becoming children of God. John 1:12 says, *"But as many as received Him* [Jesus], *to them He gave the right to become children of God."* Though they were not originally God's children, they are now full members of God's family.

The word *"adoption"* is a term used in Paul's letters. The idea was not taken from Jewish practice as much as it was from the Roman and Greek practice of adoption. It is mentioned only three times in the Old Testament (Exodus 2:7-10, 1 Kings 11:20, Esther 2:7-15), but each occurrence happened outside of Palestine. Even Paul's use of the term was always in letters to Gentile churches outside of Palestine.

According to scholars, the Greek idea of adoption was that the adopted male had the privileges of a real son, but he had to also accept the legal obligation and religious duties of a real son. Therefore, adoption carries with it the ideas of both privilege and responsibility. Christian adoption takes place at the time one is born again and culminates in the resurrection (Romans 8:23). God receives us as His sons with the full privileges and responsibilities of an adult.

THE BENEFITS OF ADOPTION

What are the benefits that we gain by being received into God's family as adult sons? We must begin with a passage in Romans.

Romans 8:15-17
15 For you have not received a spirit of slavery leading to fear again, but **you have received a spirit of adoption as sons by which we cry out, "Abba! Father!"**
16 The Spirit Himself bears witness with our spirit that we are children of God,
7 and if children, heirs also, heirs of God and fellow heirs with Christ, if indeed we suffer with Him so that we may also be glorified with Him.

Freedom from Spiritual Bondage

A great privilege of being an adult son in God's family is that of being brought out of slavery into real freedom by the Spirit of God. Before salvation we were slaves of sin, Satan, and the world. Now, we are sons of God who have been freed by royal decree. Freedom from spiritual slavery is a very real benefit of adoption. The spirit of adoption or sonship is the exact opposite of the spirit of bondage.

An Intimate Relationship with God

The Spirit of God puts in us a desire for a close relationship with God the Father. The word *"Abba"* is an

Aramaic word which can be translated as "Daddy." In English we call the same person "Father" and "Daddy." "Father" is the authority figure in the home. "Daddy" is the one we go to when we want something – money, an item, or something done for us. We do not usually say to him, "Father, will you do this?" We come as a child and say, "Daddy, will you do this for me?"

God is not only a Father who disciplines, but He is a warm, loving, and providing Daddy. Daddy is the one a little child trusts completely. God becomes our "Daddy" who supplies needs, answers questions, teaches, corrects, and trains from a heart of infinite love. If we do not listen, His training can be hard on us until we do. But, He is not a human father who makes errors, or is limited in his ability to meet our needs. He is the eternal, personal, infinite God who loves us as a daddy loves his own child.

Assurance of Salvation

There is no biblical reason why anyone who trusts the Lord Jesus Christ need worry about his relationship with God, unless he wanders far off into sin and loses the assurance of salvation. The Spirit of God Himself makes it plain within us that we are His children. Satan often tries to get us to believe that we do not belong to God, but we must refuse his lie.

THE RESULTS OF ADOPTION

Fellow-heirs with Christ

Everything God has made is given into the hands of Jesus and He shares it with those who believe in Him. He was able to say in complete truth, *"Blessed are the gentle, for they shall inherit the earth."* (Matthew 5:5). When Jesus returns we shall see that promise realized in fact. Those who submit to God shall indeed inherit the earth when He returns.

Physical Resurrection

Our adoption is a guarantee from God that we will be resurrected in a new, glorious body. Romans 8:23 says, *"we ourselves, having the first fruits of the Spirit, even we ourselves groan within ourselves, waiting eagerly for our adoption as sons, the redemption of our body."* Our body, which is still perishable, corruptible, and mortal, will be exchanged for one that is imperishable, incorruptible, and immortal on the day of resurrection. This part of our adoption is, of course, still future.

Adult Rights within the Family

Galatians tells us that we are not adopted into God's family as infants, but as full-fledged adult sons. Chapter four points out additional benefits we receive through adoption as adult sons in God's family.

Galatians 4:4-7
4 But when the fullness of the time came, God sent forth His Son, born of a woman, born under the Law,
*5 so that He might redeem those who were under the Law, **that we might receive the adoption as sons.***
*6 Because you are sons, God has sent forth the Spirit of His Son into our hearts, crying, **"Abba! Father!"***
7 Therefore you are no longer a slave, but a son; and if a son, then an heir through God.

The word in the original language for *"son"* is the one meaning an adult son. It is one thing to be a minor child, but quite another thing to be an adult son. Even though the inheritance belongs to the child, he does not have the right to use it without the agreement of his guardians and managers until he reaches adulthood.

The very point Paul makes here is that we are already adult sons in God's family. The promises of God are already ours. We do not have to wait; we are already considered adults. We already have the privilege of claiming our inheritance, provided we use it properly. For example, if we use it to take the news of God's kingdom to others, God can and will provide us with sufficient resources, health, and strength to carry out the tasks which He has called us to do.

Knowledge of God's Plans

God shares His plans with us, both for the present and the future. Jesus said in John 15:15, *"No longer do I call you slaves, for the slave does not know what his master is doing; but I have called you friends, for all things that I have heard from My Father I have made known to you."* If Jesus shares what the Father is doing with friends, how much more with His brothers, sons of His Father? God is pleased to reveal His plans for the future, as written in the Scripture, as well as His plans for us as individuals, if we follow Him and keep His commands. It is the privilege of an adult son to be informed of family plans, at least as they pertain to him.

Security in Jesus

Finally, the Word of God says in Ephesians 1:5 that God *"predestined us to adoption as sons through Jesus Christ to Himself ..."* God has always intended for those who believe in Jesus to be adult sons in His family. Therefore, He decided that our adoption should come to pass, because of His kind intentions toward us. The previous verse says that He chose us in Christ before the foundation of the world, that we should be holy and blameless before Him. He knew before the foundation of the world was laid exactly who would be adopted into His family as sons. This, again, is an indication of the eternal purpose of God which does not change. We may rest secure in Jesus Christ knowing that God planned our position in His family before the foundation of the world.

As you study the Bible for yourself, you may be able to discover other benefits we have as adopted sons of God. In the next section we will see the varied responsibilities that such a glorious position places upon us.

✝ Salvation — Duties of God's Sons

Not only are there numerous benefits which God bestowed upon us when He adopted us into His family as adult sons, but there are responsibilities that go along with the benefits. What are some of the religious duties of sonship? A number of these duties are like the duties that a child owes to his earthly father.

RELIGIOUS DUTIES OF GOD'S SONS

Honor the Father

The Bible teaches us to honor our father and obey him. Likewise, it teaches us to conduct ourselves in such a way as to guard his good reputation. One of the strong charges of sin which God has against the human race is found in Romans where Paul wrote:

> Romans 1:21-23
> *21 For even though they knew God, they did not honor Him as God or give thanks, but they became futile in their speculations, and their foolish heart was darkened.*
> *22 Professing to be wise, they became fools,*
> *23 and exchanged the glory of the incorruptible God for an image in the form of corruptible man and of birds and four-footed animals and crawling creatures.*

"They did not honor Him as God or give thanks" means they did not glorify God as God. They did not give God proper respect. God is not an old man in the sky. He is the

Creator and Sustainer of all life. He is an absolute Sovereign who wants only the best for His creatures.

God is often blamed for all the cruelty and suffering in the world. However, people have not taken to heart what the Bible says about this very idea. The verses quoted above speak of mankind deliberately turning away from God. Immediately after that Paul wrote, *"And just as they did not see fit to acknowledge God any longer, God gave them over to a depraved mind, to do those things which are not proper"* (Romans 1:28).

The problems of mankind are a result of turning away from God, not because God is cruel. Paul said men turn away from Him because they do not honor Him as God.

What does it mean to honor a person? It means to recognize the worth of an individual and hold that individual in respect and esteem because of it. As His sons, we should recognize God as the only God worthy to be served. Such service will express itself in worship and in praise. David wrote prophetically of Jesus Christ's praise of His Father, *"I will tell of Your name to my brethren; In the midst of the assembly I will praise You"* (Psalm 22:22). We are to worship and praise God because of who He is and what He has done, just as Jesus did.

Obey the Father
Obedience is another duty of a son to his father. A responsible adult son is not rebellious and disobedient to his father. The Apostle Peter said that you *"are chosen according to the foreknowledge of God the Father, by the sanctifying work of the Spirit, **to obey Jesus Christ**"* (1 Peter 1:1-2). While it is true that Jesus is not the Father, He is One with the Father (John 10:30).

According to Acts 5:32, God has given the Holy Spirit to those who obey Him. Obedience to the Father, especially when that Father is God, must be rendered immediately and without question because He is always right in what He requires. Some have imagined that obedience to God is bondage. But the Apostle John did not think so. He wrote, *"For this is the love of God, that we keep His commandments; and His commandments are not burdensome"* (1 John 5:3). In fact, to obey God's commandments is one way that we can tangibly express our love for Him. The Apostle John also wrote, *"And this is love, that we walk according to His commandments"* (2 John 6).

The commandments of God are not burdensome but rather are a means to real freedom. Jesus said, *"You will know the truth, and the truth will make you free"* (John 8:32). Only as we walk in the truth of God, obeying the laws of God, do we come into real freedom from mental and spiritual oppression. Paul and Silas demonstrated for us the freedom of a child of God. They were still free in spirit and mind even after having been beaten and thrown into prison. At midnight they were heard singing songs and praising God in their very trying circumstances (Acts 15:25). That shows the liberty of mind and spirit which believers have when they live in obedience to God.

Guard the Father's Reputation

An adult son should jealously guard the reputation of his father. God expects us, as adult sons in His family, to conduct ourselves as responsible men and women. Just as the actions of a son reflect upon his parents' reputation, so our actions reflect upon God's reputation. We are responsible to reflect God's good and gracious character to those around us.

To say we are Christians and act as though we had never come to know God is to bring dishonor upon His name. Paul wrote to Titus concerning such people. He said, *"They profess to know God, but by their deeds they deny Him, being detestable and disobedient and worthless for any good deed"* (Titus 1:16). The Corinthians were also given instruction to stop having fellowship with those who profess to know God but lived in a way which brought dishonor upon His name. Paul said to them:

1 Corinthians 5:9-11
9 I wrote you in my letter not to associate with immoral people;
10 I did not at all mean with the immoral people of this world, or with the covetous and swindlers, or with idolaters, for then you would have to go out of the world.
11 But actually, I wrote to you not to associate with any so-called brother if he is an immoral person, or covetous, or an idolater, or a reviler, or a drunkard, or a swindler – not even to eat with such a one.

LEGAL DUTIES OF GOD'S SONS

Exercise Spiritual Authority

God has bestowed authority upon His children to preach the Gospel and spread the good news of the kingdom of God. He has chosen His sons to proclaim the victory of Jesus Christ over the satanic kingdom. Jesus said that the gates of hell will not prevail against the Church (Matthew 16:18). Whatever we bind on earth shall have been bound in heaven and whatever we loose on earth shall have been loosed in heaven (Matthew 16:19). God has granted us the legal authority to be victorious over the satanic kingdom's activity against individuals, churches, cities, and even nations. We must, however, exercise such authority in extreme humility and submission to God. Otherwise, we will find ourselves against a host of hell which would overrun us except for the grace and protection of the Lord Jesus. We may exercise such authority because all authority has been given to Jesus, and He delegates it to His followers. *"All authority has been given to Me in heaven and on earth. Go therefore ..."* (Matthew 28:18-19).

209

Training to Rule

God has great plans for His children. Those plans include places of leadership in the kingdom of God on earth when Jesus returns to establish His millennial kingdom: *"they will reign upon the earth"* (Revelation 5:10). For those who know Him, this present time is a training ground in obedience and in the exercise of God's authority in the earth. Satan has been quite successful in leading the people of God away from using their authority to help push earthly events toward righteousness. We need to be constantly aware of the responsibilities God has given us and push back the evil spiritual powers through the victory that Jesus won over them.

† Salvation – Sanctification

Of all our topics, salvation is perhaps the most important for you and me, since it involves our eternal destiny. This is one of the key places Satan tries to sow error. To believe his error rather than God's truth will certainly give you many spiritual heartaches. The only way to escape stumbling spiritually is to follow the teaching of Scripture. Sanctification, the subject of this section, is one of the important truths of Scripture that believers should understand. It was briefly discussed earlier, starting on page 105.

What Is Sanctification?

Sanctification may be defined as being "set apart for God." It has to do with His ownership of that which is set apart for Him. Another meaning, coming from the first, is to become holy in everyday life. The root word from which "sanctification" comes literally means "holy." Therefore, it has two aspects in Christian teaching. First, it is a holy standing – a holy position – before God because one belongs to Him through receiving Jesus as Lord and

Savior. Second, it speaks of daily growth in maturity and holiness in living. The first is a work of God alone; the second requires the cooperation of the believer.

GOD'S PART IN SANCTIFICATION

God alone makes possible our perfect and complete standing before Him in holiness. Both Testaments verify that He is the one who sanctifies. The book of Leviticus states no fewer than seven times in three chapters that the LORD is the one who sanctifies (Leviticus 20:8; 21:8, 15, 23; 22:9, 16, 32). The first example is Leviticus 20:8 that says, *"You shall keep My statutes and practice them; I am the LORD who sanctifies you."* God sets us apart as His own personal possession (Ephesians 1:14).

The New Testament recognizes that each member of the Trinity plays a part in sanctification. Jesus asked God the Father to do the sanctifying work in John 17:17 where He prayed, *"Sanctify them in the truth; Your word is truth."* Later, Paul wrote, *"But by His* [God's] *doing you are in Christ Jesus, who became to us wisdom from God, and righteousness and sanctification, and redemption"* (1 Corinthians 1:30).

The Father Sanctifies
The way God sanctifies us is by the offering of Jesus Christ. Hebrews 10:10 speaks of God's will in this matter: *"By this* [God's] *will we have been sanctified through the offering of the body of Jesus Christ once for all."* God the Father and God the Son planned Jesus' death, burial, and resurrection as the means of redemption and sanctification. One can easily see that sanctification is a work of God the Father. It is clearly His will that we be separated from evil unto Him.

211

The Son Sanctifies

Jesus Christ's participation in our sanctification is clearly stated a number of times. As an example, Paul wrote to the Ephesians:

Ephesians 5:25-26
25 ... Christ also loved the church and gave Himself up for her,
*26 so that **He might sanctify her** ...*

Likewise, Hebrews 13:12 tells us that the blood of Jesus Christ sanctifies us: *"Therefore Jesus also, **that He might sanctify the people through His own blood,** suffered outside the gate."*

The Holy Spirit Sanctifies

The Spirit is also an agent in our sanctification according to the Apostle Peter. Peter wrote that we are chosen *"according to the foreknowledge of God the Father, **by the sanctifying work of the Spirit"*** (1 Peter 1:2). Paul adds his "amen" when he wrote: *"God has chosen you from the beginning for salvation through sanctification by the Spirit and faith in the truth"* (2 Thessalonians 2:13).

This first aspect of sanctification about which we have been speaking is a total, once-for-all setting apart to God of each believer. It is already a completed work which became effective for us the moment we were born again. This is not us setting ourselves apart to God, but rather it is His setting us apart unto Himself.

OUR PART IN SANCTIFICATION

Our side of sanctification is twofold: 1) a turning to God and 2) a turning away from sin. The Christians in Thessalonica illustrate both of these. Paul said of them, *"you turned to God from idols to serve a living and true God"* (1 Thessalonians 1:9). God does not require us to turn from sin without giving us something far better in its

212

place. We not only turn *away* from sin, but we turn *to* God. Those who follow God have great blessings and pleasures; those who pursue their own sinful ways often end up with countless sorrows.

The Old Testament speaks about men sanctifying themselves and the temple of God. They were to sanctify the temple by removing all the vile things that had been introduced into the holy place and getting rid of every unclean thing. God expects sanctification to be practical. In the words of the Apostle Paul, we are to yield ourselves to God as instruments of righteousness and we are to refuse to yield ourselves to Satan as instruments of unrighteousness (Romans 6:13). Paul illustrated an area that needs sanctifying: *"For this is the will of God, your sanctification; that is, that you abstain from sexual immorality"* (1 Thessalonians 4:3). Sanctification works on a very practical level!

Who will and who will not inherit the kingdom of God? This is the Bible's statement on the matter:

1 Corinthians 6:9-11
9 Or do you not know that the unrighteous will not inherit the kingdom of God? Do not be deceived; neither fornicators, nor idolaters, nor adulterers, nor effeminate, nor homosexuals,
10 nor thieves, nor the covetous, nor drunkards, nor revilers, nor swindlers, will inherit the kingdom of God.
11 Such were some of you; but you were washed, but you were sanctified, but you were justified in the name of the Lord Jesus Christ and in the Spirit of our God.

These three verses vividly demonstrate that God expects certain standards of conduct from His children. It also shows that the sanctifying of verse 11 delivers one from the sins of verses nine and ten. Those who live according to verses nine and ten will not inherit God's kingdom. Those

213

who live according to verse 11 will inherit the kingdom of God.

According to 2 Corinthians 3:18, we are being transformed into the image of the Lord. God's eternal purpose for us is to be like Jesus Christ. It is obvious that sanctification in the experience of a Christian is a progressive matter. We are exhorted to *"grow in the grace and knowledge of our Lord and Savior Jesus Christ"* (2 Peter 3:18). The writer to the Hebrews commands us to pursue sanctification without which no one will see the Lord (Hebrews 12:14). Personal sanctification should be the goal of every believer. Without it, no one will see the Lord. First, each of us must exercise the righteousness and purity found in the Lord Jesus Christ; and second, we must rid ourselves of evil things.

Relationship Between God's Part and Ours

Many Christians desire to walk closely with God. This walk is often called a deeper life, or a sanctified life. Practically, however, one cannot have a close walk with God until he discovers that he has already been sanctified by God. As a result of understanding that sanctification is already his as a free gift, he can begin to reflect personal holiness in his Christian conduct. Since it is Jesus' blood that sanctifies us, we must rest in the work He has done on Calvary to provide everything necessary to maintain personal holiness before God. The Word of God tells us:

2 Peter 1:2-3
2 Grace and peace be multiplied to you in the knowledge of God and of Jesus our Lord;
*3 seeing that **His divine power has granted to us everything pertaining to life and godliness,** through the true knowledge of Him who called us by His own glory and excellence.*

Through the true knowledge of Jesus Christ and His Father, everything we need for a godly life has already been granted to us. We do not have to constantly search after additional remedies that will help us live godly lives pleasing to the Father.

Practical Sanctification

This kind of personal holiness must be more than mere thoughts or words; it must be a very practical outworking in deeds. The Word of God has a very good illustration of that being done on a practical level. The book of Acts relates how the Ephesian Christians actually rid themselves of evil books of magic. It says:

Acts 19:18-20
18 Many also of those who had believed kept coming, confessing and disclosing their practices.
19 And many of those who practiced magic brought their books together and began burning them in the sight of everyone; and they counted up the price of them and found it fifty thousand pieces of silver.
20 So the word of the Lord was growing mightily and prevailing.

They sanctified themselves **from** the practice of magic **to** the service of God. First, they confessed and disclosed their practices, then they burned their books of magic openly for all to see. As a result, the Word of the Lord grew mightily and prevailed. As we separate ourselves from evil and yield to God for personal cleansing, we, too, will experience the growth that comes from Him.

† Salvation – Glorification of the Believer

One of the most precious truths concerning salvation and the believer is the Bible's teaching on glorification. Jesus said, *"The glory which You have given Me I have given to them"* (John 17:22). Like many truths in the New Testament, glorification has both a present aspect and a future aspect. Therefore, we will deal with the question of glorification under two headings: Spiritual Glorification at Salvation and Physical Glorification at Christ's Coming.

SPIRITUAL GLORIFICATION AT SALVATION

It is easier to understand glorification of the believer at the second coming of Christ than it is to understand the glorification of the believer at salvation. We expect to see the believer glorified in a new body when he appears with Christ in glory (Col. 3:4). However, when we look around at believers now, we see no radiant light of glory; rather we see them in the same light as the unsaved.

Present Spiritual Glorification

Paul teaches in Romans 8 that there are several parts to complete salvation.

Romans 8:29-30
29 For those whom He foreknew, He also predestined to become conformed to the image of His Son, so that He would be the firstborn among many brethren;
30   and these whom He predestined, He also called; and these whom He called, He also justified; and these whom He justified, **He also glorified.**

We are not concerned in this section with foreknew, predestined, called, or justified. However, we are concerned with the final phrase of Romans 8:30 that reads: *"and whom He justified, these He also glorified."* Many people explain *"glorified"* in this passage as something to look forward to in the future, and there is certainly that aspect to it. They believe it is in the past tense because it is an accomplished fact "in the mind of God." However, a good case can be made for something more – that is, an accomplished present spiritual glorification. Believers are already spiritually glorified.

Ephesians Teaching on the Glorification of Christ

In Ephesians 1:19-23 we have these words concerning the exaltation of Christ:

Ephesians 1:19-23
19 [I pray that you may know] ... what is the surpassing greatness of His power toward us who believe. These are in accordance with the working of the strength of His might
20 which He brought about in Christ, when He raised Him from the dead, and seated Him at His right hand in the heavenly places,
21 far above all rule and authority and power and dominion, and every name that is named, not only in this age but also in the one to come.
22 And He put all things in subjection under His feet, and gave Him as head over all things to the church,
23 which is His body, the fulness of Him who fills all in all.

Note in verse 20 that God raised Christ from the dead and seated Him at His right hand in heavenly places. A glorified Man now sits at the right hand of the Majesty on High! That exalted position is *"far above all rule and authority and power and dominion, and every name that is named, not only in this age but also in the one to come."* Verse 23 goes on to say that the Church is His fulness. That is absolutely amazing!

Ephesians on the Glorification of Believers

But, even more amazing is Ephesians 2:6 which states that God *"raised us up with Him, and seated us with Him in the heavenly places in Christ Jesus."* God, in His kindness, has seated us spiritually in heavenly places in Christ. What does that mean? It means that we have been raised up

217

spiritually to a place superior to the principalities and powers. In a spiritual sense, we have been glorified with Jesus because we sit with Him on the throne in heaven.

Furthermore, Paul continues in Ephesians 3 to clarify the reason God has done such a marvelous work for us:

Ephesians 3:9-10
9 and to bring to light what is the administration of the mystery which for ages has been hidden in God who created all things;
10 so that the manifold wisdom of God might now be made known through the church to the rulers and the authorities in the heavenly places.

God's purpose through the Church is to demonstrate His manifold wisdom *"to the rulers and the authorities in the heavenly places,"* another way of describing angelic beings. Satan did his best to destroy mankind in the fall. God took the worst Satan could do, turned it around through His grace, and made redeemed man superior to the angels by seating them with Christ in the heavenlies.

Because of this present, spiritually-glorified position of believers in heaven, they have been granted authority to resist Satan in the name of Christ. It is not by any virtue in them that gives them authority; it is purely by the grace of God in raising them up with Christ.

PHYSICAL GLORIFICATION AT CHRIST'S COMING

Future Glorification of the Body

It is certainly clear that believers who have died in Christ will be raised at His second coming, and those who remain alive until then will be instantly changed into His likeness: *"Then we who are alive and remain will be caught up together with them in the clouds to meet the Lord in the air, and so we shall always be with the Lord"* (1 Thessalonians 4:17).

The new resurrection body will be raised incorruptible, in glory, and power – a spiritual body that will be like unto Jesus' resurrected body. Several New Testament Scriptures testify to that fact:

1 Corinthians 15:42-44
*42 So also is the resurrection of the dead. It is sown a perishable body, **it is raised an imperishable body;***
*43 it is sown in dishonor, **it is raised in glory**; it is sown in weakness, **it is raised in power**;*
*44 it is sown a natural body, **it is raised a spiritual body.** If there is a natural body, there is also a spiritual body.*

1 John 3:2
*2 Beloved, now we are children of God, and it has not appeared as yet what we will be. We know that when He appears, **we will be like Him,** because we will see Him just as He is.*

Philippians 3:20-21
20 For our citizenship is in heaven, from which also we eagerly wait for a Savior, the Lord Jesus Christ;
21 who will transform the body of our humble state into conformity with the body of His glory, by the exertion of the power that He has even to subject all things to Himself.

In other words, when Jesus comes, we shall shed this vile, corrupt body in exchange for a glorious body that will be like His glorious body that shall never die again. It will radiate the glory of God for all to see.

Romans 8:16-17
16 The Spirit Himself testifies with our spirit that we are children of God,
17 and if children, heirs also, heirs of God and fellow heirs with Christ, if indeed we suffer with Him so that we may also be glorified with Him.

Public Glorification with Christ at His Appearing

According to the gospel of Mark, Jesus is coming again in the glory of God His Father: *"For whoever is ashamed of Me and My words in this adulterous and sinful generation, the Son of Man will also be ashamed of him when He comes in the glory of His Father with the holy angels"* (Mark 8:38).

According to Paul, when Jesus appears, He will reveal His glory to His saints: *"For I consider that the sufferings of this present time are not worthy to be compared with the glory that is to be revealed to us"* (Romans 8:18). Likewise, on that wonderful occasion, believers will be associated with Him in His glory: *"When Christ, who is our life, is revealed, then **you also will be revealed with Him in glory**"* (Colossians 3:4).

Second Thessalonians states that Jesus will be glorified "in," or because of, His saints. The trophies of His grace will be used to bring glory to the Savior, ***"when He comes to be glorified in His saints** on that day, and to be marveled at among all who have believed – for our testimony to you was believed"* (2 Thessalonians 1:10).

Glorification's Eternal Outcome

The believer will live in a state of glorification for all eternity. Peter tells us that God has called us to His eternal glory: *"After you have suffered for a little while, the God of all grace, **who called you to His eternal glory** in Christ, will Himself perfect, confirm, strengthen and establish you"* (1 Peter 5:10).

That glory will be manifested in the new heaven and new earth where we shall walk in the light of the glory of God: *"And the city has no need of the sun or of the moon to shine on it, for the glory of God has illumined it, and its lamp is the Lamb"* (Revelation 21:23).

What a joy and a glory it shall be to walk the street of gold (Revelation 21:21) and see the magnificence in store for us. We shall also see the glory of the kings and nations of the earth brought into new Jerusalem:

Revelation 21:24 & 26
24 The nations will walk by its light, and the kings of the earth will bring their glory into it.

26 and they will bring the glory and the honor of the nations into it;

MAKE SALVATION PERSONAL

In summary, speaking of God, the Scripture says, *"without faith it is impossible to please Him"* (Hebrews 11:6). You must believe God who cannot lie and His Son who gave Himself for your sins. Once you have made the step of acknowledging the truth of the Scripture about salvation, then you must repent, i.e., turn your back on the sin that sent Jesus to the Cross. That does not mean you will never sin again. However, your desire must be to please the One who died for you.

You may say, "I cannot live up to what God expects. I cannot turn from my sin; therefore, I cannot be saved." Keep in mind that God said that if you come to Him, He will give you His Holy Spirit to help you. He will enable you to overcome the sin in your life. If you fall, He will not cast you out. He will pick you up. It is not your responsibility to produce the power to overcome sin. It is only your responsibility to believe God and to be willing in your heart to turn away from the sin. He has promised you the ability to overcome. *"This is the victory that has overcome the world – our faith"* (1 John 5:4). Turn from your sin and turn to the living God that you may have the eternal life which He has promised in Jesus Christ our Lord. If you will do that, all the wonders of salvation that God has provided will be yours.

These things being true, then it is easy to see that salvation is a matter of pure grace. Because it is of grace and not of works, everyone has an equal opportunity of having eternal life. No one is barred because of past sin. No one is excluded because of the lack of education. No one is kept out because of the lack of money to pay for priestly services or to do good works by giving to the poor. Rich man, beggar man, poor man, thief – all may be saved by turning from sin to God through Jesus Christ with a heart willing to trust Him. If you have never made that step of faith, do it right now – do it today. Put your faith in Jesus Christ. Trust Him to forgive your sins. Trust Him to take you to heaven. Trust Him because He paid for your sins on Calvary. And then you will see what Paul meant when he wrote:

Ephesians 2:8-9
8 For by grace you have been saved through faith; and that not of yourselves, it is the gift of God;
9 not as a result of works, that no one should boast.

Chapter 9

Prayer
† How God Responds

Prayer – talking with and listening to God – is a subject of great interest and vital importance. We need to know how God responds to prayer and why, it seems, He often does not respond when we pray.

Prayer – A Great Privilege

Prayer is one of the greatest privileges we have as believers. Those who know Jesus have a tremendous treasure in God's invitation to come directly into His presence to worship and talk with Him concerning their needs and those of others. It is not necessary to come to Him through a saint, a priest, or a pastor. God invites us to come directly to His throne for grace to help in time of need (Hebrews 4:16).

Jesus spoke to His disciples just before His crucifixion saying, *"if you ask the Father for anything in My name, He will give it to you."* (John 16:23). This is a great promise given to us by Jesus. He invites us to come directly to God. We may come for the little things we need in our lives, as well as the big things. Nothing is too small for God to care about or too large for Him to handle.

How God Responds to Prayer

One common question many new Christians ask about prayer is, "Why does God not respond immediately when I pray? After all, didn't Jesus promise us that?" The answer is that God responds in at least three ways: "Yes, your request is granted immediately;" "Yes, your request is granted but you must wait for a time;" or "No, your request is not granted because it is not in your best interest." And sometimes He may not respond at all because of sin!

Yes, Your Request Is Granted Immediately

The first response, "Yes, your request is granted immediately," has been experienced by believers from the beginning. It is very well illustrated in Acts where the disciples were praying because they had been told by the authorities not to preach and teach in the name of Jesus:

> Acts 4:23-24 and 29-31
> *23 When they had been released, they went to their own companions, and reported all that the chief priests and the elders had said to them.*
> *24 And when they heard this, they lifted their voices to God with one accord and said ...*
>
> *29 "And now, Lord, take note of their threats, and grant that Your bond-servants may speak Your word with all confidence,*
> *30 while You extend Your hand to heal, and signs and wonders take place through the name of Your holy servant Jesus."*
> *31 And when they had prayed, the place where they had gathered together was shaken, and they were all filled with the Holy Spirit and began to speak the word of God with boldness.*

That must have been some prayer meeting! The servants of God, under threat of persecution, and without worldly resources, turned directly to their heavenly Father. They simply laid their problem before Him. They did not ask to be spared from persecution; they asked to speak the Word of God with boldness and were filled with the Holy Spirit to do so.

That kind of prayer is answered immediately. Notice they were not concerned for their own interests. They were concerned about the kingdom of God. Their prayer was not self-centered; rather, it was Christ-centered. They were intent upon fulfilling the command which Jesus had given them to preach the Gospel. Notice in the second place, they recognized their own weakness and inability. They knew that in face of threats and persecution they might not be able to remain bold and faithful in the preaching of the Gospel. Therefore, they asked God to supply their lack by granting them the ability to speak the Word with all confidence. In the third place, they asked God to grant signs, wonders, and healings to validate their message as they preached the Gospel.

The outcome of their prayer was that the power of God came down upon them in such a mighty filling of the Holy Spirit that even the place where they were gathered was literally shaken. Would that God would grant us the purity of life, the consecration of obedience, and the humility of spirit necessary to receive answers like that!

Yes, But You Must Wait for a Time

The second way God may respond to our prayers is to say, "Yes, your request is granted, but you must wait for a time for it to be answered." Some requests of necessity take time to fulfill. When we pray about things in which other people must play a part, it may take time for the prayer to be answered. It is entirely possible, of course, for God to make people do whatever He wants them to do. However, He normally will not overrule their will. He will take time to work with them to bring them to the place of doing His will without being forced into it.

The life of Abraham illustrates how God may take time to answer prayer. Abraham lived about 2,000 years before Christ. God asked him to leave his home at the age of 75 and live in Palestine (Genesis 12:4). He promised Abraham that He would make him a great nation, bless him, and make his name great. Some years later, the Lord came to Abraham in a vision. At that time his name was still Abram. The Scripture says:

Genesis 15:2-4
2 Abram said, "O Lord GOD, what will You give me, since I am childless, and the heir of my house is Eliezer of Damascus?"
3 And Abram said, "Since You have given no offspring to me, one born in my house is my heir."
4 Then behold, the word of the LORD came to him, saying, "This man will not be your heir; but one who will come forth from your own body, he shall be your heir."

God expanded the promise that He first made to Abraham when he was 75 years old. He said specifically that one from Abraham's own body – his own son – would be his heir. After Abraham lived 10 years in Palestine, he still had no children. Thus, he had not begun to see the fulfillment of God's promise to make him a great nation even though he was already 85 years old. But it was still another 15 years before Isaac was born. According to Genesis 21:5, *"Abraham was one hundred years old when his son Isaac was born to him."*

Putting all this together, 25 years passed from the time Abraham left his home in Haran (Genesis 12:4) until his son Isaac was born. It is interesting that the book of Romans says that Abraham did not waver in unbelief, but grew strong in faith because he believed that God was able to do what He had promised (Romans 4:20). Rather than his faith growing weak during that 25 years, it kept increasing in strength.

We read more about the faith of Abraham in Romans 4:

Romans 4:18-22
18 In hope against hope he believed, so that he might become a father of many nations according to that which had been spoken, "SO SHALL YOUR DESCENDANTS BE."
19 Without becoming weak in faith he contemplated his own body, now as good as dead since he was about a hundred years old, and the deadness of Sarah's womb;
20 yet, with respect to the promise of God, he did not waver in unbelief but grew strong in faith, giving glory to God,
21 and being fully assured that what God had promised, He was able also to perform.
22 Therefore IT WAS ALSO CREDITED TO HIM AS RIGHTEOUSNESS.

In this passage Abraham believed God's promise for an heir when all around him the evidence said it should not happen. Abraham was 99 years old and Sarah was already past the age of child bearing. He would be 100 and Sarah 90 when Isaac was to be born. And yet, in hope against hope, he believed and God fulfilled his request.

No, Your Request Is Denied

Sometimes God simply has to say, "No." At times He must deny a request because it is not in our best interest or in the best interest of His kingdom to grant it. For example, the Apostle Paul prayed concerning a problem which gave him much trouble in his Christian life:

2 Corinthians 12:7-9
7 Because of the surpassing greatness of the revelations, for this reason, to keep me from exalting

myself, there was given me a thorn in the flesh, a messenger of Satan to torment me--to keep me from exalting myself!
8 Concerning this I implored the Lord three times that it might leave me.
9 And He has said to me, "My grace is sufficient for you, for power is perfected in weakness." ...

Paul prayed three times for this messenger of Satan to be taken away from him. God told him the problem was permitted to keep him from becoming proud over the great revelations given to him. The Lord refused his request because it would have been bad for Paul to have it granted.

The important thing is, God made it absolutely clear to Paul his request was denied, and told him why. God must sometimes deny our requests for our own good. However, please notice that "no" is as clear and definite an answer as "yes."

Sometimes, God does not say, "Yes, I will do it now." "Yes, I will do it later." or, "No, it is not good for you." He does not say anything! The heavens appear to be silent. If you do not receive either a "yes" or a "no," God has other reasons for not responding. The question is, "Why?"

† Prayer – Why God May Not Answer

The Bible gives at least eleven reasons why God may not answer prayer. It is important to know these, particularly if our prayers are not being answered. When God does not answer either "yes," "yes, but wait," or "no," it is usually because of sin. The Scripture reveals a number of specific sins which keep our prayers from being answered.

Idols in the Heart

Idolatry is a great sin, whether it be the outward worship of false gods or idols in the heart. The concept of idols in the heart is found in the Old Testament:

> Ezekiel 14:1-3
> *1 Then some elders of Israel came to me and sat down before me.*
> *2 And the word of the LORD came to me, saying,*
> *3 "Son of man, **these men have set up their idols in their hearts** and have put right before their faces the stumbling block of their iniquity. Should I be consulted by them at all?"*

God says clearly that He will not respond to the prayers of those who set up idols in their hearts. What does it mean to set up idols in the heart? It means that some person or thing comes before God in your heart; God does not have first place. An idol is worshiped and served rather than God. A husband, a wife, or children are idols in the heart if they are put before God. Any time a home, money, or any other thing is placed before God they become idols. If you placed anything above God, it must be removed from first place because only God should have first place in your heart.

Sin in the Heart

Another hindrance to prayer is found in Psalm 66:18. There the Psalmist said, *"If I regard wickedness in my heart, The Lord will not hear."* Likewise Isaiah wrote:

> Isaiah 59:1-2
> *1 Behold, the LORD's hand is not so short*
> *That it cannot save;*
> *Nor is His ear so dull*
> *That it cannot hear.*
> *2 But your iniquities have made a separation between you and your God,*
> ***And your sins have hidden His face from you so that He does not hear.***

These two passages make it clear that sin harbored in the heart stops prayer from being answered. Most sins have to do with relationships with other people. If you have wronged someone and never made it right, or if you have hatred in your heart toward someone, then God simply may not answer your prayers. It must be made right before you can expect your prayers to be answered.

Wrong Motives

James 4:3 says, *"You ask and do not receive, because you ask with wrong motives, so that you may spend it on your pleasures."* God may not answer prayer based on a desire for selfish advantage, advancement, comfort, or pleasure. This does not mean we cannot pray for our needs. The Lord taught us to do that in Matthew 6:11 when He said, *"Give us this day our daily bread."* Bread is a necessity of life; therefore, it is not wrong to request things we need.

Holding a Grudge or Unforgiving Spirit

In the Gospel of Mark, the Lord gives us another reason why God may not hear and respond to our prayers.

Mark 11:25-26
25 "Whenever you stand praying, forgive, if you have anything against anyone, so that your Father also who is in heaven may forgive you your transgressions.
26 ["But if you do not forgive, neither will your Father who is in heaven forgive your transgressions."]

It is clearly evident that we must not hold a grudge or an unforgiving spirit. Many of us forgive when a person has wronged us if he or she apologizes to us. However, the Lord expects us to forgive even when that does not happen.

This does not mean we should tolerate sin. But it does mean we should maintain an attitude of love and forgiveness toward all men. Humanly speaking, it cannot be done, but God can enable us to do it. Jesus is our example. He forgave those crucifying Him, even while they were in the very act. Even Stephen, the first Christian martyr, forgave those who were killing him while they were still casting stones. Both Jesus and Stephen demonstrated the spirit of forgiveness which God expects us to have. If you hold a grudge or have a difficult time forgiving, then by all means ask God to enable you to do what is right, even if you do not feel like it.

Poor Marital Relationship

Another hindrance to prayer is a poor relationship in a marriage. Peter wrote, *"You husbands in the same way, live with your wives in an understanding way, as with someone weaker, since she is a woman; and show her honor as a fellow heir of the grace of life, so that your prayers will not be hindered"* (1 Peter 3:7). The point is that marriage must be kept by God's standards if prayer is to be answered. Husbands and wives cannot have hatred and bitterness toward one another without suffering spiritually. This does not mean, of course, that a person married to a bitter unbeliever does not have his prayers answered. You must strive to keep a right attitude toward your mate regardless of his or her attitude.

Unbelief

One of the greatest hindrances to prayer is unbelief. James speaks about prayer in chapter one where he says:

James 1:6-7
6 But let him ask in faith without any doubting, for the one who doubts is like the surf of the sea, driven and tossed by the wind.
7 For that man ought not to expect that he will receive anything from the Lord.

231

Mark tells us that Jesus said it is important to believe God will answer when we pray: *"Therefore I say to you, all things for which you pray and ask, believe that you have received them, and they will be granted you"* (Mark 11:24).

The above two passages show that faith is important. We must believe that our request is granted even before the answer is evident, provided other conditions of Scripture that we are now discussing are properly fulfilled. Many of us pray without expecting God to answer. One who asks in unbelief has no real confidence in the goodness and truthfulness of God, or else he knows already that he is asking for the wrong thing. Therefore, he will not receive an answer to his request.

Wrong Attitudes

Everyone has some bad days, but that is not what we are talking about in this instance. Wrong attitudes refer to hypocritical attitudes that some people have. Jesus said:

Matthew 6:5-6
5 "When you pray, you are not to be like the hypocrites; for they love to stand and pray in the synagogues and on the street corners so that they may be seen by men. Truly I say to you, they have their reward in full.
6 "But you, when you pray, go into your inner room, close your door and pray to your Father who is in secret, and your Father who sees what is done in secret will reward you."

Jesus taught that wrong attitudes will keep our prayers from being answered. Prayer must not be used to support pride by calling attention to oneself. In prayer before other people, we should be especially careful not to purposefully pray in order to be seen, heard, or praised by men. Remember the story of the Pharisee and publican who went down to the temple to pray (Luke 18:9-14)? The Pharisee was self-righteous; the publican was repentant and humble. The Pharisee was proud of his fasting and self-righteous life. The publican would not even lift up his head before God. He bowed his head, pounded his chest, and said, *"God, be merciful to me, the sinner!"* (Luke 18:13). His actions expressed an attitude of humility. His prayer was answered, not because of his actions, but because he had the proper inward attitude toward himself and toward God.

Bad Conscience

Have you ever had a bad conscience? That can also hinder your prayers. The Apostle John wrote:

1 John 3:21-22
21 Beloved, if our heart does not condemn us, we have confidence before God;
22 and whatever we ask we receive from Him, because we keep His commandments and do the things that are pleasing in His sight.

It is possible for our heart to condemn us over things which are not really sin. Conscience may lead us astray based on the social environment in which we have grown up. But even if it condemns us wrongly, we do not have confidence before God. Search the Scriptures so your conscience will work on the basis of the Word of God rather than on the basis of social customs. Once you determine what is right according to the Bible, then your conscience should act on that standard. If it condemns you based on a violation of God's laws, seek His forgiveness and make right the wrong done. With your conscience cleansed, you can pray to God with confidence.

Against God's Will

Not only is a clear conscience necessary to have confidence before God, but one must also pray according to God's will. The Apostle John also wrote:

1 John 5:14-15
14 This is the confidence which we have before Him, that, if we ask anything according to His will, He hears us.
15 And if we know that He hears us in whatever we ask, we know that we have the requests which we have asked from Him.

A prayer must be according to God's will in order for it to be answered. This does not mean that we must always say "if it be Your will." Sometimes we use that little phrase to hide our own unbelief.

Remember, we should not ask anything against the will of God as revealed in the Bible. A woman once told me that following her husband's death, she asked God to let him appear and talk with her for a few minutes. When she did that, according to her testimony, the room went black and a figure claiming to be her husband appeared and told her that everything was fine. At the time, the woman may not have known that her prayer was directly against the will of God. The Old Testament book of Deuteronomy expressly forbids calling up the dead to talk with them. Therefore, her prayer could not have been in God's will as is evident from this Scripture:

Deuteronomy 18:9-11
*9 "When you enter the land which the Lord your God gives you, **you shall not learn to imitate the detestable things of those nations.***
10 "There shall not be found among you anyone who makes his son or his daughter pass through the fire, one who uses divination, one who practices witchcraft, or one who interprets omens, or a sorcerer,
*11 or one who casts a spell, or a medium, or a spiritist, **or one who calls up the dead."***

234

She had a difficult problem later because Satan had gained an advantage through her ignorance. She struggled for quite a long time against a temptation which she knew was absolutely wrong. Because of her experience, she was tempted to hold seances to help other people contact their dead loved ones. This, of course, is absolutely against God's will; other Scriptures are clear – the dead do not return to talk with the living, except in one special case. In the Old Testament, Samuel returned to talk to Saul. However, there are demons who say they are the dead person. Still, she struggled against the temptation until she finally went to her pastor. After they prayed together against the temptation, it ceased. But she had given entrance to the tempter through violating God's will which is clearly revealed in the Bible.

Do not let yourself fall into a similar trap. Do not pray for something that is not according to God's will, or worse yet, something that is definitely against God's revealed will already made clear in His Word.

Disobedience to God's Directives
Another thing that greatly hinders prayer is refusing to heed God when He speaks. Today, God most often speaks through His Word. We know that certain things are His will. Sometimes we simply do not listen to what He says. Therefore, He simply will not hear what we have to say. The Lord Himself confirms that: *"'And just as He called and they would not listen, so they called and I would not listen,' says the LORD of hosts"* (Zechariah 7:13).

Furthermore, Proverbs says, *"He who turns away his ear from listening to the law, even his prayer is an abomination"* (Proverbs 28:9). Did you know that your prayer can become an abomination to God? If you refuse to heed God's voice, not only does your prayer go unheard, but it becomes a thing hated by God. Therefore, you must be obedient to the Word of God and to His Spirit day by day.

235

However, a word of caution must be given. One should not get in the habit of obeying all internal compulsions to do something. Satan will take advantage of such blind obedience to whatever comes into one's mind. Some Christians believe that any internal impression must be from God. But that is not the case. The Holy Spirit will never lead a person to do something against the Word of God. Therefore, inner suggestions and compulsions must always be in agreement with the teaching of the written Word of God in order to keep from going astray.

Without Mercy

Believers must show mercy and compassion toward other people. Proverbs 21:13 states, *"He who shuts his ear to the cry of the poor will also cry himself and not be answered."* It is God's will to help those who are helpless or in need of food and clothing. It is His will for us to express the love of Christ toward people in need. If you turn your ear away from the poor who need help, when it is in your power to help them, then you should not be upset if God does not hear your cry!

MAKE PRAYER PERSONAL

If you do not know the only true God and Jesus Christ whom He has sent, you have no ground on which to request anything from God at all. If your prayers are not answered, then turn to God today, confess your sin and your need of Jesus Christ as Lord and Savior. Then your heavenly Father will hear you when you pray.

Even if you are saved, your prayers may still be hindered by any of the sins just discussed. Thankfully, it is very unlikely that a believing person would have all of those problems at one time! However, it is possible that you have permitted one or two of those sins to creep into your life.

236

It is quite evident that none can live a perfect and sinless life. You are not required to be sinless in order to have your prayers answered. But if you do not see God answer your prayers regularly, consider some of the things that have been said to see whether or not there may be hindrances in your life. God will point out the hindrances if you will see to it that they are corrected. Then you will be on a good, solid footing for an effective prayer life.

Hebrews 4:16
16 Therefore let us draw near with confidence to the throne of grace, so that we may receive mercy and find grace to help in time of need.

Chapter 10

The Church
† Its Identity

God has chosen the New Testament Church to be the *"pillar and support of the truth"* (1 Timothy 3:15). The Church, therefore, is very important in the work of the Lord. We need to know the identity of the Church – what it is, what it is not, and who its members are.

What Is "the Church"?

The word "Church" comes from the Greek word "ecclesia" which means "to call out from." In secular literature at the time of the New Testament the word meant an assembly of people. It was used for a town assembly or other gathering of people for a specific purpose. In the New Testament it is used especially to designate a local congregation of Christian believers meeting together for the purpose of worship, for instruction, and for spreading the Gospel of Jesus Christ. It is likewise used to refer to the entire worldwide body of believers as the Body of Christ from Pentecost until the Second Coming of the Lord Jesus. The context of the word shows which is meant.

God is now saving the Jew by faith in Jesus Christ as well as *"taking from among the Gentiles a people for His name"* (Acts 15:14). The Church is composed of both Jews and Gentiles who have been called by God from among their countrymen into a special relationship with Himself through Jesus Christ. The Church is a body of believers who have trusted in the Lord Jesus Christ for eternal salvation and are voluntarily under His dominion and authority. It is spoken of figuratively in the Bible as the body of which Jesus is the Head, the temple in which God now dwells, and a building for God in the Holy Spirit.

Not a Meeting Place

It is interesting to note that the term "church" in the New Testament is not applied to a literal building or a place of meeting. It is used to describe the people who meet together and belong to Jesus Christ. The Church, then, is not a meeting place or building, but it is rather the New Testament people of God.

The New Testament Church

The Church, in the New Testament sense, did not exist before the day of Pentecost. Before His crucifixion, Jesus spoke of His Church as still in the future. Notice the future tense Jesus used when He said to Peter, *"upon this rock I will build My church; and the gates of hell will not overpower it"* (Matthew 16:18).

While the nation of Israel was an assembly in the wilderness (Acts 7:38), it did not have the same meaning and relationship to God that the New Testament Church does. The nation of Israel was made up of all who were born into the nation by natural birth. Obviously, some trusted in God and others did not believe in Him. In the New Testament, while there are unbelievers coming to Christian meetings, the Church itself is spoken of as being composed only of those who have been born again by the Spirit of God and are in proper relationship with God through Jesus Christ.

The Church began on the day of Pentecost when the Holy Spirit came upon the 120 disciples who were awaiting the fulfillment of the promise of God. Jesus had promised His apostles that the Father would send the Spirit of God upon them so they would receive power to witness. In keeping with the promise of God, the Holy Spirit came upon them on the day of Pentecost, uniting them into one body of believers called the Church.

The first local church met in different homes in Jerusalem, but it is referred to as one church with one roll of members. Even as it continued to grow it remained one church. In Acts 1:15 there were 120 gathered to await Pentecost and the coming of the Holy Spirit. In Acts 2:41, 3,000 were added and by Acts 4:4 there were 5,000 men in addition to women and young people. Daily additions were being made to the Church by the Lord (Acts 2:47).

Local Congregations and the Worldwide Church
Later, the word "church" was used to describe local congregations in various places, such as Jerusalem, Antioch, Galatia, Ephesus, and Corinth. The primary use of the word in the New Testament is in reference to these local assemblies. It does, however, have a more extended meaning in passages like 1 Corinthians 15:9, Galatians 1:13, and Matthew 16:18. In these passages the Church is spoken of as one body of Christ throughout the whole earth. Paul said, *"For I am the least of the apostles, and not fit to be called an apostle, because I persecuted the church of God"* (1 Corinthians 15:9). He wrote to the Galatians, *"For you have heard of my former manner of life in Judaism, how I used to persecute the church of God beyond measure and tried to destroy it"* (Galatians 1:13). Paul persecuted the Christians in Jerusalem and was on his way to Damascus to persecute them when he was converted. He wrote about persecuting the Church of God – speaking of Christians in Jerusalem and elsewhere.

The Church, Christendom, and the Kingdom of God
While studying the New Testament, it should be kept in mind that the Church is not all of Christendom, nor is it

240

all of the kingdom of God. The kingdom of God is a term used to designate the rule of God over all, both good and evil. Jesus said:

Matthew 13:41-42
41 "The Son of Man will send forth His angels, and they will gather out of His kingdom all stumbling blocks, and those who commit lawlessness, 42 and will throw them into the furnace of fire; in that place there shall be weeping and gnashing of teeth."

Therefore, both good and bad people are included in the sphere of the kingdom of God.

Christendom is a term including every group of people who call themselves Christian. It does not have to be based on the pattern of the New Testament Church in order to be part of Christendom. Many groups in Christendom do not hold to the teachings of Jesus Christ although they use His name and refer to themselves as Christians. Jesus implies this in Matthew:

Matthew 7:21-23
21 "Not everyone who says to Me, 'Lord, Lord,' will enter the kingdom of heaven, but he who does the will of My Father who is in heaven will enter. 22 "Many will say to Me on that day, 'Lord, Lord, did we not prophesy in Your name, and in Your name cast out demons, and in Your name perform many miracles?' 23 "And then I will declare to them, 'I never knew you; DEPART FROM ME, YOU WHO PRACTICE LAWLESSNESS.'"

The Church is distinct from both the kingdom of God and Christendom. The real Church is made up of people who have genuine faith in Jesus Christ as Lord.

Membership Requirements

Membership in the New Testament Church is limited to those who have repentance toward God and faith in our Lord Jesus Christ (Acts 20:20-21). We have already studied at some length about repentance, so we will not repeat that except to say one cannot become a member of the genuine Church without a change of heart attitude toward God. Neither can he become a member without really trusting in Jesus Christ as Lord and Savior. When those two requirements are met, the Lord Himself adds that person to His Church (Acts 2:47). Local churches may have additional requirements to join their particular assembly. As an example, most churches require water baptism for church membership. Many churches require baptism by immersion, while others accept baptism by sprinkling. (See "Baptism" on page 244). But nonetheless, the Lord requires there be a trust in the Lord Jesus Christ as Savior and a repentance toward God the Father who is in heaven.

A Paraphrase Helps Distinguish

What is your personal relationship to Jesus Christ? Paul makes a distinction in Romans 2 between a spiritual Jew and a nominal Jew. A professor in a Bible college once said that we could tell much about our Christianity by paraphrasing Romans 2 to see the difference between the genuine and the nominal Christian. Below is the passage with the words "Christian" substituted for "Jew," "Gospel" for "Law," and "baptism" for "circumcision."

Keep in mind that a paraphrase is not consistent if carried beyond its intended purpose. For example, verses 28 and 29 below do not rule out water baptism after conversion to Christ.

Romans 2:17-29 (Paraphrased for Application)
17 But if you bear the name Christian, and rely upon the Gospel, and boast in God,

18 and know His will, and approve the things that are essential, being instructed out of the Gospel,

19 and are confident that you yourself are a guide to the blind, a light to those who are in darkness,

20 a corrector of the foolish, a teacher of the immature, having in the Gospel the embodiment of knowledge and of the truth,

21 you, therefore, who teach another, do you not teach yourself? You who preach that one should not steal, do you steal?

22 You who say that one should not commit adultery, do you commit adultery? You who abhor idols, do you rob temples?

23 You who boast in the Gospel, through your breaking of the Gospel, do you dishonor God?

24 For "the name of God is blasphemed among the Gentiles because of you," just as it is written.

25 For indeed baptism is of value, if you practice the Gospel; but if you are a transgressor of the Gospel, your baptism has become as one being unbaptized.

26 If therefore the unbaptized man keeps the requirements of the Gospel, will not his lack of baptism be regarded as baptism?

27 And will not he who is physically unbaptized, if he keeps the Gospel, will he not judge you who though having the letter of the Gospel and baptism are a transgressor of the Gospel?

28 For he is not a Christian who is one outwardly; neither is baptism that which is outward in the flesh.

29 But he is a Christian who is one inwardly; and baptism is that which is of the heart, by the Spirit, not by the letter; and his praise is not from men, but from God.

This paraphrase demonstrates that you may call yourself a Christian and say you are a member of the church, but unless there has been a heart conversion to Jesus Christ as Lord and Savior, you are not really a member of God's Church.

† The Church – Its Ordinances

As God's heavenly people, the Church is not tied to earthly holidays or religious festivals (Colossians 2:16-17). That is not to say holidays and festivals should not be observed by members of a local church, nor is it to say they are wrong. It is clear, however, the churches have not been given any special feasts like Israel was given in the Old Testament. Most Christians celebrate Christmas and Easter, but the New Testament does not tell us to do so. The Lord asked us to do two things. New believers are to be baptized and all believers who walk in fellowship with Him are to observe the Lord's Supper. These two commands of the Lord are called ordinances.

What Is an Ordinance?

An ordinance is a command or an order given with authority. Before Jesus returned to heaven after His first coming, He left orders concerning two ordinances which were to be followed by the apostles in both teaching and practice. These were passed on in the New Testament and have been followed by Bible-believing churches since that time. Those two ordinances are: baptism and the Lord's Supper.

BAPTISM

How Was It Done in the New Testament?

Meaning of the Word – The English word "baptism" comes from a Greek word that means to dip or immerse. It was used to describe the dying of cloth and the sinking of ships. When cloth was dyed or ships sank, they were completely under water, i.e., they were immersed in water.

The Baptism of Jesus – In the New Testament the form of baptism used was immersion in water as is apparent in the baptism of Jesus. Look at how He was baptized by John the Baptist:

244

Mark 1:9-11

*9 In those days Jesus came from Nazareth in
Galilee and was baptized by John **in the Jordan.**
10 Immediately **coming up out of the water,** He
saw the heavens opening, and the Spirit like a
dove descending upon Him;
11 and a voice came out of the heavens: "You are
My beloved Son, in You I am well-pleased."*

Here we see that Mark referred to the baptism of Jesus as
being *"in the Jordan"* in verse nine; and then in verse ten,
that Jesus was *"immediately coming up out of the water."*

The account of Jesus' baptism by Matthew in his
Gospel is similar to Mark's account:

Matthew 3:13-17

*13 Then Jesus arrived from Galilee at the Jordan
coming to John, to be baptized by him.
14 But John tried to prevent Him, saying, "I have
need to be baptized by You, and do You come to
me?"
15 But Jesus answering said to him, "Permit it at
this time; for in this way it is fitting for us to fulfill
all righteousness." Then he permitted Him.
16 And after being baptized, **Jesus came up immediately from the water;** and behold, the heavens
were opened, and he saw the Spirit of God
descending as a dove, and lighting on Him,
17 and behold, a voice out of the heavens, said,
"This is My beloved Son, in whom I am well-
pleased."*

Notice again that verse 16 says, *"Jesus came up immediately
from the water."* Matthew and Mark agree on the fact that
Jesus came up out of the water; therefore, He must have
been **in** the water. Why else would He have been in the
water except to be immersed in it?

245

You may wonder what Luke has to say about this. Luke 3:21-22 tells us about the baptism of Jesus. But, there is nothing said there about how He was baptized or where He was baptized, only that Jesus was baptized. It is interesting that John's Gospel does not record the baptism of Jesus. Why? Because John is emphasizing that Jesus is God come in the flesh. As God, He did not need to be baptized. His baptism is recorded in the Gospels of Matthew, Mark, and Luke because He was identified with the human race as a man in them.

Baptism in John's Gospel – John 3:23 gives an indication of the manner of baptism being used at that time. Concerning John the Baptist, the Apostle John wrote, *"John also was baptizing in Aenon near Salim, because there was much water there; and people were coming and were being baptized"* (John 3:23). Likely, he was baptizing in a place with much water because he was baptizing by immersion. He would not have needed a great deal of water if he were sprinkling or pouring. I believe he was there because he needed enough water to baptize by immersion.

Jesus was obviously in the water when He came up out of the water; and John was in a place where there was much water for baptizing which would not have been necessary had he been baptizing in some other way. These two arguments, along with the use of the word in cloth dyeing and ship sinking, strongly supports baptism by immersion.

Its Symbolism
Water baptism is used as an important symbol to illustrate spiritual truth. Water baptism by immersion best fits Paul's explanation of genuine spiritual baptism in Romans 6, of which water baptism is an outward symbol:

Romans 6:4-5
4 Therefore we have been buried with Him through baptism into death, so that as Christ was

raised from the dead through the glory of the Father, so we too might walk in newness of life.
5 For if we have become united with Him in the likeness of His death, certainly we shall be also in the likeness of His resurrection.

Baptism is a symbol of the believer's union with Jesus Christ in His death, burial, and resurrection, represented by the believer being put under water and by coming up out of the waters of baptism. The New Testament standard is baptism of believers upon their profession of faith in Jesus Christ as Lord and Savior, in other words, believers' baptism. It is a one-time event in the life of a believer signifying his permanent spiritual union with Jesus Christ.

One of the most significant things about the Church is its spiritual union with Jesus Christ represented by baptism. Paul goes to some length in Corinthians and Ephesians to describe the union of the risen Lord with His Church. He wrote, *"the one who joins himself to the Lord is one spirit with Him"* (1 Corinthians 6:17). Furthermore, there is a union between Jew and Gentile in the Church. Paul says in Ephesians, speaking of Jesus Christ:

Ephesians 2:14-15
14 For He Himself is our peace, who made both groups [Jews and Gentiles] *into one, and broke down the barrier of the dividing wall,*
15 by abolishing in His flesh the enmity, which is the Law of commandments contained in ordinances, so that in Himself He might make the two [Jew and Gentile] *into one new man, thus establishing peace.*

The great mystery of the Church is that God would bring both Jew and Gentile into proper relationship with Himself through Jesus Christ, and make both groups into one new group called the Church.

The Church's union with Jesus Christ gives her His authority (see pages 209-210). The Church is the mouth, hands, and feet of Jesus on earth, to speak for Him, to work for Him, and to go for Him wherever He directs. The union between the believer and Christ gives the believer authority over Satan and over sin in his own life. This enables each believer, who wills to do so, to live above sin and above the world, in the sense of not being a partaker of the evil in it. The problem is many Christians do not know that they have such authority and some who do know it choose not to exercise it for one reason or another. However, by entering into baptism, the believer is saying, "I am united to Jesus Christ and I intend to live for Him."

THE LORD'S SUPPER

The second ordinance the church is to observe is the Lord's Supper, or known to some as Communion. Jesus initiated it Himself on the night before His trial and cruci-fixion. It was later explained by Paul in 1 Corinthians 11. It is made up of bread and wine, which many believe is the unfermented juice of the grape. It is clear in the New Testament that the ordinances themselves do not impart saving grace. Rather, they represent in outward form the spiritual reality that has already taken place in the life of a believer through faith in Christ. The bread, which repre-sents Jesus' body, signifies the believer's partaking of His life and nature through faith. The fruit of the vine repre-sents His blood shed on Calvary for the payment for our sins.

How Often Should It Be Observed?
The Lord's Supper may be observed as often as desired until Jesus returns. Paul wrote:

> 1 Corinthians 11:25-26
> *25 In the same way He took the cup also after supper, saying, "This cup is the new covenant in My blood; do this, as often as you drink it, in remembrance of Me."*

26 For as often as you eat this bread and drink the cup, you proclaim the Lord's death until He comes.

Thus, the Lord's Supper spans this entire age from Jesus' death *"until He comes"* again. The Church's one great hope is the return of Jesus Christ, at which time she will be raptured to be with Him where He is. Jesus promised to come again to resurrect all who died in faith. He will give new, glorified bodies both to resurrected believers and to believers still alive when He comes.

Respect for the Lord's Supper

It is dangerous to partake of the Lord's Supper unless you are a genuine believer in fellowship with Jesus. When Paul wrote to the Corinthians he said that many of them were sick and some had even died because they were partaking of the Lord's Supper in an unworthy manner (1 Corinthians 11:27-30). They did not understand the meaning of the Lord's Supper. They were sinning by partaking of it without due respect.

It is impossible to hold onto your sin and properly partake of the bread and cup. You should not constantly examine yourself because that leads to defeat. On the other hand, the observance of the Lord's Supper gives an occasional opportunity to examine yourself with a view to repenting and changing.

† The Church – Its Destiny

One of the key promises to the Church concerns its future destiny. The Apostle John wrote: *"Beloved, now we are children of God, and it has not appeared as yet what we will be. We know that when He appears, we will be like Him, because we will see Him just as He is"* (1 John 3:2).

Destined for Marriage – Bride of Christ

The Bible often uses human relationships to explain and illustrate the relationship between God and His people. For example, in the Old Testament, Israel is referred to as the wife of Jehovah. When the nation went into idolatry, she was charged as an adulteress before God. In the New Testament, the Church is referred to as the bride of Christ, and the same example of faithfulness and the possibility of unfaithfulness is used. Paul wrote to the church in Corinth:

> 2 Corinthians 11:2-4
> *2 For I am jealous for you with a godly jealousy; for I betrothed you to one husband, so that to Christ I might present you as a pure virgin.*
> *3 But I am afraid that, as the serpent deceived Eve by his craftiness, your minds will be led astray from the simplicity and purity of devotion to Christ.*
> *4 For if one comes and preaches another Jesus whom we have not preached, or you receive a different spirit which you have not received, or a different gospel which you have not accepted, you bear this beautifully.*

Paul speaks of the Church as a virgin engaged to Jesus Christ. He does not want the Church to be enticed and led astray from purity of devotion to her bridegroom, the Lord Jesus Christ.

Satan is a seducer who tries to deceive the bride so that she does not correctly understand Jesus and the Gospel of the grace of God. When one embraces false doctrine, it could be likened to a virgin being seduced and giving up her purity to the filth and vileness of the seducer. This is where one can truly stumble spiritually! As true Christian believers, let us guard our spiritual faithfulness to Jesus Christ at all costs, lest we become spiritual adulteresses.

The idea of the Church as the bride of Christ is also discussed by Paul in his letter to the Ephesians. Beginning at Ephesians 5:22, the Apostle writes about the relationship between a husband and wife. That relationship is one of mutual love and respect with each having a proper area of responsibility. The wife is to be subject to her husband as to the Lord; the husband is to love his wife so much that he puts her ahead of himself, just as Christ loved the Church and died for her. Then Paul concludes his teaching with these words:

Ephesians 5:32-33
32 This mystery is great; but I am speaking with reference to Christ and the church.
33 Nevertheless, each individual among you also is to love his own wife even as himself, and the wife must see to it that she respects her husband.

Following the explanation of husband-wife relationships, Paul says that he is really talking about Christ and the Church. Earthly relationships are important, but not as important as our spiritual relationship with Jesus. It is by far the most important relationship we can have.

Destined for the Marriage Supper
The Church is destined to join Christ at the marriage supper of the Lamb as His bride. The Apostle John speaks of the blessedness of those who will rejoice and participate in the marriage supper when Jesus comes to take His bride, the Church, to Himself. He wrote about this glorious event in Revelation 19 where Jesus is called the Lamb of God, a reference to His death for our sins. Remember what John the Baptist said when Jesus appeared on the banks of the Jordan where John was baptizing, *"Behold, the Lamb of God who takes away the sin of the world!"* (John 1:29). John the Apostle wrote in Revelation:

251

Revelation 19:6-9
6 ..."Hallelujah! For the Lord our God, the Almighty, reigns.
7 "Let us rejoice and be glad and give the glory to Him, for the marriage of the Lamb has come and His bride has made herself ready."
8 It was given to her to clothe herself in fine linen, bright and clean; for the fine linen is the righteous acts of the saints.
9 Then he said to me, "Write, 'Blessed are those who are invited to the marriage supper of the Lamb.'" And he said to me, "These are true words of God."

When a person receives Jesus Christ as personal Lord and Savior he becomes spiritually united to Him. Our present state is like one engaged to be married; but our destiny is to be forever spiritually joined with the Son of God, much like a man and wife are one. He is the Bridegroom, and we, the Church, are His bride forever. The idea of marriage gives a little better understanding of the love the Lord has for His own people! He loves us just as strongly as any man ever loved his bride.

Destined to Share in Christ's Glory

Another part of our destiny is hard to imagine, but is nevertheless true; we shall share in His glory. We spoke of this in the last section of the chapter on salvation. In a sense, we already share in Christ's glory. In Romans 8:29-30 the Apostle teaches that those whom God foreknew, He predestined to be like Jesus; and those whom He so predestined, He called. Those whom He called, He also justified. Finally, those whom He justified, He has also glorified. The tense of the verbs in the sentence indicates something that has already been done: foreknew, predestined, called, justified, glorified. We have already been glorified with Jesus. This position of exaltation gives the

Christian his position of spiritual power and authority. That is why God makes it possible for a Christian to cast out demons in Jesus' name. He already shares in the authority of Jesus Christ as the risen Son of God.

Ephesians and Colossians, as well as other books in the New Testament, teach that Jesus Christ was raised from the dead and ascended to heaven – to the right hand of God. Furthermore, it is written that God *"raised us up with Him, and seated us with Him in the heavenly places in Christ Jesus"* (Ephesians 2:6). In a very real sense, we now share in the glorified position of Jesus Christ in heavenly places.

However, there will come a time when we will share in His manifested glory right here on earth. Romans 8:18-25 teaches that the sons of God will be revealed with Him to the world. At that time our bodies will be redeemed from corruption and mortality, because this corruption must put on incorruption and this mortal must put on immortality (1 Corinthians 15:53). When that happens, *"the creation itself also will be set free from its slavery to corruption into the freedom of the glory of the children of God"* (Romans 8:21). When Christ, who is our life, appears, then we also will appear with Him in glory (Colossians 3:4). Paul wrote to the Thessalonians:

> 2 Thessalonians 1:9-10
> *9 These* [unsaved] *will pay the penalty of eternal destruction, away from the presence of the Lord and from the glory of His power,*
> *10 when He comes to be glorified in His saints on that day, and to be marveled at among all who have believed ...*

These are only a few of the Scriptures that teach that the destiny of the Church is to share in the glory of Jesus Christ when He comes again.

Destined to Inherit the Earth

The Church will be at Christ's side when He takes complete and total possession of the earth for the glory of God. Jesus Himself taught in the Sermon on the Mount, *"Blessed are the gentle, for they shall inherit the earth"* (Matthew 5:5). God owns the earth by right of creation (Revelation 4) and by right of redemption (Revelation 5). He has given the title deed to Jesus Christ who will reign on the throne of David when He returns to earth. At His side will be the Church, who will rule and reign with Him upon the earth (Revelation 5:10).

This is borne out in several passages in the book of Revelation. Jesus addresses the church of Thyatira in chapter two. There He promises the saints who overcome something special. Jesus said,

> Revelation 2:26-27
> *26 'He who overcomes, and he who keeps My deeds until the end, TO HIM I WILL GIVE AUTHORITY OVER THE NATIONS;*
> *27 AND HE SHALL RULE THEM WITH A ROD OF IRON, AS THE VESSELS OF THE POTTER ARE BROKEN TO PIECES, as I also have received authority from My Father.'*

Jesus will rule over the nations with a rod of iron during the millennium and ruling with Him will be the saints of God. Jesus received authority from His Father and will delegate that authority to His Church. Therefore, He could tell the believers in Thyatira they would rule the nations with a rod of iron.

Revelation 5 also teaches the same concept:

> Revelation 5:9-10
> *9 And they sang a new song, saying, "Worthy are You to take the book and to break its seals; for You were slain, and purchased for God with Your*

blood men from every tribe and tongue and people
and nation.
10 "You have made them to be a kingdom and
priests to our God; and they will reign upon the
earth."

Again, it is stated that those purchased for God with the
blood of Christ will reign upon the earth. In these two
places it is clearly taught that the Church will be associated
with Jesus Christ in His reign over the earth.

Destined to Judge Angels and the World

Following the millennial kingdom of Christ on earth,
there will be a judgment of the unsaved called the Great
White Throne judgment. There will also be a judgment of
the angels.

Did you know that if you believe in Jesus Christ you
will be associated with Him in those judgments? Paul
wrote to the church in Corinth:

1 Corinthians 6:2-3
*2 Or do you not know that **the saints will judge***
***the world?** If the world is judged by you, are you*
not competent to constitute the smallest law
courts?
*3 Do you not know that **we will judge angels?***
How much more matters of this life?

Incredible as it may seem, Christian believers are going to
be associated with Jesus in the judgment of the unsaved and
the judgment of angels!

MAKE THE CHURCH PERSONAL

Jesus made it clear that the Church is the institution He
founded against which the "gates of hell" will not prevail.
Too many of God's people think that they are "stand alone"
Christians who can flourish apart from the rest of the body

of Christ. Because the Lord has designed the Church as a spiritual organism, each member is designed to provide help to the rest of the body and to receive help from other members of the body.

The Church can be compared to a campfire of glowing embers. If one ember is separated from the rest, it will soon grow cold, even while the rest remain glowing hot. Put the cold ember back in the hot bed and it starts to glow again. Believers are like that ember. They need to be baptized, active members of a local church if they are to grow in the grace and knowledge of our Lord Jesus Christ.

Our present life is a training ground for the future. A great deal of our usefulness in the future kingdom of God will depend upon the degree of our faithfulness now. Jesus taught this in the parable of the talents in Matthew 25. In view of the great destiny of the Church to be next to Jesus as He rules over all, and to be next to Him in judgment, should we not be all the more diligent to be found faithful today in our relationship to Him and His Church body?

2 Corinthians 7:1
1   Therefore, having these promises, beloved, let us cleanse ourselves from all defilement of flesh and spirit, perfecting holiness in the fear of God.

Chapter 11

The Future
† Jesus Is Coming!

Hope is one of the three foundational Christian virtues. Paul wrote, *"But now abide faith, hope, love, these three; but the greatest of these is love"* (1 Corinthians 13:13). Faith, hope, and love do indeed make the Christian life worth living. In previous chapters, we have studied about faith and love a great deal. Hope is the subject of this chapter about the Second Coming of Jesus.

What Is Hope?
Hope is faith firmly planted in the future. Hope in the Scripture is different than hope as we normally think of it in the English language. When we use the word "hope" there is an element of doubt. For example, "I hope the sun will shine today," meaning it would be nice if the sun would shine, but in actual fact, it may not. In the Scripture, however, hope is sure because it's based upon the unfailing promises of God – promises that are still to be fulfilled when Jesus returns.

The Blessed Hope
The hope we have is based on many promises of God found in the New Testament. Perhaps the most blessed of these is found in John's Gospel, where Jesus promised to return for those who believe in Him:

John 14:1-3

1 "Do not let your heart be troubled; believe in God, believe also in Me.

2 "In My Father's house are many dwelling places; if it were not so, I would have told you; for I go to prepare a place for you.

3 "If I go and prepare a place for you, I will come again and receive you to Myself, that where I am, there you may be also."

Jesus definitely promised that He will return so those who are His may be with Him.

WILL JESUS LITERALLY COME AGAIN?

The above promise is repeated in Acts 1 by angels who were present when Christ left earth to ascend into heaven:

Acts 1:9-11

9 And after He [Jesus] had said these things, He was lifted up while they were looking on, and a cloud received Him out of their sight.

10 And as they were gazing intently into the sky while He was going, behold, two men in white clothing stood beside them.

11 They also said, "Men of Galilee, why do you stand looking into the sky? This Jesus, who has been taken up from you into heaven, will come in just the same way as you have watched Him go into heaven."

A question naturally comes to mind when thinking about this Scripture. The two men in white said that Jesus would come in just the same way as He went into heaven. The question is, "How did Jesus go into heaven?" According to these three verses, His departure was visible, physical, and personal – therefore it was literal.

His Return Will Be Visible

While they were looking at Him, a cloud took Him out of their sight. It was the same Jesus with whom they had walked and talked during the three and a half years of His ministry. It was the same Jesus who had been raised from the dead and had walked among them for forty days following His crucifixion and resurrection. It was this same Jesus who was literally taken up into heaven in full view of all the apostles. While they were **looking on** a cloud received Him out of their sight. His departure was visible – they could see Him go. His return will be in just the same way – He will return visibly. John wrote, *"BEHOLD, HE IS COMING WITH THE CLOUDS, and every eye will see Him"* (Revelation 1:7). Jesus said earlier during His trial, *"I tell you, hereafter you will see THE SON OF MAN SITTING AT THE RIGHT HAND OF POWER, and COMING ON THE CLOUDS OF HEAVEN"* (Matthew 26:64). It is clear from many Scriptures that Jesus' coming will be literal and visible.

His Return Will Be Physical

Some people believe incorrectly that Jesus was raised only in a spiritual or figurative sense. It is clear in Luke that He was raised from the dead in a physical body that could be seen and touched. Keep in mind that the following event took place after His resurrection. Jesus said:

Luke 24:39-43
39 "See My hands and My feet, that it is I Myself; touch Me and see, for a spirit does not have flesh and bones as you see that I have."
40 And when He had said this, He showed them His hands and His feet.
41 While they still could not believe it because of their joy and amazement, He said to them, "Have you anything here to eat?"
42 They gave Him a piece of a broiled fish;
43 and He took it and ate it before them.

Jesus was raised from the dead in a physical body of flesh and bones which the disciples could both see and feel. Thus, the second thing we learn from the Scriptures about the return of Jesus is that it will be physical – just as physical as His ascension.

His Return Will Be Personal

Some have taught that His prophecy of a second coming was fulfilled by the coming of the Holy Spirit. It was not! It is true that the Holy Spirit is the Spirit of Christ, but His coming at Pentecost in no way fulfills the second coming of Jesus Christ. The Bible says *"this Jesus"* who was taken up from you into heaven will come in just the same way as you have watched Him go into heaven. It is not the Holy Spirit who is being spoken of, nor is it an angel, but it is precisely *"this Jesus."* At the second coming, Jesus will personally return to earth to set up a kingdom of righteousness which shall never end.

We read in the Old Testament book of Zechariah, a prophecy about the coming again of Jesus Christ. When He comes He will go forth to fight against the nations that come to wage war against Jerusalem. Zechariah wrote:

> Zechariah 14:3-4
> *3 Then the LORD will go forth and fight against those nations, as when He fights on a day of battle.*
> *4 In that day His feet will stand on the Mount of Olives, which is in front of Jerusalem on the east; and the Mount of Olives will be split in its middle from east to west by a very large valley, so that half of the mountain will move toward the north and the other half toward the south.*

Thus, we see that Jesus is coming physically and His return will be personal because His feet will stand on the Mount of Olives east of Jerusalem.

The Apostle Paul made it clear that the Lord Jesus Himself would come again personally when he wrote, *"For the Lord Himself will descend from heaven with a shout, with the voice of the archangel and with the trumpet of God, and the dead in Christ will rise first"* (1 Thessalonians 4:16). He calls the second coming of Jesus *"the blessed hope"* in Titus, where he says that we are to be:

Titus 2:13-14
13 looking for the blessed hope and the appearing of the glory of our great God and Savior, Christ Jesus,
14 who gave Himself for us to redeem us from every lawless deed, and to purify for Himself a people for His own possession, zealous for good deeds.

Yes, Jesus Christ died, was buried, raised from the grave, and ascended into heaven. But the most joyous future prospect is that He will return. His coming will be just as real and just as literal the second time as it was the first time. The difference will be in the job He has to do when He comes. His first coming was in humility for the purpose of paying for our sins. The second coming will be in great power and great glory for the purpose of destroying all opposition and rendering just judgment against the wicked.

† The Future – The Glorious Hope

The promise of Jesus to return has been the hope of Christians through the centuries. Let us examine several things Christian believers may expect when Jesus returns to call them to Himself.

WHAT BELIEVERS EXPECT

A Resurrection into New, Glorified Bodies

The coming of Jesus Christ is a glorious hope for the Church in at least two ways. First, His coming will mean the resurrection of those believers who have died during past centuries. Paul wrote that when the Lord comes, *"the dead in Christ will rise first"* (1 Thessalonians 4:16). We believe and firmly fix our hope upon the fact that, if we should die before Jesus comes, we will yet see Him in our own resurrected body. It is written:

1 Corinthians 15:50-54
50 Now I say this, brethren, that flesh and blood cannot inherit the kingdom of God; nor does the perishable inherit the imperishable.
51 Behold, I tell you a mystery; we will not all sleep, but we will all be changed,
52 in a moment, in the twinkling of an eye, at the last trumpet; for the trumpet will sound, and the dead will be raised imperishable, and we will be changed.
53 For this perishable must put on the imperishable, and this mortal must put on immortality.
54 But when this perishable will have put on the imperishable, and this mortal will have put on immortality, then will come about the saying that is written, "DEATH IS SWALLOWED UP in victory."

The hope of the resurrection has lived long in the hearts of men who have trusted in God. In the book of Job, which is believed to be the oldest book in the Bible, Job is reported as saying:

Job 19:25-27
25 "As for me, I know that my Redeemer lives, And at the last He will take His stand on the earth.

26 "Even after my skin is destroyed,
Yet from my flesh I shall see God;
27 Whom I myself shall behold,
And whom my eyes will see and not another. ..."

The Apostle Paul made much of the resurrection of believers when Jesus comes. In his personal defense before King Agrippa, he asks a very simple but very important question, *"Why is it considered incredible among you people if God does raise the dead?"* (Acts 26:8). If God is able to create the universe and to bring every soul to account unto Himself, why would He not have the power to raise the dead?

That is why Christians hold firmly to the truth of the resurrection at Jesus' coming. He will raise those of our believing loved ones who have already died. Therefore, we need not grieve at the death of our loved ones as others who have no hope (1 Thessalonians 4:13).

Relief from Persecution
Hope is also for believers who will be living when Jesus returns. Life is often full of sorrow, pain, and tribulation. But, thank God, we all have some periods of peace, joy, and happiness. Nonetheless, we all experience trying times in our lives. The Scripture teaches that Christians will suffer persecution for their belief in God and in Jesus Christ. However, it holds out to the Christian the hope of Jesus' coming as a time of blessed relief from trying and difficult circumstances.

Several Scriptures mention this, but two stand out above the others. One is found in 2 Thessalonians:

2 Thessalonians 1:5-8
5 This is a plain indication of God's righteous judgment so that you will be considered worthy of the kingdom of God, for which indeed you are suffering.

263

6 For after all it is only just for God to repay with affliction those who afflict you,
7 and to give relief to you who are afflicted and to us as well when the Lord Jesus will be revealed from heaven with His mighty angels in flaming fire,
8 dealing out retribution to those who do not know God and to those who do not obey the gospel of our Lord Jesus.

The hope Paul holds out to the Thessalonian believers is the revelation of the Lord Jesus Christ *"from heaven with His mighty angels in flaming fire."* At that time, he says in verse seven, Christian believers will be given relief from persecution.

The second outstanding passage is in 1 Peter:

1 Peter 4:12-13
12 Beloved, do not be surprised at the fiery ordeal among you, which comes upon you for your testing, as though some strange thing were happening to you;
13 but to the degree that you share the sufferings of Christ, keep on rejoicing, so that also at the revelation of His glory you may rejoice with exultation.

In these two passages, the second coming of Jesus Christ is held out as an object of desire, of hope, and of salvation from great suffering, which Peter calls a *"fiery ordeal."* The blessed hope for which all God's people wait is the return of Jesus to earth. Peter exhorts us, *"Therefore, prepare your minds for action, keep sober in spirit, fix your hope completely on the grace to be brought to you at the revelation of Jesus Christ"* (1 Peter 1:13).

RAPTURE AND TRANSFORMATION

We have spoken about the resurrection of those who have died in Jesus; and we have spoken about the relief that will be given to Christians when Jesus comes. However, we have not spoken about exactly what takes place at the resurrection. Paul talks about this in 1 Thessalonians where he speaks of the coming rapture:

> 1 Thessalonians 4:15-18
> *15 For this we say to you by the word of the Lord, that we who are alive, and remain until the coming of the Lord, will not precede those who have fallen asleep.*
> *16 For the Lord Himself will descend from heaven with a shout, with the voice of the archangel and with the trumpet of God, and the dead in Christ will rise first.*
> *17 Then we who are alive and remain will be caught up together with them in the clouds to meet the Lord in the air, and so we shall always be with the Lord.*
> *18 Therefore comfort one another with these words.*

According to the above verses, the principle elements involved with the return of Jesus are as follows:

- Three sounds will be heard:
  1) Jesus gives a command (meaning of "shout"),
  2) the voice of the archangel will be heard
  3) the sound of the trumpet will be heard;
- the resurrection of believers; glorified bodies reunited with their souls and spirits;
- living believers' bodies will be changed into the same kind of glorified body; together they will rise to meet the Lord in the air.

For believers, the hope of reunion with the resurrected loved one is a source of comfort for those left at their death.

Paul teaches in 1 Corinthians 15 that the immortal body will bear the same relationship to the present body as a fully mature plant bears to the seed from which it came. It will not be the exact same body, because the body decays in the grave. There will be, however, a connection between the two bodies. Paul goes to some length in 1 Corinthians to describe what will happen to the body:

1 Corinthians 15:35-39
35 But someone will say, "How are the dead raised? And with what kind of body do they come?"
36 You fool! That which you sow does not come to life unless it dies;
37 and that which you sow, you do not sow the body which is to be, but a bare grain, perhaps of wheat or of something else.
38 But God gives it a body just as He wished, and to each of the seeds a body of its own.
39 All flesh is not the same flesh, but there is one flesh of men, and another flesh of beasts, and another flesh of birds, and another of fish.

Paul uses an illustration that is common in human experience. Beef has a different taste and texture than chicken. Yet both beef and chicken are flesh. That is exactly what Paul is saying in the above passage of Scripture. There is one flesh of men, another flesh of beasts, another flesh of birds. Of course, when we eat fish it is different from beef or chicken. Paul uses a common experience to explain the difference between the earthly body we have now and the heavenly body we will have in the resurrection.

The Apostle goes on to say this:

1 Corinthians 15:40-44
40 There are also heavenly bodies and earthly bodies, but the glory of the heavenly is one, and the glory of the earthly is another.

41 There is one glory of the sun, and another glory of the moon, and another glory of the stars; for star differs from star in glory.
42 So also is the resurrection of the dead. It is sown a perishable body, it is raised an imperishable body;
43 it is sown in dishonor, it is raised in glory; it is sown in weakness, it is raised in power;
44 it is sown a natural body, it is raised a spiritual body. If there is a natural body, there is also a spiritual body.

Thus, there is a connection between the two bodies though they will not be the exact same body.

As the resurrection is taking place, those who are living when Jesus comes will immediately receive their new immortal bodies without dying. There will be great reunions between those who have died and those who have remained alive until Jesus comes. After the living are changed and the dead are raised, then both will be lifted up into the air to meet Jesus. *"And so,"* the Scripture says, *"we shall always be with the Lord"* (1 Thessalonians 4:17). The joy of seeing the risen and glorified Lord in person will be beyond description. What a glorious day of rejoicing that will be!

† The Future – Rewards and Wrath

The future holds an unusually strong attraction for mankind. We want to know what is going to happen. That is the allure of fortunetellers and psychics. Those who know the Bible have certain knowledge about many future events. God's promise that Jesus would return has been the hope of the Church throughout this age. Several things will be realized when He comes:

- Our dead loved ones who died in faith will be resurrected (1 Thessalonians 4:13-18),
- Those who are suffering persecution for their faith will be given relief (2 Thessa. 2:5-10),
- Living believers will be changed and given immortal bodies (1 Corinthians 15:51-52),
- All Christians will be raptured to meet the Lord in the air (1 Thessalonians 4:13-18).

Both those who are resurrected, and those who are living and changed when Jesus comes, will go together to meet the Lord in the air before God's wrath is poured out on the ungodly.

Consider what both the saved and the unsaved will receive from the hand of the Lord when He returns. First, we will deal with the saints and then with the unsaved.

Rewards for Christians When Jesus Comes
When Jesus comes there will be an examination of each Christian to determine which rewards, if any, he is to receive based upon how he lived his life as a Christian. Paul wrote to the Christians in Rome:

Romans 14:10-12
10 ... we will all stand before the judgment seat of God.
11 For it is written,
"As I live, says the Lord, every knee shall bow to Me,
And every tongue shall give praise to God."
12 So then each one of us shall give account of himself to God.

This theme is further enlarged upon in 2 Corinthians where Paul wrote:

2 Corinthians 5:9-10
9 Therefore we also have as our ambition, whether at home or absent, to be pleasing to Him.

10   For we must all appear before the judgment seat of Christ, so that each one may be recompensed for his deeds in the body, according to what he has done, whether good or bad.

It should be noted that the judgment of Christians has nothing to do with their eternal destination.   Whether eternity is to be spent in heaven or hell is fixed before one dies by the decision one makes about Jesus Christ. He who receives Jesus as Lord and Savior is given a place in heaven with the Father and the Son. He who rejects Jesus will spend eternity in the Lake of Fire, forever separated from God who is the source of eternal life.

Therefore, the outcome of this particular judgment is based on how faithful the believer has been in carrying out the responsibilities which God gave him as a Christian. This will determine the place of service he or she is given in Christ's kingdom after He returns.

Paul wrote this about the basis of Christian rewards:

1 Corinthians 3:9-15
9 For we are God's fellow workers; you are God's field, God's building.
10 According to the grace of God which was given to me, like a wise master builder I laid a foundation, and another is building on it. But each man must be careful how he builds on it.
11 For no man can lay a foundation other than the one which is laid, which is Jesus Christ.
12 Now if any man builds on the foundation with gold, silver, precious stones, wood, hay, straw,
13 each man's work will become evident; for the day will show it because it is to be revealed with fire, and the fire itself will test the quality of each man's work.
14 If any man's work which he has built on it remains, he will receive a reward.

15 If any man's work is burned up, he will suffer loss; but he himself will be saved, yet so as through fire.

The judgment of Christians has more to do with the quality of work than it does with the quantity of work. Some people are trying to do so much that they do not put much quality into what they are doing. Whether or not it is quality work depends upon whether it was done under the direction and leadership of the Holy Spirit for the glory of God or led by one's own desire and motivation. If your work is done with wrong motives under your own direction and planning to satisfy your own pride, it will not stand the test. Based on that standard, the least of God's saints – who seem as nothing in the eyes of the world and perhaps very little in the eyes of the church – may well be at the forefront in the day of reward.

The New Testament speaks of five crowns which will be given when Jesus returns for different types of Christian service and faithfulness. Those who are interested and have a Bible should search out the different crowns mentioned and examine their own lives to see if they are living up to that which God requires in each case. Read more about Christian rewards in chapter 12.

Wrath for the Ungodly When Jesus Comes

What will happen to the ungodly when Jesus returns? There is a dramatic difference between what the Christian can expect and that which the unbeliever can expect. The ungodly will experience the wrath of God reserved for them. His wrath is poured out on them after believers are raptured to be with Jesus where He is. Unlike the believer, who has a great hope and joy at the prospect of Jesus' coming, the unbeliever has a sure expectation of judgment and wrath. Following the beautiful passage in 1 Thessalonians 4 about the rapture of Christians to be with Jesus, Paul wrote in chapter five:

1 Thessalonians 5:2-3
2 For you yourselves know full well that the day of the Lord will come just like a thief in the night.
3 While they are saying, "Peace and safety!" then **destruction will come upon them suddenly** *like labor pains upon a woman with child, and they will not escape.*

This thought of sudden and unexpected judgment coming upon the ungodly is the same truth that Jesus Himself taught:

Matthew 24:38-39
38 "For as in those days before the flood they were eating and drinking, marrying and giving in marriage, until the day that Noah entered the ark,
*39 and they did not understand until **the flood came and took them all away; so will the coming of the Son of Man be.***

And again, Paul states in 2 Thessalonians that:

2 Thessalonians 1:7-9
7 ... the Lord Jesus will be revealed from heaven with His mighty angels in flaming fire,
8 dealing out retribution to those who do not know God and to those who do not obey the gospel of our Lord Jesus.
*9 **These will pay the penalty of eternal destruction,** away from the presence of the Lord and from the glory of His power,*

According to 2 Thessalonians, at the very end of this age an exceptionally evil man called Antichrist will appear on the world scene:

2 Thessalonians 2:9-10
9 ... the one whose coming is in accord with the activity of Satan, with all power and signs and false wonders,

271

10 and with all the deception of wickedness for those who perish, because they did not receive the love of the truth so as to be saved.

Because ungodly men will not receive the love of the truth, God will send an influence upon them that will cause them to believe the lie of Antichrist, *"in order that they all may be judged who did not believe the truth, but took pleasure in wickedness"* (2 Thessalonians 2:12).

Indeed, the second coming of the Lord Jesus, the Lamb of God, will be with so much glory that ungodly mankind will flee in terror to hide from His presence: *"and they said to the mountains and to the rocks, "Fall on us and **hide us from the presence of Him who sits on the throne, and from the wrath of the Lamb"*** (Revelation 6:16). This only begins their ordeal; the resurrection and final judgment of the ungodly will come 1,000 years later. Jesus must reign during the millennium, after which comes the judgment of the ungodly at the Great White Throne (see chapter 12).

The message about the coming wrath of God upon the ungodly is not well received. Many preachers avoid this unpleasant subject because they are afraid of driving people away from their church. They will answer to the Chief Shepherd, the Lord Jesus, for not preaching the whole counsel of God.

Paul wrote about people who do not accept the truth:

1 Timothy 4:3-4
3 For the time will come when they will not endure sound doctrine; but wanting to have their ears tickled, they will accumulate for themselves teachers in accordance to their own desires,
4 and will turn away their ears from the truth and will turn aside to myths.

If you are one who turns away from the truth, remember, the Word of God says there remains for you only *"a*

terrifying expectation of judgment and THE FURY OF A FIRE
WHICH WILL CONSUME THE ADVERSARIES" (Hebrews 10:27). A
momentary life of sinful pleasure is not worth the gamble of
counting on the goodness and love of God to escape the
wrath He says is coming. Only Jesus can save you from
God's wrath. We all need to be the like the believers in
Thessalonica who *"turned to God from idols to serve a
living and true God, and to wait for His Son from heaven,
whom He raised from the dead, that is Jesus, who rescues us
from the wrath to come"* (1 Thessalonians 1:9-10, see 5:9).

† The Future – The Millennial Kingdom

No discussion of the end times and the future would be
complete without a brief study about the millennium.

What Is the Millennium?

The word "millennium" comes from the Latin language
and means one thousand. It refers to a beautiful time of
peace and prosperity when Jesus Christ will personally reign
upon the throne of David in Israel, and from there over the
entire earth. Isaiah 11:9 says, *"the earth will be full of the
knowledge of the LORD as the waters cover the sea."*

The Millennium in the Revelation

The millennial period of one thousand years is
mentioned no fewer than six times in Revelation 20. Some
people believe this is figurative because the book of
Revelation is filled with figures of speech, types, and
symbols. However, many believe that it is speaking of a
definite period of time because it has been the subject of
much prophecy in the Old Testament. It has been a longing
in the hearts of God's people from ancient times.

Revelation 20 tells us about the millennium. It follows
the passage about the second coming of Christ that says,

"on His robe and on His thigh He has a name written, '*KING OF KINGS, AND LORD OF LORDS*'" (Revelation 19:16). Revelation 20 begins with *"an angel coming down from heaven, holding the key of the abyss and a great chain in his hand"* (Revelation 20:1). The abyss is sometimes called the bottomless pit, the place where fallen angels are kept in bondage waiting for the day of judgment. A holy angel from heaven is seen coming down from heaven with the key of the abyss and a great chain in his hand. The angel binds Satan and throws him into the abyss:

> Revelation 20:2-3
> *2 And he laid hold of the dragon, the serpent of old, who is the devil and Satan, and bound him for a thousand years;*
> *3 and he threw him into the abyss, and shut it and sealed it over him, so that he would not deceive the nations any longer, until the thousand years were completed; after these things he must be released for a short time.*

Satan is bound in the abyss during the 1,000 year reign of Christ so that he cannot interfere.

Following the verses about the binding of Satan in the abyss is a brief description of the resurrection of believers martyred during the final great tribulation. John explains that the resurrection of the just at the coming of Christ is separated from the resurrection of the wicked by the space of 1,000 years. During that interval of time, those who have been resurrected will reign with Christ:

> Revelation 20:4-6
> *4 Then I saw thrones, and they sat on them, and judgment was given to them. And I saw the souls of those who had been beheaded because of their testimony of Jesus and because of the word of God, and those who had not worshiped the beast or his image, and had not received the mark on*

*their forehead and on their hand; and **they came to life and reigned with Christ for a thousand years.***
*5 The rest of the dead did not come to life **until the thousand years were completed.** This is the first resurrection.*
6 Blessed and holy is the one who has a part in the first resurrection; over these the second death has no power, but they will be priests of God and of Christ and will reign with Him for a thousand years.

People born during the millennium will still have a sin nature. Even though Satan is bound and will not be on earth to tempt them, they will still sin. The human heart is desperately wicked even without the influence of evil from outside. That is seen in the rebellion that takes place once Satan is released from the abyss:

Revelation 20:7-10
7 When the thousand years are completed, Satan will be released from his prison,
8 and will come out to deceive the nations which are in the four corners of the earth, Gog and Magog, to gather them together for the war; the number of them is like the sand of the seashore.
*9 **And they came up on the broad plain of the earth and surrounded the camp of the saints and the beloved city, and fire came down from heaven and devoured them.***
10 And the devil who deceived them was thrown into the lake of fire and brimstone, where the beast and the false prophet are also; and they will be tormented day and night forever and ever.

In the next section we will discuss the period of final rebellion in more detail.

NATURE OF THE MILLENNIUM

The Millennium Will Be a Theocracy

What will Christ's rule be like? It will be a theocracy – a government in which God is the ruler. Since Jesus Christ is God in the flesh, He is the King who will rule over the earth. Jeremiah prophesied about those days:

Jeremiah 23:5-6
5 *"Behold, the days are coming," declares the* LORD,
"When I will raise up for David a righteous Branch;
And He will reign as king and act wisely
And do justice and righteousness in the land.
6 *"In His days Judah will be saved,*
And Israel will dwell securely;
And this is His name by which He will be called,
'The LORD *our righteousness.'"*

Saved and Unsaved Will Be There

In the New Testament the angel Gabriel, in announcing the coming birth of Jesus Christ to His mother Mary, said to her in Luke:

Luke 1:31-33
31 "And behold, you will conceive in your womb and bear a son, and you shall name Him Jesus.
32 "He will be great and will be called the Son of the Most High; and the Lord God will give Him the throne of His father David;
*33 and **He will reign over the house of Jacob forever, and His kingdom will have no end.**"*

Because Gabriel said that Christ's kingdom will have no end, some people do not see how Christ can rule for a millennium that ends in a revolt led by Satan. The answer is that the kingdom of Jesus Christ is eternal but it has different manifestations.

276

When Jesus returns, He will establish a literal, physical, political kingdom over which He will reign for a thousand years. People will be born just as they are now during His reign. And, like now, some will trust Him as Savior and Lord, and others will not.

At the end of the millennium, the unsaved will be gathered out of His kingdom. Then His kingdom will continue throughout eternity. There is a distinction between the millennial period on earth, during which time Christ will rule over Israel and the Gentile nations, including saved and unsaved, and His eternal rule over the saved. His kingdom will have no end, regardless of the different forms in which it will be manifested.

God's Glory Will Be Seen
Some of the characteristics of the Millennium are given in the Old Testament. It will be a time in which the knowledge of the Lord will cover the earth as water covers the sea (Isaiah 11:1-9). God said in Isaiah:

Isaiah 66:18-19
18 "... the time is coming to gather all nations and tongues. And they shall come and see My glory.
19 "I will set a sign among them and will send survivors from them to the nations: Tarshish, Put, Lud, Meshech, Rosh, Tubal and Javan, to the distant coastlands that have neither heard My fame nor seen My glory. And they will declare My glory among the nations."

During the millennium, the children of Israel will be sent throughout the earth as God's representatives to declare His name and to show forth His glory.

A Time of Worldwide Peace
Worldwide peace will prevail. It is written, *"I will abolish the bow, the sword and war from the land, and will make them lie down in safety"* (Hosea 2:18). From Zechariah 9:10 we read *"the bow of war will be cut off.*

And He will speak peace to the nations." The prophet Isaiah said, *"He will judge between the nations, and will render decisions for many peoples; and they will hammer their swords into plowshares and their spears into pruning hooks.* **Nation will not lift up sword against nation, and never again will they learn war"** (Isaiah 2:4).

A Time of Universal Righteousness

Not only will the millennium be a time of universal peace, but it will also be a time of universal righteousness (Psalm 72:7-8). There will be great joy, good health, and long life for those born during that time (Isaiah 25:6-8; 65:20-23). Holiness and justice will be the order of the day (Psalm 72:2-4, 12-14).

So we can see that the promise of a righteous reign of Jesus Christ over the earth is a happy prospect. The words used in the Old Testament to describe that period of time show that it has not yet been fulfilled. Therefore, part of the hope which God gives us is for a golden age of a thousand years over which Jesus will rule in righteousness.

The problem is that those who do not know Jesus Christ, and die before the millennium, have no hope of ever experiencing its joys. On the other hand, the dead in Christ will be resurrected before the millennium and will enjoy it with God's people who are alive when Jesus comes. We will be present with the Lord and reigning with Him when He sits on the throne of David.

People from Every Nation There

Revelation speaks of those from every nation who will be associated with Jesus in that glorious day.

Revelation 5:9-10
9 ... they sang a new song, saying,
"Worthy are You to take the book and to break its seals; for You were slain, and purchased for God

with Your blood men from every tribe and tongue and people and nation.
10 "You have made them to be a kingdom and priests to our God; and they will reign upon the earth."

Here is the promise of reigning upon the earth with Jesus Christ. Jesus Himself gave a promise to those who overcome in Revelation 3:21: *"He who overcomes, I will grant to him to sit down with Me on My throne, as I also overcame and sat down with My Father on His throne."* Thus the Church, made up of people from all nations on earth, will be associated with Him as He rules over the ages to come.

† The Future – The Final Rebellion

The reign of the Lord Jesus from the throne of David in Jerusalem will be an unparalleled time of joy, peace, prosperity, health, and overall blessing. That makes it all the more incredible that mankind will rise up in rebellion against His righteous rule. It serves to demonstrate the incorrigible wickedness of the human heart. At the end of the millennium, wicked men will echo the cry of 3,000 years before: *"We do not want this man to reign over us"* (Luke 19:14).

Satan Bound During the Millennium

In the previous section we did not include details about what happens to the satanic principalities and powers during the millennium. However, we did mention Satan's imprisonment. Let us review the passage that deals with that subject:

Revelation 20:1-3
1 Then I saw an angel coming down from heaven, holding the key of the abyss and a great chain in his hand.

2 And he laid hold of the dragon, the serpent of old, who is the devil and Satan, and bound him for a thousand years;
3 and he threw him into the abyss, and shut it and sealed it over him, so that he would not deceive the nations any longer, until the thousand years were completed; after these things he must be released for a short time.

In addition to the express blessing of the Lord and the return of the earth to the condition before man sinned, Satan will be bound in the abyss so that he will no longer have access to the human race. He will not be able to tempt them nor will he be able to lead them into sin. To be sure, an unsaved human being can conceive and commit sins without number. However, the torment and the oppression of Satan certainly add to the miserable condition of our world. His being bound for a thousand years will add to the beauty and rest of that time.

The word "apocalypse," another name for the book of Revelation, means a prophetic disclosure or unveiling. The book of Isaiah has what is known as "the little apocalypse" in chapters 24 to 27. These chapters tell us what will happen at the second coming of Jesus Christ. In short, God will bring judgment upon the ungodly when Jesus comes. Isaiah wrote, *"Behold, the LORD lays the earth waste, devastates it, distorts its surface and scatters its inhabitants"* (Isaiah 24:1). Then, in verses five and six, God brings a charge against the inhabitants of the earth and follows up with the coming judgment:

Isaiah 24:5-6
5 The earth is also polluted by its inhabitants, for they transgressed laws, violated statutes, broke the everlasting covenant.
6 Therefore, a curse devours the earth, and those who live in it are held guilty. Therefore, the

*inhabitants of the earth are burned, and few men
are left.*

Then Isaiah goes on to tell us about God's judgment
against the satanic host of heaven:

Isaiah 24:21-22
21 *So it will happen in that day,
    That the LORD will punish the host of heaven,
    on high,
    And the kings of the earth on earth.*
22 *And they will be gathered together
    Like prisoners in the dungeon,
    And will be confined in prison;
    And after many days they will be punished.*

In this context the term *"host of heaven"* refers to the
satanic principalities and powers. According to verse 22,
they, along with the kings of the earth, will be gathered
together like prisoners in a dungeon. *"After many days they
will be punished,"* a likely reference to the thousand year
millennial reign of Christ. That agrees with what John
teaches in Revelation 20 about the binding of Satan for a
thousand years, after which he will be released for a short
time.

The release of the satanic host, according to the
passage in Isaiah, is for the express purpose of bringing
them to judgment and punishment. Notice that Satan does
not escape from the dungeon prison, but he will be released
(Revelation 20:3). He will likely be accompanied by his
evil host.

The Final Rebellion
The punishment spoken of is recorded in Revelation 20
and has to do with the final rebellion which will take place
at the end of the millennium. Revelation records this
rebellion:

Revelation 20:9-10

9 And they came up on the broad plain of the earth and surrounded the camp of the saints and the beloved city, and fire came down from heaven and devoured them.

10 And the devil who deceived them was thrown into the lake of fire and brimstone, where the beast and the false prophet are also; and they will be tormented day and night forever and ever.

Notice that the devil is thrown into the Lake of Fire where the beast and the false prophet are. They were thrown in at the beginning of the millennium a thousand years before. A thousand years later the beast (Antichrist) and the false prophet who worked with him are still in torment day and night. So much for the idea of annihilation!

Children born during the millennial reign of Christ will have sinful natures just as people born now have. Some of them will come to acknowledge the Lordship of Jesus Christ and voluntarily accept the sacrifice of Calvary as the basis for their own salvation. Others, however, just like today, will not accept Him. While they will enjoy the benefits of the millennial golden age, nevertheless they will rebel against God. Revelation 20 says that Satan will once again deceive the nations of the earth.

In spite of the great benefits of being under the rule of Christ, the number of men involved in the rebellion will be as the sand of the seashore. They will try to bring the kingdom of God to an end by destroying Jerusalem and the camp of the saints. The battle will not be long and drawn out. Fire will come down from heaven and devour them. The final judgment on Satan and his kingdom is recorded in one short verse: *"And the devil who deceived them was thrown into the lake of fire and brimstone, where the beast and the false prophet are also; and they will be tormented day and night forever and ever"* (Revelation 20:10). *"Forever and ever"* is a long time to be tormented; and those who follow Satan will be tormented with him.

Gog and Magog

Gog and Magog are people who will try to destroy Jerusalem at the end of the millennium. Mentioned in Ezekiel 38 and 39, they live to the north of Palestine; the nations who join with them are situated around Israel. It is not possible to say with absolute certainty who Gog and Magog are today. However, we do know they stand for people who are opposed to the rule and kingdom of God and are, therefore, opposed to the people of God.

Some question whether there will be one or two invasions of Palestine by Gog and Magog. Some students of the Bible believe that the invasion of Ezekiel 38 is identical with the one spoken of in Revelation as Armageddon. If that is the case, one invasion will take place during the second coming of Jesus Christ. That necessitates a second invasion of Palestine by Gog and Magog at the end of the millennium to fulfill Revelation 20.

Gog may be the title to the ruler of the people of Magog. This would explain the use of the name "Gog" for two different men, living 1,000 years apart, both energized by Satan to attack God's people. Whether there will be one or two invasions of Palestine by Gog and Magog is not as important as the fact that the Lord Jesus saves His people from them.

Gog and Magog will be miraculously stopped by the intervention of Jesus. The battle of Armageddon is brought to a swift and sure conclusion by the appearance of Jesus Christ. The last great rebellion will likewise be put down by Jesus Christ as the fire of the wrath of God falls from heaven and devours the enemy.

MAKE THE FUTURE PERSONAL

Jesus is coming – what a glorious hope that is for those who know Him – what a fearsome expectation of fiery judgment for those who do not. Before all is said and done, this world is destined to go through seven terrible years of tribulation and final wrath before Jesus sets up His thousand-year reign of righteousness.

Only two sides are laid out for us in Scripture regarding the coming of Jesus Christ – His side and the opposing side. His is the victorious side; the other is the side of defeat and judgment. The question is, "Whose side are you on?"

Notice carefully what Paul wrote about God's love for us and His desire to deliver us from the wrath to come:

Romans 5:8-10
8 But God demonstrates His own love toward us, in that while we were yet sinners, Christ died for us.
9 Much more then, having now been justified by His blood, we shall be saved from the wrath of God through Him.
10 For if while we were enemies, we were reconciled to God through the death of His Son, much more, having been reconciled, we shall be saved by His life.

If you do not know Jesus Christ, you must turn to Jesus who lives forevermore. You may live in a place where there are no carved idols, but you may be sure if you do not trust in Jesus Christ, you do have idols in your heart. They may be idols of money, gold, silver, or whatever else takes first place in your heart and mind. But you must turn from all of them to Jesus. Ask Him for cleansing and trust Him to rule your life for your good and His glory. He will deliver you from the wrath to come and give you a glorious future in the millennium and the eternal ages to come!

1 Thessalonians 1:10; 5:9

1:10 ... wait for His Son from heaven, whom He raised from the dead, that is Jesus, who delivers us from the wrath to come.

5:9 For God has not destined us for wrath, but for obtaining salvation through our Lord Jesus Christ.

Chapter 12

Judgment to Come
† The Basis of Judgment

A basic truth is that judgment will come for all unsaved people. Acts 17:31 says that God *"has fixed a day in which He will judge the world."* And the book of Hebrews says, *"it is appointed for men to die once and after this comes judgment"* (Hebrews 9:27).

The Most Important Judgment

The most important judgment is God's judgment on sin when Jesus died on the Cross. The question of first importance is, "What have you done with Jesus?" Did you receive Him or reject Him? By the time you stand in judgment, that question will have already been answered. Those who receive Jesus as Lord and Savior, trusting His payment for their sins, will spend eternity with God. Peter said in the book of Acts, *"There is salvation in no one else; for there is no other name under heaven that has been given among men, by which we must be saved"* (Acts 4:12). Those who reject Jesus Christ will be judged at the Great White Throne and spend eternity separated from God in the place prepared for the devil and his angels (Matthew 25:41).

Different Judgments

Several different types of judgment are mentioned in the Bible, but we will study only those that come after death. The saved will appear before the Judgment Seat of Christ, and the unsaved will appear before the Great White

Throne. The purpose of the first is to determine the rewards that will be given to believers for their service and the second is to determine the degree of punishment for those who die in rebellion against God. Neither of these determines a person's eternal destiny. That is settled during this lifetime by how one responds to God's offer of salvation through His Son.

STANDARDS OF JUDGMENT

What are the standards by which God will judge mankind? If you were to be tried in a human court, you would want to know the exact charges to be brought against you before the trial begins. You would also want to know the law to be used as a standard by which you are to be judged. In the same way, we should know the standards which God will use in judgment. They are found in Romans 2:1-16.

The Standard of Truth
The first standard of judgment God will use is absolute truth:

Romans 2:1-2
1 Therefore you have no excuse, everyone of you who passes judgment, for in that which you judge another, you condemn yourself; for you who judge practice the same things.
2 And we know that the judgment of God *rightly falls upon those who practice such things.

Another reading: "is according to truth against those who practice such things" (see marginal note).

You may ask the question *"What is truth?"* as did the Roman governor, Pontius Pilate, who sat in judgment of Jesus. John's Gospel gives the answer to that question in at least two places. Jesus said, *"I am the way, and the truth,*

and the life; no one comes to the Father but through Me"
(John 14:6). In this instance truth is embodied in the
person of Jesus Christ. Jesus taught us by His word and by
His conduct. It is safe to say that God will judge men both
by what Jesus said and by what He did.

Jesus said something else about truth relating to our
subject. In a prayer to His Father He said, *"Your word is
truth"* (John 17:17). Jesus equated *"truth"* with *"Your
word."* Men, therefore, will be judged by the Word of
God, the Bible. Exodus 20 contains the Ten Commandments which give us some of the truth by which actions
will be judged. However, Jesus expanded on the meaning
of the commandments beyond the letter of the law. When
dealing with the seventh commandment, He said,

> Matthew 5:27-28
> 27 *"You have heard that it was said, 'YOU SHALL
> NOT COMMIT ADULTERY';*
> 28 *but I say to you that everyone who looks at a
> woman with lust for her has already committed
> adultery with her in his heart."*

Jesus goes deeper than the outward act of adultery. He
goes to thought and intent of the heart. The lust that drives
the actual adultery is within; it is in the heart of men. It is
that which comes from within that defiles a person (Mark
7:20-23).

Paul makes it clear that no one will escape the
judgment of God. He wrote, *"do you suppose this, O man,
when you pass judgment on those who practice such things
and do the same yourself, that you will escape the judgment
of God?"* (Romans 2:3). The answer is, "Certainly not!"
Because God's judgment has not already fallen does not
mean that it will not fall. But, on the contrary, verse four
teaches that God's kindness and patience in withholding
judgment should lead us to repentance.

288

On judgment day no one will be able to hide his real motives nor twist the facts of his sin to suit himself. Responsibility cannot be denied or be passed to someone else. Truth alone will be the standard.

The Standard of Works

God will also judge on the basis of good and bad deeds. Speaking about God, Paul wrote that He:

Romans 2:6-8

6 ... WILL RENDER TO EACH PERSON ACCORDING TO HIS DEEDS:

7 to those who by perseverance in doing good seek for glory and honor and immortality, eternal life;

8 but to those who are selfishly ambitious and do not obey the truth, but obey unrighteousness, wrath and indignation.

Paul is not teaching salvation by works in these verses. Keep in mind that judgment comes after one's life has ended. Looking back, it is evident who did the "good" deeds in God's eyes. It is clear from other Scripture that believers are the only people who qualify for salvation because *"without faith it is impossible to please Him"* (Hebrews 11:6). Earlier in Romans, Paul said he had *"received grace and apostleship to bring about the obedience of faith among all the Gentiles* (Romans 1:5).

If taken out of context this passage seems to teach that one is given eternal life for good works and punishment for bad works. However, the Apostle Paul never teaches that salvation is earned by good works. If he had, he would have contradicted himself within the same book, teaching two different doctrines. Later on in Romans it is made very clear that salvation is not on the basis of works. He wrote: *"But if it is by grace, it is no longer on the basis of works, otherwise grace is no longer grace"* (Romans 11:6). In

Romans 2 Paul makes a general statement of truth about those who persevere in doing good, but he does not say how one gains such faithfulness in doing good. One can only persevere through faith in Jesus Christ. It is a result of salvation and not the reason for it.

However, God is not so unjust as to punish all men alike, regardless of the degree of their evil. Nor will He reward all men alike regardless of the degree of their good deeds. Those whose deeds are very evil will bear a heavier punishment than those whose deeds are not. Likewise, believers who do the will of God in their good works will receive a proper reward. It does make a difference how you live, even though good works do not earn salvation.

The Standard of Opportunity and Inner Moral Law

A third basis of judgment is the spiritual opportunity one has had and the inner moral law written in his heart:

Romans 2:12-15
12 For all who have sinned without the Law will also perish without the Law, and all who have sinned under the Law will be judged by the Law;
13 for it is not the hearers of the Law who are just before God, but the doers of the Law will be justi-fied.
14 For when Gentiles who do not have the Law do instinctively the things of the Law, these, not having the Law, are a law to themselves,
15 in that they show the work of the Law written in their hearts, their conscience bearing witness and their thoughts alternately accusing or else defend-ing them.

God will consider both the opportunity people have of hearing the Word of God and their response to it. If they continued in sin, rejecting faith in Christ after hearing much of the Word of God, their punishment will be greater. Jesus once said to Pilate, *"You would have no authority over Me, unless it had been given you from above; for this reason he who delivered Me to you has the greater sin"* (John 19:11). Judas Iscariot, who betrayed Jesus, had a greater opportunity and moral responsibility because he had been one of the twelve apostles of Jesus Christ. Therefore, his sin was greater than Pilate's.

The Standard of the Gospel

Finally, men will be judged by the Gospel of Jesus Christ. Paul said that the conscience of men would bear them witness and their thoughts would accuse or defend them *"on the day when, according to my gospel, God will judge the secrets of men through Christ Jesus"* (Romans 2:16). The sin of rejecting Jesus Christ is the only unpardonable sin today. To reject Jesus is to reject the Holy Spirit as He convicts of sin, of righteousness, and of judgment to come.

† Judgment – The Judgment Seat of Christ

The Judgment Seat (or Bema) of Christ is the place where the good and bad deeds of believers will be weighed to determine their rewards or lack of rewards. It takes place shortly after the rapture of believers when Jesus Christ comes again. The Great White Throne judgment of unbelievers is a thousand years after believers are examined, those two events being separated by the millennium.

The Purpose of the Judgment of Believers

Christian believers will never be judged for the purpose of determining their eternal destiny. That was settled the day and hour they trusted Jesus Christ as their own personal Lord and Savior. Therefore, the believer will never come into judgment (John 5:24) at the Great White Throne.

Believers will, however, answer for the deeds they did on earth for the purpose of determining the merit of their service. It cannot be over emphasized that good works never secure salvation, or even contribute to it. Isaiah said, *"all our righteous deeds are like a filthy garment; And all of us wither like a leaf, And our iniquities, like the wind, take us away"* (Isaiah 64:6).

The purpose of the Judgment Seat of Christ is expressed in at least two passages: 1 Corinthians 3:8-15 and 2 Corinthians 5:9-10. We will examine those two to see what they teach us about examining believer's works.

The Certainty of Judgment

But first, let us deal with the certainty of believers having to give an account of their deeds. Paul wrote:

Romans 14:10-12
10 ... we will all stand before the judgment seat of God.
11 For it is written,
"AS I LIVE, SAYS THE LORD, EVERY KNEE SHALL BOW TO ME,
AND EVERY TONGUE SHALL GIVE PRAISE TO GOD."
12 So then each one of us will give an account of himself to God.

Many believers live their life as if they will never have to answer to the Lord for their deeds. Nothing could be further from the truth! It is certain that each of us will give an account to the Lord for what he has done. This is not contrary to John 5:24 in which Jesus says that the one who believes will not come into judgment. Jesus was speaking of a judgment of condemnation to hell; Paul, on the other hand, was speaking of an evaluation of service to determine rewards or lack thereof.

292

EXAMINING THE SAVED

In 1 Corinthians 3, Paul deals with the quality of each Christian's work:

1 Corinthians 3:8, 12-15
8 ... but each will receive his own reward according to his own labor.

12 Now if any man builds on the foundation with gold, silver, precious stones, wood, hay, straw,
13 each man's work will become evident; for the day will show it because it is to be revealed with fire, and the fire itself will test the quality of each man's work.
14 If any man's work which he has built on it remains, he will receive a reward.
15 If any man's work is burned up, he will suffer loss; but he himself will be saved, yet so as through fire.

Notice that the entire context deals with those who are fellow workers with God. The construction of a building is symbolically used to describe the Christian's service to Christ. Believers will be judged as to how they build upon the foundation of Jesus Christ. Paul's instruction in verse 10 is, *"each man must be careful how he builds on it."* The foundation is laid; it is up to us to build properly.

Symbolically, six different materials can be used to build. The first three are gold, silver, and precious stones. Gold represents deity. The book of Job uses gold as a symbol for deity: *"the Almighty will be your gold"* (Job 22:25). Likewise, silver stands for redemption. Silver was the price paid for the redemption of a slave. The Old Testament tabernacle, which illustrated redemption by substitution, rested upon a foundation of silver. The precious stones represent those who are redeemed. Malachi speaks of God's people as being precious stones in His treasure chest. Malachi wrote, *"they shall be mine, saith the LORD of hosts, in that day when I make up my jewels"* (Malachi 3:17 KJV).

Gold, silver, and precious stones are symbolic of work done in and through the power of the Holy Spirit. God, working in us through the redemption in Christ, produces precious jewels for His treasure chest. These first three symbols represent deeds done by the power of God, to the glory of God, not deeds done in pride or in self-service. These materials, and the works they represent, cannot be burned up.

The next three materials are wood, hay, and straw, symbolic of deeds originating with our human nature. Again, the Old Testament tabernacle reveals the symbolic meaning of wood. Christ was pictured by the wooden boards of the tabernacle covered by gold. It shows the unique character of Jesus as being both man and God. Wood, hay, and straw will burn up because the quality of each man's work will be revealed with fire, according to what we read in 1 Corinthians 3:13.

Notice that the quality of work will be judged rather than the quantity. Some Christians live long and fruitful lives while others are converted and die shortly thereafter. Therefore, the quantity of work which one does is not the issue, but rather the quality of the work. Let me ask you a question, "Is your work for God led by the Spirit of God based on His Word, or is it based on your own ideas, producing nothing but that which can be burned?" The work that stands the test of fire and remains shall receive a reward.

Notice that 1 Corinthians 3:15 emphasizes that this judgment is not to determine heaven or hell, but to determine reward. If a man's work is burned up, he shall suffer loss, but he himself shall be saved. Those who have done their work in the energy of the flesh for personal gain will end up with no reward from the Lord. However, they themselves will still be saved because of the work of Jesus Christ.

Good and Bad Works to Be Judged

The second passage dealing with the Judgment Seat of Christ is 2 Corinthians 5:10. Paul says that *"we must all appear before the judgment seat of Christ, so that each one may be recompensed for his deeds in the body, according to what he has done, whether good or bad."* What we do now does make a difference in eternity. Each one will be repaid for what he has done. Both good and bad deeds will be recompensed. By comparing this with the previous passage, we can see that good deeds are those done in the power of the Holy Spirit.

As believers, we must be careful not to judge solely by outward appearance. Jesus said that men look on the outward appearance, but God looks on the heart. Much of what passes for good works would utterly fail the test before God. Likewise, some things that men might consider bad may be righteous in the sight of God. Let me illustrate. Some start a work for God that becomes very successful in the eyes of men. Perhaps a church is established and many are brought to Christ. However, the person God used to start the church may become proud and begin to take credit for it rather than giving glory to God. He begins to act in the flesh and insists on doing things his own way. When problems arise, rather than seeking God's direction and guidance, he will do all in his power to keep everything under his own control. Therefore, from the outside everything may look good, but from God's point of view it is sinful. God will give no reward because the motivation is wrong and the glory is stolen from Him.

Many times in history people have believed an error. They may have thought the man of God was wrong when he stood for the truth in the face of their opposition. He

295

must stand alone for what is right even when the majority of people are wrong and oppose him. Those who are against him will often call him judgmental or self-righteous. They may even say he is proud and arrogant because he strongly argues for truth. However, in the sight of God he may be the key to keeping the truth alive in that generation. Martin Luther was such a man. In the face of threats and strong opposition, he stood opposed to the corruption in the church. Without doubt, he will be rewarded at the Judgment Seat of Christ rather than those who opposed him. Indeed, many of those who opposed him will not stand at the judgment Beam of Christ at all, because they were unbelievers all along.

† Judgment – The Great White Throne

The Great White Throne is the place where unbelievers will be judged. The resurrection of the saved of this age comes before the thousand-year reign of Christ that we call the millennium. The resurrection and judgment of the unsaved comes after the thousand-year millennial reign of the Lord Jesus Christ.

Two Resurrections

Revelation 20 tells us about the thousand-year reign of Christ during which Satan is bound in the abyss. Verse four speaks of the resurrection of those who were beheaded because of the testimony of Jesus and the Word of God. They had not worshiped the Antichrist, or his image, and had not received his mark. They come to life and reign with Christ for a thousand years. Then Revelation 20:5 says, *"The rest of the dead did not come to life until the thousand years were completed."* This is in keeping with what Jesus taught in John's Gospel:

296

John 5:25-29

25 "Truly, truly, I say to you, an hour is coming and now is, when the dead will hear the voice of the Son of God, and those who hear will live.

26 "For just as the Father has life in Himself, even so He gave to the Son also to have life in Himself;

27 and He gave Him authority to execute judgment, because He is the Son of Man.

28 "Do not marvel at this; for an hour is coming, in which all who are in the tombs will hear His voice,

*29 and will come forth; those who did the good deeds to **a resurrection of life**, those who committed the evil deeds to **a resurrection of judgment**.*

THE JUDGMENT OF THE LOST

Revelation 20:11 to the end of the chapter records the judgment of those who are unsaved:

Revelation 20:11-12

*11 Then I saw **a great white throne** and Him who sat upon it, from whose presence earth and heaven fled away, and no place was found for them.*

12 And I saw the dead, the great and the small, standing before the throne, and books were opened; and another book was opened, which is the book of life; and the dead were judged from the things which were written in the books, according to their deeds.

Jesus Will Be the Judge

The one seated on the Great White Throne is none other than Jesus Christ Himself. He said in John 5:27 quoted above that the Father had committed all judgment to Him. The throne is white, a symbol of righteousness and holiness. Jesus Christ, God in the flesh, is the one from whom heaven and earth rushes away. Because of the majesty of almighty God, neither heaven nor earth can stand before Him. This is a description of the absolute and utter majesty of our Lord Jesus Christ.

Spiritually Dead Will Be Judged
Revelation 20:12 describes what will take place then. Those who stand before Him are called *"the dead."* Ephesians 2 speaks of the unsaved as dead. Though they are physically alive, they are spiritually dead. It says:

> Ephesians 2:1-2
> *1 And you were dead in your trespasses and sins,*
> *2 in which you formerly walked according to the course of this world, according to the prince of the power of the air, of the spirit that is now working in the sons of disobedience.*

Thus, it is entirely possible to be alive physically, but dead spiritually.

Jesus' teaching on the resurrection in John is clear. Both the saved and the unsaved will be resurrected from the dead, but one is resurrected unto everlasting life and the other is resurrected unto everlasting condemnation. Those who appear before the Great White Throne are spiritually dead, yet have been resurrected to be judged. Both *"the great and the small"* will be there. The Bible says elsewhere that God is not a respecter of persons, nor is He partial to any man (Romans 2:11). All the unsaved – the high and mighty, and the meek and lowly – will stand in that judgment. They are said to stand before the throne – the throne on which Jesus sits as judge!

The Book and the Books
Revelation goes on to explain the books from which the unsaved will be judged. *"Books"* plural, and another

"book" singular, will be used. It is written, *"And books were opened; and another book was opened, which is the book of life"* (Revelation 20:12).

The Book of Life

No one who is spiritually dead will have his name recorded in the book (singular) of life. The book is not there to determine people's eternal destiny. That was decided by their relationship to Jesus while they still lived. The book is there at the judgment of the Great White Throne merely as a proof that they are without eternal life.

The Books of Deeds

The *"books"* plural, contain a record of the deeds done by those being judged. It is evident there will be degrees of punishment in the Lake of Fire (Matthew 10:15; John 19:11), just as there will be degrees of reward in heaven. God is not so unjust as to reward every person exactly alike regardless of their deeds and attitudes when they lived. However, the least punishment will be terrible to endure with no opportunity to escape!

The Second Death

John tells us about the destination of the unsaved who are being judged:

Revelation 20:13-15
13 And the sea gave up the dead which were in it, and death and Hades gave up the dead which were in them; and they were judged, every one of them according to their deeds.
14 Then death and Hades were thrown into the lake of fire. This is the second death, the lake of fire.
15 And if anyone's name was not found written in the book of life, he was thrown into the lake of fire.

The sea will give up its dead, and death and Hades will give up the dead which are in them.

Hades is a temporary place of punishment for those who die without believing the Gospel. Jesus spoke of Hades in Luke's Gospel when He talked about the rich man and Lazarus, the poor man who died. While this is quite a long passage of Scripture, it needs to be included to show how Paradise and Hades were arranged before the crucifixion and resurrection of Jesus. Paradise is no longer opposite Hades as it is in Luke's record. After the resurrection of Jesus, it was transferred to heaven. Paul was caught **up** to Paradise (2 Corinthians 12:4). However, there appears to be no change in the place called Hades. This is what Jesus said about the rich man and Lazarus:

Luke 16:22-26
22 "Now the poor man died and was carried away by the angels to Abraham's bosom; and the rich man also died and was buried.
23 "In Hades he lifted up his eyes, being in torment, and saw Abraham far away and Lazarus in his bosom.
24 "And he cried out and said, 'Father Abraham, have mercy on me, and send Lazarus so that he may dip the tip of his finger in water and cool off my tongue, for I am in agony in this flame.'
25 "But Abraham said, 'Child, remember that during your life you received your good things, and likewise Lazarus bad things; but now he is being comforted here, and you are in agony.
26 'And besides all this, between us and you there is a great chasm fixed, so that those who wish to come over from here to you will not be able, and that none may cross over from there to us.'"

Thus, Hades is a place of torment – a place where the rich man desired just a drop of water to cool off his tongue because of his agony. A great chasm or gulf was fixed between Paradise and Hades so that no one could cross over from one side to the other. Neither could anyone return to the land of the living from Hades. Notice carefully what the Scripture says,

Luke 16:27-31
27 "And he [the rich man] *said, 'Then I beg you, father, that you send him to my father's house –*
28 for I have five brothers – in order that he may warn them, so that they will not also come to this place of torment.'
29 "But Abraham said, 'They have Moses and the Prophets; let them hear them.'
30 "But he said, 'No, father Abraham, but if someone goes to them from the dead, they will repent!'
31 "But he said to him, 'If they do not listen to Moses and the Prophets, they will not be persuaded even if someone rises from the dead.'"

The last verse tells it like it is! Jesus has risen from the dead and there are still millions of people who will not be persuaded though One has risen from the dead. Thus, we learn from Revelation 20 that Hades, already a place of torment, is one of the places from which the dead will be gathered for the Great White Throne judgment.

The Final Sentence

The sentence handed down by the Judge in Revelation 20 is for the unsaved to be put into the Lake of Fire, which is the second death. The second death is not ceasing to exist, but it is eternal separation from God who is the source of eternal life. Men who spurn God now, will not be in heaven with Him later. They will be forever separated from Him because they turned away from His love.

The place they will spend eternity is called *"the lake of fire."* It is a place prepared for the devil and his angels

(Matthew 25:41); those who die in rebellion against God will also be there. Revelation 20:15 concludes, *"if anyone's name was not found written in the book of life, he was thrown into the lake of fire."* It is clear that these dead do not have their names in the book of life. Everyone who appears before the Great White Throne for judgment will be put in the Lake of Fire. The next chapter will discuss in more detail the Lake of Fire and the condition of those who die without Jesus Christ.

MAKE JUDGMENT TO COME PERSONAL

It is important to make sure of your eternal destiny before it is too late. If the Spirit of God has been dealing with your heart, and yet you have not yielded to God's call to salvation in Jesus Christ, I beg you to consider seriously the consequences involved. You must make a firm and unchanging commitment to trust Jesus Christ as your own Lord and Savior.

He has already done His part. He came from heaven to earth and gave His life on the Cross to pay the penalty for your sin. If you will receive Him as Lord and Savior, that payment will be counted on your behalf and you will be set free from the penalty of sin. You shall never come into the judgment of the Great White Throne and be sentenced to the Lake of Fire. I beg you by the grace of God in Christ Jesus to be reconciled to God who has already offered you His hand of peace.

2 Corinthians 5:19-20
19 ... God was in Christ reconciling the world to Himself, not counting their trespasses against them, and He has committed to us the word of reconciliation.
20 Therefore, we are ambassadors for Christ, as though God were making an appeal through us; we beg you on behalf of Christ, be reconciled to God.

Chapter 13

The Eternal State
† Unsaved: The Lake of Fire

It is only fitting to conclude these studies with the Bible's teaching about the eternal condition of the saved and the lost. A separate destiny awaits each group. There is a heaven to gain and a Lake of Fire to escape. Heaven is gained by trusting God to remove your sin through the sacrifice of Jesus on the Cross and His resurrection from the dead to live forevermore.

The Lake of Fire is gained by doing nothing! According to God's Word, you need do nothing more than you have already done to go to a Christless eternity. Paul wrote that *"all have sinned and fall short of the glory of God"* (Romans 3:23). And John's Gospel tells us, *"He who believes in Him [Jesus] is not judged; he who does not believe has been judged already, because he has not believed in the name of the only begotten Son of God"* (John 3:18). Therefore, only those who repent and trust in Jesus will be saved. All that we know for sure about the afterlife comes from the Bible, and all we know about the condition of the lost comes from Jesus. Even the book of Revelation is *"The Revelation of Jesus Christ, which God gave Him to show to His bond-servants, the things which must soon take place"* (Revelation 1:1).

TEMPORARY ABODE OF THE UNSAVED

Let us consider briefly the final destiny of those without God and without hope in the world. The word *"Hades"* is the Bible's name of the place where the souls of ungodly men stay between death and the final judgment.

The Gospel of Luke contains one of the most important passages dealing with Hades. Jesus relates a true story of a poor man, Lazarus, and a rich man. The rich man died without God, but Lazarus died in faith. Luke 16 tells the story. Concerning the rich man it says:

Luke 16:23-24
23 "In Hades he lifted up his eyes, being in torment, and saw Abraham far away and Lazarus in his bosom.
24 "And he cried out and said, 'Father Abraham, have mercy on me, and send Lazarus so that he may dip the tip of his finger in water and cool off my tongue, for I am in agony in this flame.'"

Clearly the rich man was fully conscious because he called out for mercy. Furthermore, he knew he was being punished. He wanted just a drop of water to cool off his tongue. He felt the great pain of being in flaming fire, for he said, *"I am in agony in this flame."* Therefore, Hades is a place where the ungodly dead are fully capable of reasoning, and fully conscious of their pain and agony. Certainly, it is a place to avoid. The unsaved are called from Hades to the Great White Throne Judgment. (See page 296.)

PERMANENT ABODE OF THE UNSAVED

The Furnace of Fire – The final place of punishment is referred to as both the furnace of fire and the Lake of Fire. We commonly call this place "hell."

Fire is symbolic of judgment in the Bible. Jesus Himself mentions the furnace of fire in the Gospel of Matthew:

Matthew 13:49-50
49   "So it will be at the end of the age; the angels will come forth and take out the wicked from among the righteous,
*50   and will throw them into **the furnace of fire**; there shall be weeping and gnashing of teeth."*

The furnace of fire is a place of weeping and gnashing of teeth, thus, a place of torment. Jesus said that the everlasting fire cannot be put out. In Mark 9 He speaks about the seriousness of going to the place of eternal punishment. He said:

Mark 9:43, 45, 47-48
43   "If your hand causes you to stumble, cut it off; it is better for you to enter life crippled, than, having your two hands, to go into hell, into the unquenchable fire,

45   "If your foot causes you to stumble, cut it off; it is better for you to enter life lame, than, having your two feet, to be cast into hell,

47   "If your eye causes you to stumble, throw it out; it is better for you to enter the kingdom of God with one eye, than, having two eyes, to be cast into hell,

48   where THEIR WORM DOES NOT DIE, AND THE FIRE IS NOT QUENCHED."

He used an illustration to make His point when He said, *"if your hand causes you to stumble, cut it off"* (Mark 9:43). We do not believe He meant to actually cut off a hand or foot. That would not take care of the problem, because one could sin with the other hand or foot. Even if both hands and feet were gone, one can still plan all kinds of evil. What Jesus is emphasizing is that hell should be avoided at all costs because of the great horror of eternal fire.

We all know that Jesus is a man of compassion, so He is not trying to frighten us. He teaches us that we must avoid all manner of sin. The hand represents the actual deeds of evil that one can commit, the foot represents the approach to or direction and inclination toward evil. And the eye represents the desire that pulls us toward evil. James teaches that sin is conceived through lust and the eye is the gate through which lust is fed. Therefore, we must deal with hand, foot, and eye, that is, with the deed, inclination, and inspiration to do evil. The only way to deal with evil is to submit to the Lord Jesus and permit Him to cleanse us.

How Long Is Eternal?

Do the unsaved in hell get time off for good behavior? Or, are they annihilated altogether after a period of time? Jesus teaches that the fire of punishment never goes out. The ungodly are never consumed by the fire and it is everlasting: *"THEIR WORM DOES NOT DIE, AND THE FIRE IS NOT QUENCHED."* The jokes about "partying in hell" are without basis in reality. Since the identical terms of everlasting and eternal are used for both eternal life and eternal punishment, both of them endure forever. There is no time off from the Lake of Fire for good behavior!

The fact that punishment is everlasting is also mentioned in Revelation 14. During the final days of this age, Antichrist will appear, bringing great persecution and hardship on earth. Those who submit and worship him rather than worshiping God will be judged. That judgment is described in Revelation:

Revelation 14:9-11
9 ... *"If anyone worships the beast and his image, and receives a mark on his forehead or on his hand,*

10 he also will drink of the wine of the wrath of God, which is mixed in full strength in the cup of His anger; and he will be tormented with fire and brimstone in the presence of the holy angels and in the presence of the Lamb.

*11 "And **the smoke of their torment goes up forever and ever;** they have no rest day and night, those who worship the beast and his image, and whoever receives the mark of his name."*

Many imagine that they will never be punished by a loving God. They forget that God is also a God of justice. There is no conflict between His love and His justice, both of which must be satisfied. The Bible says that *"God so loved the world, that He gave His only begotten Son, that whoever believes in Him should not perish, but have eternal life"* (John 3:16). Likewise, it proclaims that those who refuse the love of God *"will pay the penalty of eternal destruction, away from the presence of the Lord and from the glory of His power"* (2 Thessalonians 1:9). The love of God has been offered to all mankind. If they spurn His love, only a certain terrifying expectation of judgment remains:

Hebrews 10:26-27
26 For if we go on sinning willfully after receiving the knowledge of the truth, there no longer remains a sacrifice for sins,
27 but a terrifying expectation of judgment and THE FURY OF A FIRE WHICH WILL CONSUME THE ADVERSARIES.

The ungodly are said to *"pay the penalty of **eternal destruction,"*** just as the righteous are to be given ***eternal life***. Thus, the punishment of the ungodly will last as long as the blessings of the godly. If the eternal life of the righteous shall cease, then the eternal punishment of the wicked shall cease also; but the truth is both are everlasting, forever, without end.

Matthew 25:41, 46

41 ... "Depart from Me, accursed ones, into the eternal fire which has been prepared for the devil and his angels."

46 "These will go away into eternal punishment, but the righteous into eternal life!"

The Lake of Fire is the place prepared for the devil and his angels. Satan will be cast into the Lake of Fire (Revelation 20:10). He will not go voluntarily! In the same chapter ungodly men are also cast into the Lake of Fire. Both Matthew and Revelation teach that the ungodly will spend eternity with Satan in the eternal fire. It is not wise for us to take this lightly or twist the Word of God because eternal punishment and suffering are unthinkable to us. They are not pleasant thoughts for anyone; however, the fact remains that Jesus Christ Himself revealed to us the eternal destiny of the lost.

† Eternal State – Saved: Paradise with God

Paradise forever – what a happy and joyous thing it is to end our study on such a wonderful note. In this section we will review what the Bible says about the blessed prospects of the redeemed. First, we will deal with the temporary state of the saved after their death and then with their permanent destiny throughout eternity.

TEMPORARY ABODE OF THE SAVED

What happens to a believer when he dies and is buried? Where will he be between physical death and the resurrection of the body? Only two beliefs have any major following among Bible students. The first is that a believer goes to sleep and will remain unconscious until Jesus returns. It is true that the Bible often refers to death as sleep, but it is related to the body rather than to the soul. The second belief held by a large majority is that the body goes to the grave, but the spirit and soul go to be with Jesus in heaven until He returns to earth. Then the spirit, soul, and body will be united forever at the resurrection of the just when the believer will receive a new, glorified body. This view is the one actually taught in Scripture.

Absent from the Body, Present with the Lord – What are the Scriptures that indicate that believers are consciously awake and with the Lord upon their death? Paul speaks in this manner:

2 Corinthians 5:6-8
6 ... while we are at home in the body we are absent from the Lord –
7 for we walk by faith, not by sight –
8 we are of good courage, I say, and prefer rather to be absent from the body and to be at home with the Lord.

It is clear – believers go to be with the Lord immediately upon their death. Paul actually preferred to be absent from the body and to be at home with the Lord rather than to continue in the body. Therefore, the temporary state of the redeemed after death is better than our present state of life.

Paul also deals with this subject in Philippians:

Philippians 1:21-24
21 For to me, to live is Christ and to die is gain.
22 But if I am to live on in the flesh, this will mean fruitful labor for me; and I do not know which to choose.

23 But I am hard-pressed from both directions, having the desire to depart and be with Christ, for that is very much better;
24 yet to remain on in the flesh is more necessary for your sake.

Paul knew that he would continue to have fruitful ministry if he did not die, so he found himself with a problem. He saw an advantage to the Church for him to remain alive, but he also saw an advantage in dying because he would *"be with Christ, for that is very much better."* As a believer, he would go directly to Paradise in heaven to be with Jesus Christ until the resurrection. Paul already had been caught up to Paradise and had a glimpse of how wonderful it is (2 Corinthians 12:3-4).

A Place of Conscious Delight

You may ask the question, "Is the believer conscious or asleep after physical death?" Paul's desire to be with Christ certainly indicates that he expected to be fully conscious. Revelation 6:9-11 strongly implies this. It mentions the souls of those who were slain for the Gospel's sake. Verse 10 says, *"they cried out with a loud voice, saying, 'How long, O Lord, holy and true, will You refrain from judging and avenging our blood on those who dwell on the earth?'"* This makes it obvious that they were fully awake. Apparently they knew what was happening on earth because they knew that God had not yet avenged their blood, though they may have learned it in heaven. The temporary state of believers is to be with the Lord in heaven, fully conscious, able to talk and reason. They may or may not have some knowledge of what is happening on earth.

Finally, 1 Thessalonians 4 says those believers with Jesus in heaven will return with Him when He comes again. Verse 14 says, *"For if we believe that Jesus died and rose again, even so God will bring with Him those who have fallen asleep in Jesus."* The soul and spirit of those who died will be united with their resurrected and glorified bodies. Then both living believers who are changed into their new bodies and resurrected believers will be with the Lord always.

PERMANENT ABODE OF THE SAVED

Will believers spend eternity in heaven? We often speak of "going to heaven." The popular idea of heaven is a large place for spirits and angels where nothing is physical. However, the popular idea does not agree with Scripture.

New Heaven and New Earth

Revelation 21 and 22 describe the new heaven and new earth. Much of it is symbolic language, but some solid facts can be gathered. According to Peter, the present earth will be burned with fire and will be replaced with a new earth.

2 Peter 3:10-13
10 ... the heavens will pass away with a roar and the elements will be destroyed with intense heat, and the earth and its works will be burned up.
11 Since all these things are to be destroyed in this way, what sort of people ought you to be in holy conduct and godliness,
12 looking for and hastening the coming of the day of God, because of which the heavens will be destroyed by burning, and the elements will melt with intense heat!
13 But according to His promise we are looking for new heavens and a new earth, in which right-eousness dwells.

There will actually be a new earth. John wrote, *"Then I saw a new heaven and a new earth; for the first heaven and the first earth passed away, and there is no longer any sea"* (Revelation 21:1). The new earth is not the same place as the new heaven. He also wrote in Revelation 21:2, *"I saw the holy city, new Jerusalem, coming down out of heaven from God."* The new earth will be a different place from the new heaven just as the present earth is a different place from the present heaven. Our eternal dwelling place will be on the new earth. God will make His new permanent dwelling place on the new earth also:

> Revelation 21:3-4
> 3   And I heard a loud voice from the throne, saying, "Behold, the tabernacle of God is among men, and He will dwell among them, and they shall be His people, and God Himself will be among them,
> 4   and He will wipe away every tear from their eyes; and there will no longer be any death; there will no longer be any mourning, or crying, or pain; the first things have passed away."

People for New Earth

The new earth will be the dwelling place of God, of Jesus Christ, and of the redeemed. Verse three quoted above mentions people who are *"His people"* and *"God Himself."* Verse 22 says, *"I saw no temple in it, for the Lord God the Almighty and the Lamb are its temple."* The Lamb is Jesus Christ who takes away the sin of the world. The eternal temple is God Himself and the Lamb, not a building, because God will dwell with us; we will be able to come directly into His presence openly for worship and fellowship.

The Glorious Conditions

Our situation will be completely peaceful. *"He [God] will wipe away every tear from their eyes; and there will no longer be any death; there will no longer be any mourning,*

312

or crying, or pain; the first things have passed away" (Revelation 21:4). All the curse of sin will be completely removed. There will be no reason to cry, no parting of a loved one, no wayward child, no drunken husband, no treacherous wife, and no tears because all sin will be wiped away.

There will no longer be any death. The wages of sin is death and, where there is no sin, there can be no death. We will never again face mourning over the loss of a loved one. Even pain itself will be removed from the experience of the redeemed. One could not describe a more glorious place than this.

Nations of New Earth

During the eternal state there will also be nations on the earth for the Bible says:

Revelation 21:24-26
24 The nations will walk by its light, and the kings of the earth will bring their glory into it.
25 In the daytime (for there will be no night there) its gates will never be closed;
26 and they will bring the glory and the honor of the nations into it.

The picture is that of the new Jerusalem as a blessing in the earth where the Lord God and Jesus Christ Himself dwell with His people. There will be no need for the sun or the moon, according to verse 23, because the glory of God will be so bright it will illuminate everything and the Lamb will be its lamp. The nations shall walk by the light of God and all the glory of the earthly kingdoms will be brought into the city to worship the Lord God Almighty. Nothing unclean or sinful will be in it, for it is written, *"nothing unclean and no one who practices abomination and lying, shall ever come into it, but only those whose names are written in the Lamb's book of life"* (Revelation 21:27).

God's All-Sufficient Provision

Chapter 22 of Revelation shows something of how God will sustain His people:

Revelation 22:1-5

1 Then he showed me a river of the water of life, clear as crystal, coming from the throne of God and of the Lamb,

2 in the middle of its street. On either side of the river was the tree of life, bearing twelve kinds of fruit, yielding its fruit every month; and the leaves of the tree were for the healing of the nations.

3 There will no longer be any curse; and the throne of God and of the Lamb will be in it, and His bond-servants will serve Him;

4 they will see His face, and His name will be on their foreheads.

5 And there will no longer be any night; and they will not have need of the light of a lamp nor the light of the sun, because the Lord God will illumine them; and they will reign forever and ever.

Again, these may be symbolic descriptions, but whether they are actual descriptions or symbolic, the meaning is surely beyond our present understanding or imagination. Paul wrote, *"THINGS WHICH EYE HAS NOT SEEN AND EAR HAS NOT HEARD, AND* which *HAVE NOT ENTERED THE HEART OF MAN, ALL THAT GOD HAS PREPARED FOR THOSE WHO LOVE HIM"* (1 Corinthians 2:9).

MAKE YOUR ETERNAL DESTINY PERSONAL

Thank God, the good news is that no one really has to die and end up in the Lake of Fire. Remember, all you have to do to be lost is nothing more than you have done already. But what must you do in order to be saved? You must simply receive by faith the work that Jesus Christ did on Calvary for you.

The world says that the man who dies with the most toys wins at the game of life. The question is, "Who really wins in life?" Obviously, it is not the one with the most toys (material possessions), nor is it the one with the most power or fame. Actually, you cannot take any of those things with you. The one who wins is the one who gains heaven by accepting Jesus Christ as his or her own personal Savior.

Once again, I challenge you to search your own heart. Have you placed your faith in Jesus and what He did for you on Calvary? Jesus did not die on the Cross because He enjoyed it. He despised the shame, but He did it for the joy set before Him. That joy was knowing that those of us who will trust Him will escape the pain of eternal hell and spend eternity with God.

Won't you open your heart to Him now, and turn from your sins? Then you will be saved and have everlasting joy and fellowship with God who loves you.

John 3:16
"For God so loved the world, that He gave His only begotten Son, that whoever believes in Him shall not perish, but have eternal life."

END

BIBLIOGRAPHY

Evans, William, The Great Doctrines of the Bible, Moody Press, Chicago, Illinois, 1949

Fitzwater, P. B., Christian Theology, A Systematic Presentation, Wm. B. Eerdmans Publishing Co., Grand Rapids, Michigan, 1953

Gromacki, Robert G., The Modern Tongues Movement, Presbyterian and Reformed Publishing Co., Philadelphia, Pennsylvania, 1967

Lindsell, Harold and Woodbridge, Charles S., Handbook of Christian Truth, Fleming H. Revell Co., Westwood, New Jersey, 1953

Morgan, G. Campbell, The Spirit of God, Fleming H. Revell Co., Westwood, New Jersey, 1933

Morgan, G. Campbell, The Crises of the Christ, Pickering & Inglis, Ltd., London, 1945

Orr, J. Edwin, 100 Questions About God, G/L Publications, Glendale, California, 1967

Orr, James M.A., D.D., General Editor, International Standard Bible Encyclopedia, Article on Angels, E-sword Bible Software.

Priddy, Eugene, Christ and the Occult, Bible Basics International, Mt. Freedom, New Jersey, 1979

Ibid, A Fresh Look at the Holy Spirit, BBI Publications, Odessa, FL, 2004

Shaffer, Lewis Sperry, <u>Major Bible Themes</u>, The Kempen Press, Wheaton, Illinois, 1926

Stone, Nathan J., <u>Names of God</u>, Moody Press, Chicago, Illinois, 1944

Tenney, Merrill C., <u>Interpreting Revelation</u>, Wm. B. Eerdmans Publishing Co., Grand Rapids, Michigan, 1957

Ibid., <u>The Reality of the Resurrection</u>, Harper & Row, New York, 1963

Thiessen, Henry Clarence, <u>Introductory Lectures in Systematic Theology</u>, Wm. B. Eerdmans Publishing Company, Grand Rapids, Michigan, 1949

About the
Author of ...

Keep from Stumbling!
Bible Basics
for Spiritual Stability

Eugene Priddy was ordained to the Gospel ministry in 1959. He and his wife Monna Dean were missionaries in North Africa, Europe, and the USA with an international radio mission from 1959 until 1973.

They founded Bible Basics International, Inc. (BBI) in October, 1973. BBI is a faith mission dedicated to proclaiming the Gospel through radio, literature, church planting, personal evangelism, and leadership training. Eugene has written Bible studies that have been translated and broadcast in more than a score of languages. In July, 1990, Bible Basics installed regional missionary station *Radio HRGS* in Roatan, Honduras. Its broadcast target area is the Bay Islands and the coastal areas of Honduras, Guatemala, and Belize.

Eugene and his wife Monna Dean were missionaries with a major radio mission for more than a decade. While they were in Europe, Eugene had the initial idea of providing systematic, basic Bible teaching for new and untaught believers. Many languages do not have the wealth of Christian books and literature available to English speaking believers. These studies were first written specifically for translation to help meet this need.

When Eugene is speaking in Stateside churches, people often say this is exactly what they themselves need – Bible teaching stated in easy-to-understand language, clearly supported by Scripture. That is precisely what you will find inside the covers of this book.

Eugene graduated in 1959 from Piedmont Bible College in Winston-Salem, NC with a B.R.E. degree and in 1968 from Wheaton Graduate School of Theology with an M.A. in Christian Education. On the fifth anniversary of *Radio HRGS*, he was given an honorary Doctor's Degree (D.D.) by the Bay Island Baptist Association. Participating in the presentation were the Governor of the Bay Islands and other officials of government, education, and the church.

Eugene and Monna Dean have five children and thirteen grandchildren. Glenn, their oldest son, was the founding manager of *Radio HRGS* in Roatan, Honduras.

Eugene has authored a number of other books and tracts. For a complete list, see www.biblebasics.org or contact:

Bible Basics International
P.O. Box 726 • Odessa, FL 33556-0726
(813) 920-2264 • Fax: (813) 920-2265
E-mail: info@biblebasics.org